Social Work with Drug, Alcohol and Substance Misusers

Social Work with Drug, Alcohol and Substance Misusers

THIRD EDITION

ANTHONY GOODMAN

Series Editors: Jonathan Parker and Greta Bradley

Los Angeles | London | New Delhi
Singapore | Washington DC

Learning Matters
An imprint of SAGE Publications Ltd
1 Oliver's Yard
55 City Road
London EC1Y 1SP

SAGE Publications Inc.
2455 Teller Road
Thousand Oaks, California 91320

SAGE Publications India Pvt Ltd
B 1/I 1 Mohan Cooperative Industrial Area
Mathura Road
New Delhi 110 044

SAGE Asia-Pacific Pte Ltd
3 Church Street
#10-04 Samsung Hub
Singapore 049483

Editor: Luke Block
Development editor: Kate Lodge
Production controller: Chris Marke
Project management: Deer Park Productions,
Tavistock, Devon
Marketing manager: Tamara Navaratnam
Cover design: Wendy Scott
Typeset by: PDQ Typesetting Ltd
Printed and bound by Henry Ling Limited, at the
Dorset Press, Dorchester, DT1 1HD

First edition published in 2007 by Learning
Matters.
Reprinted in 2007
Second edition published in 2009
Reprinted in 2010
Third edition published in 2013 by SAGE/Learning
Matters

Professional Capabilities Framework diagram
reproduced with permission of The College of
Social Work.

Library of Congress Control Number:
2013946209

British Library Cataloguing in Publication data

A catalogue record for this book is available from
the British Library

ISBN 978 1 4462-6759-2 (pbk)
ISBN 978 1 4462-6758-5

MIX
Paper from
responsible sources
FSC
www.fsc.org
FSC® C013985

Contents

Acknowledgements

My interest in working with substance misusers started when I was a probation officer, learning how to engage positively with this challenging client group. I have worked with many social work and criminology students over the years at Middlesex University and have enjoyed and learnt from the discussions on this topic. It has also been interesting to work with students on the Advanced Modern Apprenticeship and Progression Award in substance misuse. Anecdotally, motivational interviewing and an understanding of how people can change have been well received by these students.

I would like to thank the people who have assisted me with the ideas for the book, including Fran Barry, Raj Hira, Jenni Lowe, Betsy Thom, Susanne MacGregor, and Ruth Houghton, librarian at Middlesex University. I am of course responsible for any inaccuracies.

I have had great support and advice from Kate Lodge at Learning Matters and Jonathan Parker, series editor: many thanks.

Finally, I would like to dedicate this book to Sue.

Introduction

This book is written for student social workers who are developing their skills and understanding of the requirements for practice. It is also designed for practitioners and others who are interested in how practice is changing in the field of working with substance misusers. It will encourage the student or experienced practitioner to consider engagement with hard-to-reach clients who may be very ambivalent about changing their behaviour. The social work profession adheres to a set of values and is committed to client self-determination. Nevertheless there are techniques that can be successfully employed to positively challenge clients to examine and change their behaviour and lifestyle. The area of substance misuse has been somewhat ignored by the social work profession and this gap has only been more recently acknowledged. Interest in alcohol misuse is even more recent, perhaps due to its legality and common usage. Why this should be the case is unclear, but perhaps it was because the problems of substance misusers were seen as self-inflicted or that they were a low priority.

Requirements for social work education

This book will help students to learn about working with clients who are drug and alcohol and substance misusers. Social workers will meet clients with these issues whatever area of practice they go into, so ignoring this area of practice can no longer be considered an option.

The book will also help meet the Quality Assurance Agency benchmarks for social work, including:

- social work services and service users;
- values and ethics;
- social work theory; and
- the nature of social work practice.

The National Occupational Standards set for social workers are covered and the book addresses the importance of working with individuals, carers, groups and communities. Furthermore, in the language of the Standards:

- prepare for and work with the above;
- plan, carry out review and evaluate social work practice;
- manage risk;
- manage and be accountable, with supervision and support, for one's own practice; and
- demonstrate professional competence in social work practice.

What is substance misuse?

Abusing drugs can apply to legal or illegal substances, and they can be taken in a wide variety of ways to get them into the bloodstream. DrugScope comment that addiction refers to the situation whereby most of the person's life is taken over by the need to obtain and consume drugs. They helpfully remind us that words like 'addict' or 'junkie' carry with them a negative connotation and they are a powerful label. It is better to call a person drug dependent, where dependency is the compulsion to keep taking drugs. Dependency can be physical or psychological or both. In the former case Drug-Scope points out that heavy use of drugs like alcohol, heroin or tranquillisers changes the body chemistry so that withdrawal of the drug causes symptoms that can be very severe and requires more of the drug or supportive withdrawal under medical super-vision. Gossop (2003), conversely, while acknowledging that the terms 'addiction' and 'addict' can carry a social stigma, believes that the terms are useful (indeed he uses them throughout his book) as they signify the loss of power and freedom felt by the substance misuser.

Alcohol is a drug that is called a depressant. This is due to its effect on the body rather than to the personality. It slows down the brain and the central nervous system. Alcohol gets absorbed into the bloodstream and then is broken down by the liver. People can become more tolerant to alcohol but not to the physical and psychological damage that excessive consumption creates. This can be permanent, and high-profile cases, like the footballer George Best who needed a liver transplant, demonstrate the damage this drug can cause. The general guidance is that men should drink no more than 21 units per week and women 14 units (a unit is approximately equivalent to a glass of wine or half a pint of not too strong beer). More recently the advice has changed and people are advised to have some 'dry' days each week to give the liver time to recover.

Psychological dependency can apply to a number of activities like exercise, eating chocolate or the need to take substances. With some drugs like cannabis there has been debate on long-term using, the potential for psychotic episodes and how addic-tive the drug is. Certainly for some people it has become an essential item in their lives.

Nikki Kendrick wrote a supplementary report on drugs and substance misuse in Octo-ber 1999 for the Training Organisation for the Personal Social Services (TOPSS), England (the national training organisation for social care, renamed Skills for Care in April 2005) that was designed to fit with the then latest policy document, *Tackling drugs to build a better Britain* (Home Office, 1998). This was designed to ensure that social work education fitted with the four elements of the drugs strategy, namely:

- young people – to help young people to resist drugs so that they could achieve their full potential;
- communities – to protect communities from the effects of drugs and their corrosive effect on people;
- treatment – to help people to overcome their substance misuse problems so that they could be both healthy and crime-free;
- availability – to stop the supply side of drugs.

As Kendrick commented, there are skilled professionals working in this area but also staff without any specific training, especially at management level. This might be, it was suggested, because the area of practice did not attract staff as they felt that they lacked the prerequisite knowledge and skills base. Furthermore, black and ethnic minority staff were particularly scarce as practitioners. Skills development was needed in relation to:

- basic knowledge in working with substance misusers;
- work with drug-using parents;
- work with young people who use drink or misuse drugs and other substances.

The book will cover the latest government proposals to tackle drug and alcohol misuse but at the time of writing it is not clear whether a policy of minimum alcohol pricing will be introduced.

Linking social work knowledge and skills to substance misuse

Social work is an activity that draws on its knowledge base from a number of different disciplines. The message from this book is that practitioners do have the necessary knowledge and skills to work with drug and substance misusers. They can feel that this is not the case. Working with clients who can be ambivalent about themselves and with changeable motivation can lead to a feeling of being de-skilled. However, there are techniques that can be employed. These will be highlighted in the book.

Such techniques can be used in a number of different settings and it is hoped therefore that this knowledge will appeal to professionals in a variety of settings. In addition, working with substance misusers will involve close co-operation and collaboration with colleagues in health – both physical and mental – criminal justice, employment and housing, and other agencies in the public and voluntary sectors. These colleagues will be able to gain an insight into the new requirements demanded of social workers. The companion book in the series, *Collaborative social work practice* by Anne Quinney, discusses, as the title suggests, collaborative work in a number of different settings, including health and youth work. As you will see in this book, both are central to good practice in substance misuse as both adults and young people are key targets in the government drug strategies.

There are Drugs and Alcohol National Occupational Standards (DANOS) produced by Skills for Health, the sector skills council for health, in association with the NHS, the then National Treatment Agency (now Public Health England) and the Home Office. The website is given at the end of this introduction. There is considerable overlap between the content of this book and the DANOS standards; for example, its standards include: *help individuals access substance misuse services; support individuals in difficult situations; develop practice in the delivery of services; educate people about substance use; health and social well-being; deliver services to help individuals address their substance use; help substance users address their offending behaviour; support individuals' rehabilitation*. In addition there is an emphasis on reflective practice, an essential component of social work practice. Thus we can observe from the DANOS standards what has been seen as the essential underpinning for work in the sector.

Returning to the notion of reflection, what can we learn from this concept? The social worker will often look to their knowledge and experience base to make sense of what is occurring in a current situation. This requires a transfer of knowledge and skills:

> *When a practitioner reflects in and on his practice, the possible objects of his reflection are as varied as the kinds of phenomena before him and the systems of knowing-in-practice which he brings to them. He may reflect on the tacit norms and appreciations which underlie a judgement, or on the strategies and theories implicit in a pattern of behaviour. He may reflect on the feeling for a situation which has led him to adopt a particular course of action, on the way in which he has framed the problem he is trying to solve, or on the role he has constructed for himself within a larger institutional context.* (Schön, 1991, p62)

If the new phenomenon is outside of current experience, then reflection is difficult. We will return to this in Chapter 1. The value system of the practitioner can also be challenged if the client is indulging in anti-social and self-destructive behaviour. The patience of the busy practitioner can wear thin when a client does not appreciate that their repeated behaviour is self-destructive. The practitioner needs to take on board new skills and understanding about the client and we will examine what this entails later in the book.

The process of working with a substance misuser can vary between working towards the goal of total abstinence to one of harm reduction and minimisation. As will be seen in this book, the work can be very challenging and simultaneously frustrating, as a client can nearly achieve their life changes only to relapse and then fall back on previous drug-taking lifestyles. This book will help you to make sense of this behaviour and to think about how and why it happens, enabling the client to make positive use of relapse as a 'tool' of intervention.

Book structure

It is an exciting time to be writing about working with substance misusers as it is emerging from being a Cinderella service to one that is very central to government social policy. When the author was a young probation officer over 30 years ago there were little or no facilities for the client group and their needs were largely ignored. Detox was only generally available in the locked wards of old, decrepit psychiatric hospitals and practice had not evolved to give an understanding of clients' behaviour and needs. This was a client group that was treated as being largely invisible to the helping professions.

The book will examine the nature and extent of drug taking in the United Kingdom, how it has changed over time, and the points where professionals and substance misusers meet. We will look at models of care for the treatment of substance misusers and we will draw on documents from the National Treatment Agency (NTA) (their website is given at the end of this introduction). Please note that the NTA was replaced by Public Health England from 1 April 2013. We will examine the way that drug policy has evolved and the implications for social work practice. This will be broken down further into examining good practice with older and younger clients, gender and ethnic difference. Anti-discriminatory practice was not strong in the early years and knowledge that substance misuse was not just located within the white male population is a relatively recent phenomenon. We will examine good practice techniques when working with substance-misusing clients, the need to motivate clients to change and how to work with relapse – indeed that this is to be expected and planned for – so that the client can be prepared to manage their behaviour and pressures to relapse.

The book takes an interactive approach with the reader and there will be exercises and case studies to be considered to draw out key points. Research and theory summaries will also be provided and no assumptions will be made that the reader is familiar with the field of drugs. Explanations will be given of the different types of drugs, what they do, how they are categorised in law and the penalties for possession and supply of illicit drugs. Unlike many branches of social work, this area borders on the divide between legality and illegality and this will be considered in terms of practice. It should not be forgotten that many clients with a dependency on drugs do not come into conflict with the law, and their needs should not be ignored. The emotional needs and protection of children of substance misusers will be considered an area highlighted in recent official documents, and discussed in the book as a cause for concern. Partners and the families of substance misusers are also hugely affected and there are child protection and personal issues, such as domestic violence and stress, that need to be 'on the radar'.

Chapter 1 will provide an overview of how substance misusers taking illegal drugs have been dealt with by the courts and how they have been treated by the helping professions. It will examine links with social work theory and practice. Further, in terms of good practice there will be a discussion of values and ethics and the centrality of these when working with substance misusers. From the outset the intention is to make the link between social work knowledge, values and skills and work with substance misusers.

Chapter 2 will highlight the nature and extent of drug taking in the United Kingdom. This will include data from the New English and Welsh Arrestee Drug Abuse Monitoring (NEW-ADAM). It will examine the points in the system where professionals and substance misusers meet and strategies for engaging with reluctant clients. It will describe the four-tiered models of care for treating adult substance misusers and integrated care pathways. The need for, and the different approach to, younger users will also be considered.

Chapter 3 will focus on the history of drug taking, including legislative changes that have taken place. It will look at issues of enforcement and abstinence, harm minimisation, etc. This will be linked to providing an overview of the variety of drugs available in the community and in prison. The availability of detox and rehabilitation will be discussed with the growth of drug intervention programmes and a move to a treatment model for working with substance misusers. We have now moved on to an enforcement and treatment model for offending substance misusers but as mentioned earlier, by no means do all substance misusers end up in the courts. We will consider the implications of this for practice.

Chapter 4 will focus on what is known about drug misusers and drug offenders from the research and implications for their needs: what type of drugs they use, issues of dual diagnosis, linked to mental health. There are a couple of key questions here, namely how do you recognise whether a person is likely to be taking drugs and whom can they be referred to? To answer we will examine who are the substance abusers and will consider this in terms of gender, race and age. Some examples of local services will be given and exercises in the chapter will encourage you to explore what is available in your locality.

Chapter 5 will focus on policy changes that have occurred, concentrating on the 1995, 1998 (for example with the four elements of young people, communities, treatment and availability), 2002 Updated Drug Strategy, with its emphasis on *reducing the harm that drugs cause to society – communities, individuals and their families*, and the 2008 Drug Strategy, *Drugs: protecting families and communities*.

Chapter 6 will examine the changes in policy since the change to a coalition government, which has potentially increased the concern to deal with alcohol misuse. A brief history of alcohol treatment will be given, a discussion on whether alcoholism should be treated as a disease and what can be done to deal with this. It will discuss ethnicity and alcohol and the latest strategies.

Chapter 7 will focus on professional practice issues and approaches. This will include the wheel-of-change model of Prochaska and DiClemente, motivational interviewing, pro-social modelling, what works and what doesn't work with clients. The intention of this chapter is to demonstrate that the knowledge and skills of social workers are ideally suited to working with substance-misusing clients. This chapter is very practice oriented and case examples will be used extensively.

Chapter 8 will be a conclusion, drawing the themes of the book together, in particular client empowerment with notions of enforcement and good practice. It will consider the relationship between the statutory and voluntary sector and inter-professional co-operation. It will examine ways that an understanding of substance misuse can enhance professional practice in order to further develop an understanding of the complexities of individual development and behaviour when substances are involved. Finally, it will look at how social work intervention can ultimately be empowering.

Learning features

This book is written with the aim of encouraging the reader to be an active participant. It is permeated with a variety of exercises. On occasion, it invites you as a practitioner to think about particular cases and how you would approach them.

It also, more generally, asks the reader to use the internet to discover useful sources of knowledge and information. One essential task is to reflect on the knowledge gained and to apply this to your learning.

The book brings out the tension between voluntarism and compulsion in professional practice. Further, when is it appropriate to encourage clients to abstain from substances and when should there be a move towards less harmful (harm-minimisation) techniques? Social work cannot just be about letting clients 'do their own thing' and in terms of child protection we have to take seriously the implications of what having a drug habit implies. What must not happen is that decisions are made without a full assessment out of fear or ignorance. We owe it to our clients to be professional.

This book has been carefully mapped to the new Professional Capabilities Framework for Social Workers in England and will help you to develop the appropriate standards at the right level. These standards are:

- **Professionalism**
  Identify and behave as a professional social worker committed to professional development.
- **Values and ethics**
  Apply social work ethical principles and values to guide professional practice.
- **Diversity**
  Recognise diversity and apply anti-discriminatory and anti-oppressive principles in practice.
- **Rights, justice and economic well-being**
  Advance human rights and promote social justice and economic well-being.
- **Knowledge**
  Apply knowledge of social sciences, law and social work practice theory.
- **Judgement**
  Use judgement and authority to intervene with individuals, families and communities to promote independence, provide support and prevent harm, neglect and abuse.
- **Critical reflection and analysis**
  Apply critical reflection and analysis to inform and provide a rationale for professional decision-making.
- **Contexts and organisations**
  Engage with, inform, and adapt to changing contexts that shape practice. Operate effectively within your own organisational frameworks and contribute to the development of services and organisations. Operate effectively within multi-agency and inter-professional settings.
- **Professional leadership**
  Take responsibility for the professional learning and development of others through supervision, mentoring, assessing, research, teaching, leadership and management.

References to these standards will be made throughout the text and you will find a diagram of the Professional Capability Framework in Appendix 1 at the end of the book.

The third edition takes account of the latest drug and alcohol strategies (Home Office, 2010 and 2012 respectively).

WEBSITES

www.alcohol-drugs.co.uk/DANOS.htm
This will give you details of the occupational standards for drugs and alcohol.

The National Treatment Agency (NTA) became part of Public Health England on 1 April 2013. There is a publications archive for NTA materials at **www.nta.nhs.uk/publications.aspx**.

Chapter 1

The links between social work practice and working with substance-misusing clients

Introduction

In this chapter we will examine social work theory and practice and link this to working with substance misusers. You will be encouraged to identify your preconceptions and values and to reflect on stereotypical notions around this client group.

The chapter will explore issues of values and ethics in relation to working with substance misusers and issues of discrimination and anti-discriminatory practice. We will examine the implications of these and some sociological perspectives such as labelling and subculture and the impact of these on effective practice.

Initial thoughts and perspectives on substance misusers and implications for practice

Whatever branch of social work you are involved in will lead to you meeting and getting involved with clients who have a variety of personal issues and difficulties. It is hard to imagine a situation where you will not encounter a person who takes more substances than they should. This may be legal or illegal. Examples of the former may include cigarettes, prescription drugs and alcohol and the latter cannabis and opiates like heroin or morphine. Alcoholism is very dangerous but not illegal and the likelihood is that you will know of relatives, work colleagues or friends who get intoxicated more often than is good for them or those around them. Drugs are all around us and we ignore their effects at our peril. We develop views on drugs and indeed may have tried illegal substances at raves, parties or many of the social gatherings where they are present. By far the largest group of clients passing through the drug action teams are non-offenders. In one drug action team it was 78 per cent, with 22 per cent of these being self-referrals.

Clients will bring with them a multiplicity of concerns, including relationship issues, financial problems, housing, risk of offending, health (both physical and mental), behavioural problems (including anger, aggression and other difficulties). It is the skill of the practitioner to work with the client to prioritise these and to draw on their own knowledge and skills and the knowledge and skills of others to maximise the potential of the client.

RESEARCH SUMMARY

The Department of Health supplies annual information on the drug situation in the UK to the European Monitoring Centre for Drugs and Drug Addiction (EMCDDA). The web link for this is given at the end of the chapter. What we can learn from this is that the prevalence among adults has been relatively stable in recent years in the UK. However, use of cocaine and ecstasy has increased, with young adults under the age of 35 significantly likely to use drugs. The prevalence of drug use is even higher for those under 25. What is more encouraging is that there has been a significant decline in the use of drugs by those aged 16 to 24, again with the exception of cocaine and ecstasy. Young people appear to be continuing to use drugs into their thirties. Drug use among schoolchildren doubled between the years 1998 to 2002, to a lifetime prevalence of around 20 per cent, but now appears to have stabilised.

The latest report by the EMCDDA was published in 2013, entitled European Drug Report. Trends and developments 2013. *The web link is given at the end of the chapter.*

The report details trends and changes in substance use across Europe and here the main drugs will be discussed. The age categories used are adults (15–64 years), young adults in the last 12 months (15–34 years) and lifetime of students (15–16 years).

Amphetamines: in the UK, prevalence estimates of lifetime use by adults is 11.5 per cent of the population, for young adults in the previous year, 1.4 per cent, and in the lifetime of students 2 per cent. The lifetime use by adults far exceeds any other European country. The next highest is Denmark with 6.2 per cent; most countries are significantly lower.

Continued

For ecstasy, lifetime use by adults is 8.6 per cent, young adults last 12 months 2.8 per cent and lifetime of students 3 per cent. Again, the UK is the highest, followed by Ireland 6.9 per cent and Czech Republic 5.8 per cent. All other countries have a far lower usage by adults with little difference for the other categories, which is encouraging.

For cannabis, adult lifetime use is 31 per cent, young adult 12.3 per cent and student 21 per cent. While not significantly different from other countries, it is disturbing that a fifth of 15–16 year-olds have used cannabis. This would imply it is part of normalised behaviour.

Other indicators are given: 52.3 drug induced deaths 15-64 year olds per million of the population is half the rate of Estonia; France is 7.9 per cent and Germany 17.9 per cent for comparison. HIV rates in the UK are 2.1 per cent among injecting drug users, France is 1.3 per cent and Germany 1.1 per cent. However, Estonia is 51.5 per cent, Latvia 40.4 per cent and Lithuania 26.5 per cent. There may be implications for the health needs of migrant workers. The UK is successful in seizing a huge amount of illegal drugs of all kinds. In some countries, including former Eastern bloc countries, seizures are tiny.

Particular groups report greater use, a wider range and more frequent taking of drugs than others. These include 'young offenders, children in need, care leavers, homeless young people and children of drug-using parents' (Department of Health, 2005, p27). These groups will be of deep concern to social workers.

ACTIVITY **1.1**

What views do you have about substance misusers? What would be a stereotypical image of a male and a female substance misuser? How far do you think that they are able to make rational decisions about taking these substances? How have your views been shaped? What do you do if you see cannabis being passed around at a party you are attending?

COMMENT

For many people the stereotype of the substance misuser is a person who inhabits a twilight world and is a somewhat unsavoury character. We gain our images from the media; often these are generated by 'scare' stories that are designed to increase newspaper circulation and to generate fear and anxiety and to create a media campaign to do something about it. These stories are used to sell papers and the headline 'substance misuser maintains a useful lifestyle while on long-term substitute heroin prescription' will not sell papers. In the past, government campaigns have tended to try to scare people not to take drugs. They probably work for those not inclined to take them anyway, but are not helpful in deterring those who take drugs socially and perhaps irregularly and who do not see this as a problem. For men, the typical image is of a young white male, but we know that this is not the case. As we will see, the number of black and ethnic minority substance misusers is increasing and it is essential that support services are targeted at all members of the community. For women, the image is also mainly of white and young; however, again this is too simplistic. The danger is that if we start off with any fixed ideas we will fail to be receptive to the dangers of substance misuse. This is a social problem that affects all social classes, gender and races and no assumptions should be made on the question of who abuses substances. Furthermore, the age of the onset of misuse can be frighteningly early.

Under the chilling heading 'Public gallery of dead young women', Blackman (2004) describes the newspaper treatment of Leah Betts, Julia Dawes, Lorna Spinks and Rachel Whitear. All of these four beautiful young women had their lives tragically cut short by drugs. In the newspapers pictures of them were interspersed with pictures of their grieving parents and the shock campaign that followed promoted abstinence. Nobody would want to encroach or criticise the motives of the parents and indeed abstinence from drugs like ecstasy would be ideal, but we do not live in an ideal society. Young clubbers still enjoy taking ecstasy and these tragic deaths have not stopped them from doing so. Is this rational? Perhaps a policy that gave young people advice on how much and when to drink water when taking ecstasy in clubs and testing tablets for purity might save more lives? Ideally we might want to promote abstinence, but harm minimisation is likely to save more lives.

In classical criminology, from the late eighteenth century, there was an assumption that people acted rationally and the law must apply equally to all. For Cesare Beccaria (1738–1794), human behaviour was based on the pleasure–pain principle and punishment had to be uniform and apply to all (Hopkins Burke, 2001). Punishment should be linked to the offence and not to any of the characteristics of the offender (Lilly et al., 2007). Of course this ignores differences between individuals and the rationale that the pursuit of hedonism is simply one of chasing unadulterated pleasure. Following on from the classical school came the notion of positivism, advocated by Cesare Lombroso (1835–1909), and 'multi-factual explanations of crime' to try to explain what being human means (Lilly et al., 2007). Positivism was a biological approach to deviance and was therefore at variance with the notion of free will. Positivism asserted that the origins of deviance could be located within the pathology of the individual or their families (Downes and Rock, 2011). More recently psychological positivist explanations of deviance have linked behaviour to conditioning and human development. This provides us with an understanding of how we develop into adults and the influences that shape our lives (see Crawford and Walker, 2003).

Passing around cannabis at a party is illegal and is still a serious offence (the different classes of drugs are discussed in a later chapter). The level needed before the possibility of the offence of supplying the drug is not as high as many imagine but passing drugs to friends is classed as supplying. Cannabis has been regraded to a class B drug, the maximum penalty for possession is five years and for supplying is 14 years. Both can also include an unlimited fine in addition to custody. It is doubtful whether people who take this drug appreciate the potential level of penalty, especially for supplying. There is therefore an element of risk to an individual in just being around the drug. People continue to take cannabis; many would choose to ignore seeing it at the party, some would leave, some people might report this to the police. More recent evidence is emerging of the links between using cannabis and mental illness. Certainly this is not an innocent drug and mixing it with tobacco, a carcinogen, is not a healthy option.

ACTIVITY **1.2**

Do substance-misusing clients merit the use of scarce resources from social work, health and other agencies? Should these clients be seen as responsible for their actions? Are your views the same for alcohol misusers?

COMMENT

These are not easy questions to answer, although a quick response to the first two would be yes (of course) and yes. The reality is that in the past substance-misusing clients have not received a consistent service from the helping professions. In the 1960s and 1970s attempts to understand social deviance made links with the culture of the individual, often linked to social class and conformity to a different set of cultural norms and values than the mainstream. This could result in tension and individuals feeling cut off from society, what was called 'a state of anomie or normlessness'. David Matza described 'techniques of neutralization' to overcome moral objections to deviant behaviour, i.e. overcoming lawful behaviour by rational statements like: I didn't mean to do it, everybody does it, they can afford it, nobody got hurt, I did it for my friends, and so on (Downes and Rock, 2011). Drugs can be a normal practice within a subculture where there is a rejection of the usual rules of society. This can have a two-fold effect. Firstly, it can lead to more punitive policies to counteract this but secondly, it implies that, for a large number of people, drug use is normal (Blackman, 2004). Recent research has shown that recreational use of drugs is not necessarily a short-term activity or experiment linked to peers, but is an activity that endures. Furthermore, young adults start the habit without using during their adolescence and others who had stopped decided to restart when older (Parker et al., 1998).

This normalisation of drug use has huge implications for the social work profession. Certainly drugs will be encountered by professionals in their practice and a simplistic response of 'just stop' or 'just stop or else' will not do. Drugs are a reality and social work practice needs to catch up to embrace this added complexity in its work with clients.

Gossop (2000) makes the point that the arrival of ecstasy, which quickly became a popular drug in youth dance culture, produced the same type of outrage that had occurred with cannabis and LSD in the 1960s. This was due to notions of hedonism and links to the popular music culture. Cannabis remains a popular drug among the young and Gossop also comments that cannabis users continue to be criminalised and imprisoned, which he sees as both expensive and pointless, as well as the wrong target for police intervention.

How can we apply this all to social work with substance misusers? We should not be put off working with a client simply because they are taking substances, often as a palliative to other problems in their lives. Nigel Horner gives an option for state intervention:

> *To engage with potentially vulnerable families, groups and communities – to prevent the need for statutory intervention and to address the causes of their difficulties, which may be located in discrimination, oppression, marginalisation, poverty and deprivation.* (Horner, 2003, p15)

Substance misusers need support and encouragement to gain or regain control of their lives and this will require a multiplicity of responses that will be explored through this book. They are no more or less deserving of support because of their habit but they may require additional assessment, resources and forms of intervention as a consequence. Helping clients to understand how they need to modify and maintain their lifestyle is a social work skill. Daniel Keller (2003) makes the interesting point that:

> *In working with substance abusers one is frequently impressed by the capacity of these patients to expose themselves to high-risk situations and conditioned cues with hardly the slightest awareness that they are heading for trouble ... Essentially, the patient makes a decision or set of decisions that does not appear to be related to the desire to drink or use drugs but in fact brings the patient ever closer to risky environments in which cues for cravings are likely to abound.* (Keller, 2003, p97)

Social workers can deal with situations like this and the concept of relapse is covered in Chapter 7. It is not for the social worker to moralise on the lifestyle of the client just because they are taking substances; however, it may well have a consequence on the client's ability to care for others and this may well be a concern for the social worker. The client will have to live with the consequences of their behaviour on their own lives but the social worker has a duty of care to consider the impact of this behaviour on others. However, there must be a full assessment and it has been pointed out to me by specialists working in the drugs field that social workers can get very anxious about child care, even when the client is stable on a long-term harm-minimisation programme. The concern is that anxiety and ignorance of drugs and the rehabilitation process can lead to unhelpful interventions to the detriment of the client and their family. This book will examine this further in subsequent chapters.

ACTIVITY 1.3

What is the point in working with substance-misusing clients? Is social work relevant to this group?

COMMENT

Ray Jones, chair of the British Association of Social Workers, commented on the need for the profession to stay true to its core values. He talked about what made social work distinctive, which he attributed to it having 'a cluster of values, competences and roles'. He articulated them as follows:

- having a concern for social justice;
- confronting discrimination;
- valuing people, not rejecting;

- with realism as well as idealism;
- seeing people in context;
- recognising and developing people's strengths and skills;
- problem-solving in partnership;
- enabling and facilitating;
- with a focus on relationships;
- providing structure and space within chaotic experiences;
- being an ally in promoting independence and choice;
- harnessing resources;
- taking actions to protect and control where necessary.

(Jones, 2006)

These points apply very appropriately to working with substance misusers. The first two are about fairness. When we see a group that is discriminated against, then as professionals it is our role to ensure that equal opportunities are respected. This flows into the third point that we do not reject people for what and who they are. We understand that while people make choices, often this is as a result of their life experiences and feelings of self-worth. We never write people off as 'damaged goods'. That does not mean that social work avoids tough decisions. We have to remember that we have a duty to look after the welfare of children and this might result in them being taken away permanently from their parents and carers. Furthermore, we might need to section a person because we have taken a decision that they have a mental health problem that requires compulsory treatment. We might decide that a substance misuser is not prepared to change and therefore is not amenable to being worked with at the present time. This doesn't mean that in the future the person might not be ready to change. In Chapter 7 you will learn that this time is referred to as the 'pre-contemplation' stage.

We need, as Jones says, to be realistic. For substance misusers, the amount of resources available is not bottomless and we need to be realistic in what we can achieve with the client. It is important that we do not see the client as a label relating to their substance misuse problem. Stereotyping individuals takes away their identity and encourages them to perform to the label in order to obtain a service. The term 'deviancy amplification' is linked to the concept of moral panic, a term coined by Jock Young back in 1971 when he researched recreational drug use in North London. Essentially what this means is that the media exaggerate the effects of an issue, in this case drugs, which then produces a response by policy-makers and police. The public concern generated leads to drug misusers being targeted and consequentially more arrests, which are then seen as justification for the raised concerns. The client group concerned become more marginalised and alienated in the process and fall back on their own subculture as a response (see Hopkins Burke, 2001, for a discussion on labelling theories).

Seeing people in the context of their life experiences means that we work with them to understand why they are in their present situation. Psychodynamic counselling is based on the work of Freud and his successors and assumes that behaviour stems from conscious and unconscious thought processes. Counselling that focuses on early childhood, relationships and (maternal) deprivation is derived from this approach (Payne, 1997).

What is it, therefore, that the skilled practitioner brings to working with clients? It is the ability to form a relationship with the client and through this flows: 'the mobilization of the capacities of the individual and the mobilization of community resources; through it also flow the skills in interviewing, study, diagnosis, and treatment' (Biestek, 1957, p4).

This is the basis of working with clients and drawing on their strengths to change their life situation. The essence of the relationship is to empower the client to make considered decisions and these should be working towards a 'shared higher aim' between client and practitioner. This will be discussed further in Chapter 6 but the essence is that, as in task-centred casework, the client decides on their future life plans and jointly ensures that these are realistic, achievable and how the process of change will progress. Possible pitfalls can be rehearsed and solutions found in advance to minimise the danger of failure. With substance misusers, when relapse is always possible, what to do if there is a relapse can also be discussed in advance. Working with substance misusers does not require the practitioner to have an intimate knowledge of all substances, but a clear perception of what the problems and issues are for the client.

Many substance-misusing clients do not see a solution for their difficulties or they can become 'stuck'. It is not the intention here to stereotype the client – a potential danger to avoid. They may have exhausted the patience of their partners and their families. The practitioner may be the person to give them back some feeling of self-worth. Planning detox and after-care can be achieved with people who have misused substances over many years and clients should never be written off. Referring on to agencies that can offer intensive support may be necessary if the client's time has traditionally been used to find the means to pay for drugs. If this time is liberated, something will need to fill the gap. What resources are needed will require communication with community agencies and referrals on to them. The client may need support to ensure that they get to interviews and access these resources. We will discuss in a later chapter how a client gains access to treatment.

Residential detox for opiates (including heroin and methadone) can be achieved in 14 days, for stimulants (including amphetamines and crack cocaine) it can take 7–14 days, prescription (i.e. legal) drugs (antidepressants and benzodiazepines) can take up to a month and poly drug (a combination of the above) can be even longer. Just removing the physical dependence on drugs through a detox will not stop the client from returning to drugs. It is the skill of the practitioner, working with the client, giving them the encouragement and opportunity to change that has the potential to achieve this. The client may well need to move away from former associates and start afresh. This is a prospect that most of us would find to be very daunting.

The essence of working with substance misusers is thus a mixture of social work knowledge, values and skills, where there is a need for some specific knowledge around substances. This process is not a static one. The social worker has an implicit theoretical model that they use on a daily basis but this is constantly 'reconstructed' and 'deconstructed'. It is easy for a practitioner to feel de-skilled but the confidence that the underpinning knowledge and skills are present should enable the practitioner to take on new knowledge and to incorporate this into their professional practice.

CASE STUDY

A young deaf woman with learning difficulties, in residential care, has a social worker from a disabilities team. She has been in the care of the local authority all of her life and does not have family support. She started to take crack cocaine and the residential home wanted her to leave. Her behaviour deteriorated and she started staying out all night and displayed anti-social behaviour tendencies, including shouting in the care home. The social worker, who was very committed to the client, did not have much knowledge of substance abuse and felt lost, not knowing what to do next.

The social worker contacted the local drug action team (DAT). The job of the DAT is to act as a one-stop shop for specialisms and resources and a focal point for treatment. We will discuss the different tiers of treatment later in the book. There is a need to get professions out of their silo thinking and be more strategic. The objective is to manage risk and to stabilise the client. The DAT uses a Common Assessment Framework and risk assessment tool and triage is used to provide a quick health assessment for the client. In this way the health needs can be quickly appraised and treatment started. (DATs have now been renamed Drug and Alcohol Action Teams (DAATs).)

One big problem was the accommodation and the need to sort out some support for her substance misuse. She needed to get into rehabilitation but the problem was that most residential rehab places used 'talk therapy' and she couldn't hear. The solution was to keep her in the present accommodation and to provide additional skilled support to take place in her home. There was a danger that once out of there she would become homeless and there were no other suitable places available. She had mental health issues that needed addressing also and the drug action co-ordinator put her in touch with the dual diagnosis team to address these.

This was a case that could have been akin to a merry-go-round where the different services sought to offload their responsibilities on to a different specialism. Instead the drug action team acted as a resource and advice giver to the social worker who maintained responsibility for the client, who then received the appropriate support that spanned drugs advice, counselling, housing and mental health.

CASE STUDY

Janine is a British female aged 26 years. She made contact with the drug action team in March 2005, when she received a triage assessment at the drop-in centre. Her education had been disrupted as she had had a child at the age of 15; however, she was literate and numerate. She stated that she was drug and alcohol free, but had used crack cocaine twice a week for 10 years and also alcohol daily. She was receiving income support and was currently living with a friend in the borough. She did not have contact with her family.

Janine has five children; all are in care, with the youngest being 10 weeks when she made contact. Her visit to the DAT was part of the agreement she had with Children's Services.

The local authority eligibility scheme use a standard matrix to assess eligibility. A blank matrix is provided below. Have a go at completing this for Janine. What further information would you like to have on Janine?

Eligibility matrix

Critical = 4 Substantial = 3 Moderate = 2 Low = 1 N/A = 0

Threat to life
Physical health problems
Mental health problems
Abuse or neglect
Personal care
Domestic routines
Choice and control
Family and social roles/responsibilities
Work, learning and education
Key relationships and support systems

As a result of completing this matrix a score will be generated that can affect access to treatment, especially expensive residential provision. We need to be clear about what information we need on our clients and why it is needed. This case has a number of important areas that you might like to list. Clearly child care is high on the agenda with all of Janine's children being in care and the newness of her youngest child. Is she a safe person to have care and control of this new-born baby? What is stable and what is vulnerable in her life? What about her accommodation needs? Where does she get her support from?

CASE STUDY *continued*

Janine was given a key worker immediately in the drug action team who began to work with her on her commitment to remain off drugs (relapse). The key worker discussed residential rehabilitation options, which included a preference for a mother and baby unit. Children's services stated that attendance at a mother and

CASE STUDY *continued*

baby unit had been agreed as part of an action plan for the family and this was communicated to the DAT. Unfortunately, later on, after a mix-up over funding and Janine's continued good progress, this was turned down as she scored under 30 against the eligibility criteria. Three months later Janine started at a day centre and was referred to another resource for structured counselling. She began three days per week parenting skills classes, was given formal ID and she registered with a GP. She continued with supervised access to her children. After a further two months Janine admitted to the key worker that she had been using alcohol.

In this case the relapse was short-lived. A further community care assessment was made that was turned down as the client had maintained abstinence in the community for a long time. The goal for the client was to stabilise her life. Getting her children back to live with her was not seen as realistic in the short term and she was working towards unsupervised access to them. Janine agreed to voluntarily undergo supervised urine tests, to attend crack workshops and to attend Alcoholics Anonymous meetings. The key worker continued to work with the housing department to get her a place of her own.

After a further three months she was granted unsupervised access to her youngest child, who was now aged 13 months. Children's services no longer insisted on residential rehab for Janine. Her situation was therefore not completely resolved a year after seeking support.

For crack users it may be beneficial to attend workshops to talk about crack and its effects, health, cravings and urges, life skills. A groupwork approach can be very useful for this. In terms of health, this can be divided into physical and mental. On the physical side too much smoking of crack can lead to breathing problems and there is a danger of death from overdosing, especially if the drug is mixed with other drugs, including alcohol as Janine admitted to doing. On the mental health side, frequent use of crack can bring on panic attacks and the person can develop symptoms of anxiety and paranoia. If there has been a background of mental health problems then the use of crack can result in them reappearing. How the person takes crack can affect their health also. Sharing pipes (it is predominantly smoked) can lead to increased risk of contracting the hepatitis C virus. Crack houses are unsafe places to be especially for women and there is a risk of sexual exploitation in places like this, as well as for women to fund their habit. Sexual health is an area to be explored with Janine.

At the time of writing, the cost of buying a rock of crack is between £10 and £20. It is sometimes sold cheaper by the slice, so is affordable by the young. It has an immediate effect but this is short term and can result in a craving for more. The high of exhilaration is replaced by a down that leaves the person depressed and possibly feeling sick. These cravings may be masked by other drugs such as alcohol.

For people who have taken crack it has been found that alternative therapies can be beneficial. These include acupuncture, reiki and shiatsu. Sleep techniques can also be beneficial. Within the support of the social worker and other professionals the client can be given support and counselling, and harm-reduction advice, including safer practices to minimise the dangers of infection. Clients who are injecting can get exchange needles, filters, sterile wipes and the other equipment that they need to minimise the danger of contracting hepatitis B or C or HIV through sharing. The social worker does not need to know about all the equipment and how the user takes the substance; however, they should know how to refer on to the drug action team and how the process works.

In later chapters you will learn about how services are provided; the DAT can be a direct lead into all services from general drop-in and advice to residential rehabilitation. There will be triage services on hand for fast health assessments and the DAT is likely to have formal links to children's and family teams, adult services, mental health, housing, probation and the youth offending service. The huge advance in recent years is the speed of response. In one DAT they could offer an assessment to residential drug treatment within the day, with treatment to commence in 24 hours if they were seen as high risk. This would have required a complete care plan to have been formulated within this time. The key point here is that there is active partnership, not offloading of the client. The DAT has close links to social services and works with the child protection and children and families teams. This can be a significant part of the work. In the case of Janine, that has been discussed. It is questionable whether the substance-misuse problem has been diagnosed and worked with in the past. This might have been because the client was not prepared to admit to the extent of her substance-misuse problem or it may not have been questioned.

The use of reflective practice with substance misusers

In the introduction it was mentioned that the social worker will look to their knowledge and experience to make sense of what they are experiencing in a new situation. Sometimes this can lead to a feeling of being de-skilled and so there is a need to be able to make sense of what is happening in the here and now. The DANOS occupational standards are specific on reflection and it is helpful to consider their message. In terms of one's own practice, it is important to understand the limits of the social work role and responsibilities. On a personal level, as was discussed in Activity 1.1, the behaviour of the client might be very different from that of the social worker, so it is very important to remain non-judgemental. This means that the worker must be clear about their own beliefs and feelings and how these might conflict with the client's.

There is a need therefore to reflect on the effects of the intervention on the client as well as the reasons for the intervention. This might lead the social worker to think about their training needs and also to keep up to date on the research in substance misuse – for example, the social worker might favour abstinence as an outcome, but the client might want to maintain themselves on a level of prescribed medication. There is evidence that long-term substitute prescribing is more successful as a form of maintenance than abstinence. The desire for this by the client ought to be respected.

Of central importance to the process of reflection is the use of supervision. This is contained within the DANOS occupational standards as it is in the social work ones. It is a point of common interest across the professions. It is a process to enable the practitioner to be appropriately self-critical, to develop an agenda and prioritise the effective use of time. Working with substance misusers can be frustrating, challenging yet rewarding when the client is ready to move on and face up to their personal issues. The additional knowledge about drugs should not take the place of social work's traditional skills and values. It will also need skilled supervision if the practitioner is to practise effectively:

> *Supervision as a forum for reflection allows social workers to reflect their experiences and emotions and through critical reflection to understand them in the wider context of work and thus to look for alternative methods of reaction, action and agency. The individual practical experience as the focus of reflection does not mean the exclusion of education, training, knowledge, research and science, or anything in favour of mere practical knowledge. Human action is also unavoidably complicated including different kinds of emotional, psychological, material, social and cultural dynamics, so social work supervision cannot be reduced either on cognitive or emotional sides.*
> (Karvinen-Niinikoski, 2004, p32)

CHAPTER SUMMARY

In this chapter you have been introduced to some of the complexities when working with substance misusers. We started the chapter by examining preconceived ideas about substance misusers and examined implications for practice. We learnt that much drug taking has become normalised within many people's behaviour and that simply advocating an abstinence approach does not always work. Harm-minimisation approaches can be more effective and have implications for social workers in that a substance misuser who is stable on medication can stay like this successfully for years until they finally decide to stop. Social workers have the skills to engage productively with substance misusers and examples were given on this. In the past social work did not consistently choose to do so, to the detriment of its clients. Julian Buchanan, who has researched extensively on substance misuse, concluded his article that:

> *Many problem drug users have endured a difficult and disadvantaged childhood, have been immersed in a dehumanising drug centred lifestyle for most of their adult life, and have been subject to considerable prejudice and discrimination. There is an urgent need to develop services that are able to advocate on behalf of recovering drug users, tackle discrimination and begin understanding and addressing the underlying causes that cultivate, foster and sustain problem drug use.* (Buchanan, 2006, p57)

The knowledge, skills and values advocated as being necessary for effective work with substance misusers are inextricably linked with social work.

FURTHER READING

If you have found the information on crime and rule breaking useful in putting drug misuse into context, then **Downes, D and Rock, P** (2011) *Understanding deviance* (sixth edn) Oxford: Oxford University Press, is a good book.

Two books on the normalisation of adolescent drug use are **Parker, H, Aldridge, J and Measham, F** (1998) *Illegal leisure.* London: Routledge; and **Blackman, S** (2004) *Chilling out.* Buckingham: Open University Press.
A good book to give you a balanced overview of drugs is by **Gossop, M** (2000) *Living with drugs.* Aldershot: Ashgate.

A good edited book that will introduce you to a variety of ways of working with substance-misusing clients is **Rotgers, F, Morgenstern, J and Walters, S T** (eds) (2003) *Treating substance abuse. Theory and technique.* London and New York: Guilford. This covers both the 12 steps method of Alcoholics Anonymous and also psychoanalytic (the chapter by Daniel Keller is very pertinent) and behavioural approaches.

For an interesting discussion on the 'problem drug user' and whether there should be a medical or social approach to treatment in the UK, see **Buchanan, J** (2006) Understanding problematic drug use: a medical matter or a social issue?, *British Journal of Community Justice,* 4(2), 47–57.

WEBSITES

www.talktofrank.com/
A useful starting point to gain information about drugs.

Look up some drugs, including crack, and see what information is available.

www.ukfocalpoint.org.uk
For useful information on the drug situation in the UK, the Department of Health supply annual information to the European Monitoring Centre for Drugs and Drug Addiction.

www.emcdda.europa.eu
EMCDDA website. Very useful source for information on policing and practice, legislation, etc.

www.emcdda.europa.en/publcations/edr/trends-development/2013 for the European Drug Report, Trends and Developments 2013.

Chapter 2

The nature and extent of drug taking in the United Kingdom

A C H I E V I N G   A   S O C I A L   W O R K   D E G R E E

This chapter will help you to develop the following capabilities, to the appropriate level, from the **Professional Capabilities Framework**.

- Professionalism – Identify and behave as a professional social worker, committed to professional development.
- Knowledge – Apply knowledge of social sciences, law and social work practice theory.
- Contexts and organisations – Engage with, inform, and adapt to changing contexts that shape practice. Operate effectively within your own organisational frameworks and contribute to the development of services and organisations. Operate effectively within multi-agency and inter-professional settings.
- Interventions and skills – Use judgement and authority to intervene with individuals, families and communities to promote independence, provide support and prevent harm, neglect and abuse.

See Appendix 1 for the Professional Capabilities Framework diagram.

This chapter will also introduce you to the following standards as set out in the 2008 social work subject benchmark statement.

5.1.2 The service delivery context.
5.1.4 Social work theory.
5.1.5 The nature of social work practice.

Introduction

In this chapter you will learn about the nature and extent of drug taking in the United Kingdom. This is essential knowledge as you will undoubtedly encounter clients who have used and abused substances in their lives (including alcohol). We will examine the available data, including the Home Office, the New English and Welsh Arrestee Drug Abuse Monitoring (NEW-ADAM) and make some comparisons with other European countries.

We will examine the points where professionals and substance abusers meet and what strategies will be useful to engage with reluctant clients. We will look at models of care for the treatment of adult drug misusers, drawing on documents from the National Treatment Agency, and also examine the differences in approach when working with younger people.

The nature and extent of drug taking in the United Kingdom

RESEARCH SUMMARY

A report undertaken on behalf of the Home Office by the University of Essex examined the use of substances by young people drawing on extended self-report questionnaires. The cohort was predominantly white, male and aged 15 and 16. Black and Asian ethnicities were 'deliberately over-represented'. The final sample also over-represented those with longer offending histories and it was accepted that this was 'likely to exaggerate the severity of substance abuse and offending amongst young offenders'.

It found that a large minority of the sample suffered from low self-esteem, especially women. Many of the cohort did not have effective coping mechanisms and used alcohol or drugs as a form of escape. Over 20 per cent reported committing drug dealing type offences at least 20 times in the past 12 months. The drugs of choice tended to be alcohol, cannabis and tobacco. There were signs of a normalised use of these drugs and young people were using a wider range of drugs than had been the case 20 years before. There was no evidence that the age of informants on trying drugs for the first time was getting younger, nor that heroin and cocaine dependence had become commonplace among those under the age of 16. Users might use alcohol, cannabis and tobacco more heavily than hitherto but this did not show an escalation to Class A or Class B drugs. Forty per cent or more of the cohort acknowledged the link between their substance use and their offending (Hammersley et al., 2003, ppviii–ix).

The 2008/9 British Crime Survey estimates that 18.7 per cent of 16-to 24-year-olds used cannabis in the last year; this was around 84 per cent of last year's illicit drug users (Hoare, 2009). The British Crime Survey in 2000 estimated that 34 per cent of those aged between 16 and 59 had tried an illegal drug, 11 per cent of these in the last year. The New English and Welsh Arrestee Drug Abuse Monitoring (NEW-ADAM) programme in its first two years showed that 80 per cent of those arrested had used an illegal drug in the past 12 months. The level in the general population is 12 per cent (Bennett and Holloway, 2005). Clearly drug taking is an activity indulged in by many people in the United Kingdom. It is a serious problem that cannot be ignored, especially by social workers.

When do clients with substance-misuse problems come to the attention of social workers?

It is essential that no assumptions are made about the likelihood that clients are unlikely to be taking any substances, although in some circumstances substance mis-use could be as a result of taking an excess of licit drugs rather than illicit ones. It is also important to include the possibility of alcohol misuse as well as drugs. Remember that drugs and alcohol misuse are not limited to any social class and other aspects like employment and health. Social workers need to be sensitive to the possibility of substance misuse and not to discount it.

ACTIVITY 2.1

Think of a situation where the possibility of substance misuse might not be immediately apparent. What assumptions might the social worker make in order to ignore the possibility of substance misuse?

COMMENT

It is easy to produce a stereotype of the substance misuser but in truth anybody can be susceptible. It is not helpful to make assumptions about who might or might not take substances and in this context the report by the Advisory Council on the Misuse of Drugs (2003) contains some worrying statistics. It estimated that in England and Wales there are between 200,000 and 300,000 children where one or both parents have serious drug problems. This is 2–3 per cent of children under the age of 16. Furthermore, only 64 per cent of mothers and 37 per cent of fathers were still living with their children. Perhaps not surprisingly this was skewed towards those with the most serious problems. Although relatives cared for most of these children, about 5 per cent ended up in care. In Scotland the report estimated that between 41,000 and 59,000 children had a problem drug-using parent, which represents 4–6 per cent of all children under 16.

The report further points out that multiple drug use is associated with socioeconomic deprivation and other factors that affect the ability to parent a child and this can lead to referrals to social services in a number of different contexts. The child's personal health and development can also be affected at all stages. The risk of harm might be direct in terms of inadequate supervision or there might be a history of separation and poor accommodation. The consequences might include a failure to thrive, poor health, cognitive and/or behavioural difficulties, poor educational attainment, etc.

CASE STUDY

John, a young deaf boy, refuses to go to school and his parents are worried. They like the school and can't understand what is going wrong. They take him to the school and bring him home and you understand that they are very supportive of him and encourage him to bring friends home. As the social worker you have been pleased that he has adapted to the mainstream school.

You question your assumption that John has adapted to the school and after conversing with him you discover that he feels excluded from some activities. A couple of the teachers fail to ensure that he can follow what they are saying in the class. They do not look at him directly when they speak and they do not give him written details of when activities that he would like to join in are taking place. He is too embarrassed to ask them himself. John doesn't want to admit it, but the social worker also begins to suspect that he is being bullied by some of the older children.

As the DrugScope DrugData Update report from 12 May 2006 comments, some people might imagine that young deaf people are unlikely to get involved in drugs and the first reaction to the above short case study is not to think about possible drug issues. However, in terms of vulnerability the possibility of developing drug problems might be more severe than in the case of their hearing peers, with the additional problem of facing more barriers to accessing information and support. The risk of isolation can be more severe and the pressure to join in with the school culture can lead to stress, isolation, bullying, etc. Taking drugs may seem a way to gain acceptance. Valentine et al. (2003), cited in the above DrugScope report, confirmed that young deaf people found it difficult to participate in school culture. There was a high level of distress, bullying and other problems. Acceptance and recognition could be gained from misuse of alcohol and drugs. Cox and Jackson (1998), also cited in the above DrugScope report, found in a survey of 11–24 year olds who were profoundly deaf that 8 in 10 had been offered drugs at some point in their lives and 54 per cent had taken up drug offers, most commonly cannabis. Fifteen per cent had used drugs while taking alcohol.

The parents/carers may not know about drugs nor be aware of the symptoms of substance misuse. As the report points out, it is difficult for deaf people to 'overhear' conversations in the same way as their hearing peers. As a result DrugScope and the National Deaf Children's Society have co-operated to assess drug educational needs and to produce specific educational materials.

Models of care for treating adult substance misusers

Models of care, published by the National Treatment Agency (NTA) in 2002, is the national framework for the commissioning of drug treatment for adults in England. It is designed to meet the needs of local diverse communities and is based on a systems approach that links the key agencies that come into contact with substance misusers. The NTA is responsible for monitoring its national implementation. The primary focus is on adult drug users rather than alcohol service provision although the framework is relevant to alcohol treatment services. The project was set up to meet the objectives of the 1998 10-year drug strategy to get more users into treatment. It also sought 'to enhance the planning, commissioning and provision of drug treatment services' (NTA, 2002, p8).

Drug treatment services appeared for the first time in the NHS in 1998 and similarly has the goal of 'putting patients at the heart of the health service' (NTA, 2002, p8). The national target from 1998 was to increase the numbers of people in treatment by 100 per cent by 2008. Drug action teams (DATs) have the role of co-ordinating the strategic response to meet the national drugs strategy. DATs also work closely with crime and disorder reduction partnerships (CDRPs). At the time that *Models of care* was published the role of the primary care trusts became central in the provision of drug and alcohol treatment. PCTs were abolished on 1 April 2013 and responsibility now resides in Public Health England, Public Health Wales, NHS Health Scotland and the Public Health Agency for Northern Ireland.

What is the four-tiered model that operates in England?

Services to drug and alcohol misusers have been arranged into four tiers of service provision. These apply to all types of substance misuser. Levels of need will vary and the service includes those with dual diagnosis, i.e. drug and mental health needs. The DATs have access to all four levels.

Tier 1 is for services that are available for a wide range of clients and are not necessarily solely for drug and alcohol treatment. This tier will also include assessment and referral to tiers 2 and 3 specialist services. The tier 1 service may be used in conjunction with more specialised services in tiers 2 and 3. Tier 1 services are offered by a number of different professionals including social workers, teachers, probation officers, housing, homeless persons units, medical services, etc. In terms of the need for specialist knowledge for professionals (in the context of this book), it is worth quoting from the *Models of care* (2002) NTA publication:

> *Such professionals need to be sufficiently trained and supported to work with drug (and alcohol) misusers who, as a group, are often marginalised from, and find difficulty in, accessing generic health and social care services.*
> (Models of care, 2002, p12)

It is suggested that tier 1 professionals should have links with professionals in tiers 2 and 3 for support and training purposes. The following list is given as the tier 1 services that drug misusers must have access to within health and social care:

- a full range of health (primary and secondary), social care, housing, vocational and other services;
- drug and alcohol screening, assessment and referral mechanisms to drug treatment services from generic, health, social care, housing and criminal justice services;
- the management of drug misusers in generic health, social care and criminal justice settings (e.g. police custody);
- health promotion advice and information;
- hepatitis B vaccination programmes for drug misusers and their families.

(Source: *Models of care*, 2002)

Tier 2 is for drug and alcohol services that have a low threshold to access and it includes self-referrals. These services include information and advice, needle exchange and general support that does not form part of a care plan. The services within this tier may be supplied by specialist workers, including social workers, with the same knowledge and skills base as those practising in tiers 3 and 4. Social workers can offer their expertise in areas like child care and parenting and social care needs assessment. The following list is the services that drug misusers must have access to within their local area at this level:

- drug- and alcohol-related advice, information and referral services for misusers (and their families), including easy access or drop-in facilities;
- services to reduce risks caused by injecting drug misuse, including needle

exchange facilities (in drug treatment services and pharmacy-based schemes);
- other services that minimise the spread of blood-borne diseases to drug misusers, including service-based and outreach facilities;
- services that minimise the risk of overdose and other drug- and alcohol-related harm;
- outreach services (detached, peripatetic and domiciliary) targeting high-risk and local priority groups;
- specialist drug and alcohol screening and assessment, care planning and management;
- criminal justice screening, assessment and referral services (e.g. arrest referral, CARATS*);
- motivational and brief interventions for drug and alcohol service users;
- community-based, low-threshold prescribing services.

(Source: *Models of care*, 2002)

* CARATS is the acronym for Counselling, assessment, referral, advice and through-care services – it is the foundation of the drug treatment framework available in all prisons (for more detail on prison drug policy, see Duke, 2003).

Tier 3 services are reserved for drug and alcohol misusers in structured programmes. It includes psychotherapeutic interventions as detailed in Chapter 7, e.g. cognitive-behavioural interventions, motivational interviewing, structured counselling, methadone maintenance programmes, community detoxification, or day care. After-care programmes and post residential rehabilitation or prison also fit in this tier.

All drug and alcohol misusers must have a drug assessment and a care plan, which will be provided by an agreed agency. If the plan crosses a number of domains then there will need to be a care co-ordinator who will work and liaise with the appropriate agencies. In this respect clients who have a dual diagnosis (i.e. a drug and a psychiatric diagnosis) will need to have both conditions treated in line with good practice guidelines and appropriate specialist input.

The following list is the services that drug misusers must have access to within their local area at this level:

- specific community care assessment and care management;
- new care co-ordination services for drug misusers with complex needs (provided by suitably trained practitioners);
- specialist structured community-based detoxification services;
- a range of specialist structured community-based stabilisation and maintenance prescribing services;
- shared-care prescribing and support treatment via primary care;
- a range of structured, care planned counselling and therapies;
- community-based drug treatment and testing order drug treatment (now can be incorporated into community orders following the Criminal Justice Act 2003);
- structured day programmes (in urban and semi-urban areas);
- other structured community-based drug misuse services targeting specific groups (e.g. stimulant misusers, young people in transition to adulthood, black

and minority ethnic groups, women drug misusers, drug-misusing offenders, those with HIV and AIDS, drug misusers with psychiatric problems);
- liaison drug misuse services for local social services and social care sectors (e.g. child protection, housing and homelessness, family services);
- through-care and after-care programmes or support.

(Source: *Models of care*, 2002)

Tier 4 services are divided into 4a and 4b. Tier 4a is residential drug and alcohol misuse specific services aimed at individuals with a high level of need. This level of services is usually accessed via tiers 2 and 3 and requires strong commitment by the client. Services include inpatient detoxification, residential rehabilitation and residential crisis intervention. Clients might be stabilised on substitute drugs, and be supported prior to being placed in a drug- and alcohol-free residential environment. Programmes in these establishments are usually highly structured and the drug or alcohol misuser will be allocated a care co-ordinator prior to entry to this tier. Some of these provisions have been located in psychiatric wards and it appears, not surprisingly, that specialist provision for the client is more effective than this.

Tier 4b is for highly specialist non-substance misuse specific services. There are some similarities with tier 1, as the services are non-substance misuse specific. Clients may have problematic health issues, e.g. liver damage or infectious diseases (HIV, genito-urinary, etc), and/or need forensic support for mental illness and offending behaviour. Thus in tier 4b there may be links to all the other tiers.

The following list is the services that drug misusers must have access to within their local area at this level:

- specialist drug and alcohol residential rehabilitation programmes (including a range of 12-step, faith-based and eclectic programmes);
- generic and drug specialist semi-structured residential care (e.g. half-way houses, semi-supported accommodation);
- specialist drug treatment and testing order treatment (residential options);
- inpatient drug misuse treatment, ideally provided by specialist drug misuse units, or alternatively by designated beds in generic (mental) health services;
- highly specialist forms of residential units or other residential services (in-patient, prison) with a drug misuse treatment component (e.g. women and children, crisis intervention, dual diagnosis);
- relevant tier 4b services, including HIV or liver disease units, vein clinics, residential services for young people and so forth.

(Source: *Models of care*, 2002)

In 2006 the NTA updated the *Models of care for treatment of adult drug misusers*. This had a greater focus on improving the client's treatment by viewing this as a dynamic process rather than a static one. It acknowledged that each individual journey is different, will be a process that takes place over a number of years, is often episodic, and personal factors such as health, relationships, drugs of choice, etc. will be significant. Treatment will therefore need to encompass a range of problems including alcohol and other health issues.

What this updated model did not envisage but is currently a major change in process is the inclusion of payment by results (PbR), which is favoured by the coalition government. This may have implications for the time frame over which treatment is delivered and payment will only follow on from successful short-term targets being met. The 2006 model emphasises the importance of client retention and clearly this will be essential for PbR also.

www.nta.nhs.uk/uploads/nta_modelsofcare_update_2006_moc3.pdf

Integrated care pathways

Integrated care pathways (ICPs) are designed to standardise the elements of care to ensure that treatment is both effective and efficient. It is important that there are agreed standards between the different protocols if the delivery of services is going to be seamless as clients move up and down between the different tiers. ICPs for drug and alcohol misusers have been developed for the following reasons:

- drug and alcohol misusers often have multiple problems which require effective co-ordination of treatment;
- several specialist and generic service providers may be involved in the care of a drug and alcohol misuser simultaneously or consecutively;
- a drug and alcohol misuser may have continuing and evolving care needs requiring referral to different tiers of service over time;
- ICPs ensure consistency and parity of approach nationally (i.e. a drug misuser accessing a particular treatment modality should receive the same response wherever they access care);
- ICPs ensure that access to care is not based on individual clinical decisions or historical arrangements.

(Source: *Models of care*, 2002)

Effective practice, harm minimisation and care planning

The level and intensity of treatment needs to be matched to the needs of the substance-misusing client and ranges from crisis intervention requiring urgent or emergency treatment to planned opportunities to ending substance use. It might entail something in the middle, e.g. harm minimisation, but all interventions require a care plan worked out with the client to initiate structured treatment.

Hunt (2003) reviewed the evidence on harm reduction relating to drug use, which is concerned with the reduction of harm rather than stopping the use of drugs. There is no formal definition of harm reduction but its ethos is clear. This approach, as well as doing what it says, has the goal of treating drug users with dignity, maximising the options for treatment available to the client that are achievable, and does not take a stance on the debate on decriminalising of drugs. Hunt concluded that 'methadone and other replacement therapies' did work, and this included needle exchanges. Other programmes like heroin prescribing showed promise and other approaches needed still to be evaluated. More recently, Nordt and Stohler (2006) examined the liberal stance to heroin in Zurich, Switzerland, with harm reduction measures where:

> *drug consumption rooms, needle-exchange services, low-threshold methadone programmes and heroin assisted treatments have been thought to make potential users think that harm will not arise from use of illicit drugs.*
> (Nordt and Stohler, 2006, pp1830–1834)

The results have been encouraging with a stable population of heroin users since 1994. The policy of harm reduction was supported by the population and the authors postulated that taking heroin had ceased to become an act of rebellion and instead became a manifestation of 'illness that needs therapy'. In short, it was a 'loser drug' (Nordt and Stohler, 2006, p1834). The paper, published in the *Lancet*, resulted in an editorial that declared that the refusal by the UK government to try safe injecting rooms in this country, now called drug consumption rooms (DCRs), had resulted in thousands of needless drug-related deaths in the four years since the UK Home Affairs Select Committee had recommended them in 2002. This is a situation where politics, and the need not to be seen as 'soft on drugs', could have affected the health of many injecting substance misusers. Working with these clients may put social workers in some ethical difficulty when the client is having trouble maintaining their habit and is unwilling to switch from injecting.

Buchanan has characterised UK drug policy as one 'dominated by the prohibition agenda primarily concerned with reducing the supply of drugs and strengthening deterrence' (Buchanan, 2006, p49). Under the sub-heading 'Tough on drugs, tough on drug users?' he continues by saying that the status of illicit marginalised drug users makes 'reintegration and recovery less likely' (Buchanan, 2006, p49). With the number of people that have tried an illicit drug estimated at between 3.1 and 3.7 million, there is the potential to criminalise a huge number of the population. Those who do enter the criminal justice system are likely to be pushed towards abstinence. Whatever way the client enters the treatment system, they will need to be assessed, which may be at three different levels:

- Level 1 is screening and referral assessment (tiers 1 and 4b).
- Level 2 is drug and alcohol misuse triage assessment (tiers 2, 3 and 4).
- Level 3 is comprehensive drug and alcohol misuse assessment (tiers 3 and 4a and some tier 2).

(Source: *Models of care*, 2002)

Care plans should be structured, written down, agreed with the client and regularly reviewed. This should ensure that services are joined up between agencies and ensure that there is best practice. Hopefully also clients that drop out can be re-engaged when they are ready for this (see Chapter 7 for discussion on working with relapse).

ACTIVITY 2.2

How would you start to plan with a client how they can engage with their substance misuse problem? Draw up a list of questions that you would wish to work through with the client.

What are you trying to achieve with the client? You need to form an assessment about the level and frequency of their substance misuse if you are going to be able to refer them to organisations that they can engage with. You will need to ascertain the level, frequency and extent of their use of substances. Do they take drugs regularly or as a response to stress? You could get them to keep a drugs diary of when, where and why they take drugs. What factors trigger their use?

ACTIVITY 2.3

Draw up an inventory of what is available in your local area and think about what agencies might be useful for your work with clients.

COMMENT

What is available in your local area? I conducted a review of my local area, Newham in East London, and downloaded from the internet 'a guide to Newham Alcohol and Drug Services'. This helpful document listed more than 20 agencies available in the borough. The document gave their contact details, services offered, who was eligible for their services and how to access the service or make a referral. It also included the borough substance-misuse strategy, strategic priorities and statement of intent. The tier system for treatment services was clearly explained and the agencies were clear on whether they were for self-referrals or were there to gain access to tiers 3 and 4 services.

To give two examples: In-volve offered a comprehensive service including six-days-a-week opening hours and direct access to service users as well as to those referred by professionals. There were a drop-in service, holistic assessment, links to detox services, ethnic minority project workers, harm-reduction services, hepatitis and HIV testing, specific services to women, assessment for residential detox and rehabilitation and further advice.

The 409 Project Specialist Substance Misuse Team offered comprehensive needs assessment and care and after-care packages, substitute opiate prescribing, crack interventions, psychiatric and dual diagnosis, primary health care and many other options. For clients who needed access to tiers 3 and 4 this would be a referral point.

There were a large number of different agencies working within the borough and the range of services on offer was very diverse, including alternative therapies. Many agencies encouraged self-referrals. The lead-in time for access has also become quicker, as can be seen from details present on the National Treatment Agency website.

Local systems for monitoring drug treatment and outcomes

Within local areas it is important that there are commonly agreed standards of good practice. The ethnic and cultural diversity of local areas and what this means for service provision needs to be carefully established and kept up to date. Thus this is a dynamic and not a static process. This will be reflected in general health and mental health service provision. The commissioners of local services need to ensure that within their local area there are:

- clear and standardised screening assessment processes used across all agencies;
- clear criteria for referral and eligibility for entry to each part of the drug treatment system;
- a directory of services for drug and alcohol misusers;
- clear criteria for priority treatment entry and emergency access;
- adequate training of personnel carrying out screening assessment at each level;
- adequate sharing of appropriate information between agencies in the drug treatment system;
- a system of monitoring, auditing and reviewing of the screening and assessment system.

(Source: *Models of care*, 2002)

Models of care for treating young substance misusers

Since the publication of *Every child matters: change for children,* there has been a new approach to the well-being of young people up to the age of 19. The first Children's Commissioner was appointed in March 2005 and with the formation of Children's Trusts the organisation of young people's services is changing. There is an acknowledgement that whatever their circumstances, children need to:

- be healthy;
- stay safe;
- enjoy and achieve;
- make a positive contribution;
- achieve economic well-being.

Every child matters: change for children in the criminal justice system comments that the Criminal Justice System (CJS) has a key focus on making a positive contribution (choosing to be law-abiding) and staying safe. Many young people who take illicit drugs will put themselves into situations where they break the law. The document also comments that 'the Home Office and the Youth Justice Board are developing end-to-end programmes of interventions to address drug, volatile substance and alcohol misuse by children and young people at each stage of the CJS'.

The document also paints a broader picture of the context within which substance misuse takes place:

> *Substance misuse does not occur in isolation and is often associated with other problems such as truancy, school exclusion or family problems. Identification, screening assessment and onward case management take account of that broader picture so that the child or young person is offered the most appropriate support.*

Young people should have their drug problems dealt with within young people's services although there will be a need for specialist treatment on occasion. Funding for this client group increased in England from £19.5 million in 2003/4 to £23 million in 2004/5. In this last time period over 10,000 young people received treatment, up 60 per cent from the previous year.

Why is a separate focus needed for younger people?

The Home Office published guidance back in 1999 on drugs and young offenders with the stated aim of offering guidance to both drug action teams and youth offending teams. It commented that both the Health Advisory Service and the Standing Conference on Drug Abuse strongly advocated that the needs of young people in relation to substance misuse had to be addressed both 'separately and differently from services and interventions developed for adults' (DPAS, 1999, p8).

The report makes the point that although delinquent behaviour often starts before drug taking, these two phenomena are likely to be mutually reinforcing and as the level of drug taking increases so does the likelihood of problematic behaviour. One of the landmark documents on youth justice, the Audit Commission Report *Misspent youth* published in 1996, found that in a sample of 600 young offenders, 15 per cent had a 'problem' with drink or drugs, rising to 37 per cent for those classed as persistent or serious offenders.

When the Social Services Inspectorate surveyed all local authorities in 1997 they also visited eight of them and in three of these sites the number of young offenders that were heroin users was over 70 per cent. More worryingly, 'one court referral scheme had seen 41 clients aged between 11 and 16 within six weeks, 78 per cent of whom were using heroin. Most local authorities did not have any systematic assessment or monitoring of involvement with drugs among those they looked after' (DPAS, 1999, p10).

RESEARCH SUMMARY

No assumptions should be made that the factors relevant to those young people who experiment with substances are the same as the factors relevant to problematic involvement. How useful general lists of risk factors are in informing social workers of whom to be concerned about is debatable. The Home Office guidance from 1999 cites an earlier report by the Health Advisory Service (1996), Children and young people: substance misuse services, that examined risk and protective factors. It commented that significant factors could be 'physiological, family, psychological and/or economic/social factors' (DPAS, 1999, p11).

Parker et al. (1998), in a 'unique' five year longitudinal study, tracked several hundred young people through their adolescence. By the age of 15 most of the respondents had been in situations where they could try or buy drugs and certainly by 18 almost all of them had. Almost a quarter of the sample became regular drug users and social class and gender were no longer indicators of abstinence. What was of interest was some of the risk-taking indicators. For example, young people who abstained from taking drugs were much less likely to have had early sexual experiences before the age of 16 (76 per cent abstainers compared to 41 per cent of current users). In the fifth year, 46 per cent of the study had been stopped by the police, which included 72 per cent of current users. However, 81 per cent of the abstainers had never been stopped by the police.

It is interesting to note that hardly any of the cohort were seriously delinquent and over two-thirds of current users had no convictions or cautions. This tells us that the 'war on drugs' will not be won by trying to work only with known offenders, but also that as social workers, teachers or other professionals with contact with young people or adults we should not make any assumptions that lack of convictions or cautions, social class or respectability of the parents/guardians/carers is a sure signal or indicator that the young person or the adult does not use and/or have a problem with substances, including alcohol. The study by Parker et al. tells us that much drug taking may be recreational and may be 'normalised' in that unlike subcultural explanations of drug taking, young people were not spending all of their time being preoccupied with drugs, including how to fund them, get hold of them and then take them, etc. This might become true if the young people moved on to more dangerous and addictive drugs like heroin and crack cocaine. Young people in the study moved from 'abstainers' to 'triers', from 'triers' to 'users'. This was a dynamic process with young people moving in and out of active use of drugs.

Needs and risk assessment

The Drugs Prevention Advisory Service (1999) document lays down 10 key principles that adhere to the general principles of the Children Act 1989. These are relevant for all young people whether they are offenders or not.

1. A child or adolescent is not an adult: therefore their age will be significant, but not only this, also their maturity and degree of development.

2. The welfare of the child is paramount: this requires multi-agency co-operation especially as agencies may well have different goals, methodologies and philosophies.

3. The views of the young person are of central importance, and should always be sought and considered: this is integral to the Children Act.

4. Services must respect parental responsibility when working with a young person: this may well include education as well as support for parents, certainly it must include consultation and involvement.

5. Services should recognise and co-operate with the local authority in carrying out its responsibilities towards children and young people: this relates to responsibilities under the Children Act to provide services to children 'in need' and to protect children 'at risk'. The Crime and Disorder Act also places responsibilities on the youth offending team to ensure the availability of youth justice services to prevent offending/re-offending.

6. A holistic approach is vital at all levels, as young people's problems do not respect professional boundaries: this refers to the need to provide and promote drug

education, prevention and treatment to address the multi-faceted needs of young people. Strategically responsibility will be within drug action teams and the youth offending teams.

7. Services must be child centred: the intervention with a young person, whether it is focused on education, information and/or treatment must be appropriate to their age, maturity and experiences, etc.

8. A comprehensive range of services needs to be provided: schools may be a good venue for providing education and prevention services but for those who miss out on this, the youth offending team might offer the opportunity to offer this to young people who did not attend for any reason. The court process is an opportunity to assess the young person and intervene possibly at a time of crisis with a reluctant client.

9. Services must be competent to respond to the needs of the young person: drug awareness, knowledge and skills for effective interventions need to be taught to frontline practitioners to give them the confidence to engage effectively with young people and their families.

10. Services should aim to operate according to best practice principles: interventions with young people must be lawful and effective and respond to the young person's needs.

(Source: DPAS, 1999)

Young people might undergo a variety of assessments by a number of different agencies depending on their circumstances. However, although agencies will have their own agendas, it is important that when there are evidence or concerns about substance taking/misuse a thorough assessment is made in this respect. This should cover: their personal history and development; type and frequency of substance taking, including alcohol, volatile substances, etc.; family details including drug histories within the family; physical, emotional and mental health issues; education, employment and training; etc. The young person will need a risk assessment to identify the factors that make that person a risk to themselves and/or to others. From the assessment(s) a treatment package will need to be agreed and sourced, with regular reviews built in to ensure that it remains effective for that young person as their circumstances change. With the increased knowledge about relapse, this can be planned and risks minimised over time.

It will also be appropriate to establish the level and suitability of services to meet the young person's needs. This might include (not in order of priorities) detoxification, substitute prescriptions, harm minimisation (such as needle exchange), counselling including motivational interviewing, cognitive behavioural therapy, support to prevent relapse.

Finally, the Drugs Prevention Advisory Service (1999) provides a list that all young people should be provided with, that it believes is common to all:

• awareness and education about the use of drugs, solvents and alcohol;
• awareness of the laws relating to the possession and supply of drugs;

- information about sources of help for themselves; and, where needed support and advice in coping with drug taking in relation to offending;
- access to services that may help them address other factors or problems.

(DPAS, 1999)

More recently the Department for Education and Skills (DfES 2005) (now the Department for Education) published *Every child matters: change for children: young people and drugs.* It remains government policy. This document, which links to the government's updated drug strategy, has as its mission reducing the level of drug use by young people. It is holistic and envisages close co-operation between the drug action team's children's services. It comments:

> *Drugs are closely linked to poor outcomes among young people. Children's services already know many of those at greatest risk.*

ACTIVITY 2.4

Look at the extract from the DfES (2005) above. What would you put in place to work most effectively with young people and their families on problems of substance misuse? Do these indicate potential problems of drug misuse or do they indicate more general issues/concerns?

COMMENT

The drugs strategy for the coalition government recognises the need to reduce the demand for drugs for young people and envisages an increase in the number of health visitors in support of this. It has also retained the Family Nurse partnership. The emphasis will be on abstinence as a goal of treatment.

The above document discusses targeted interventions with vulnerable young people and comments that there needs to be in place:

- early assessment of all vulnerable children and young people;
- care management and appointment of a lead professional for all children and young people who need support and intervention on drug misuse;
- integrated information systems to help agencies work together to track interventions on individual children and young people.

(Sources: DfES, 2005)

The document identifies groups that it considers to be at risk:

- children of problem drug misusers (often linked to poor outcomes for their children);
- persistent truants and school excludees (likely to be linked to higher drug misuse and includes pupil referral units, etc.);
- looked-after children (need for early identification and assessment);
- young people in contact with the criminal justice system (high level of risk of drug misuse);
- other groups identified from research, e.g. homeless, those involved in teenage prostitution, etc.

(Source: DfES, 2005)

In 2009 the NTA published *Getting to grips with substance misuse among young people*. It highlights progress made by treatment services and locates the substance misuse in the context of the family, social pressures and emotional issues. It is available as a download.

CHAPTER SUMMARY

In this chapter we have looked at the numbers of people who take drugs and then we have looked at the pathways into treatment. Since the development of the National Treatment Agency we have seen a growth in the number of agencies that offer support and treatment to substance users and an integration of local systems to ensure a more 'joined-up' approach.

As a social worker it is important that you should be aware of the services available in your area so that you can encourage your clients to refer themselves or be referred by you for the appropriate treatment. Above all else it is vital that as social workers we do not opt out of working with substance misusers because we somehow feel that it is not part of our work or that we do not have the necessary knowledge and skills to do so.

FURTHER READING

Audit Commission (2004) *Drug misuse 2004. Reducing the local impact.* London: Audit Commission.

The Audit Commission (AC) report, available on the web, is aimed at policy-makers and gives much useful information on the impact of drugs on local communities. The need for a multi-agency approach can be seen from the contents and the abstract on the AC website is worth quoting at length:

> The report contains key messages for local authorities, health services, police and probation partners as they prepare the drug misuse component of local crime and disorder strategies for 2005 to 2008. Local leaders can use the sets of key questions and wall chart to improve their performance and make best use of resources to meet the needs of the whole person rather than tackling the user's drug problem alone. This in turn will help make communities safer for everyone.

Home Office (2004a) *Tackling drugs: Changing lives: Every child matters: Change for children: Young people and drugs.* London: Home Office.

This publication is the official policy to prevent drug harm to young people and is a joint approach by the Department for Education and Skills, the Home Office and the Department of Health. Like the other *Every child matters* documents, it should be required reading for any professional working with, or interested in, young people.

McIntosh, J and McKeganey, N (2000) The recovery from dependent drug use: addicts' strategies for reducing the risk of relapse, *Drugs: Education, Prevention and Policy*, 7(2), 179–192.

The journal *Drugs: Education, Prevention and Policy* is excellent for articles relevant to practitioners interested in substance misuse and is generally recommended. McIntosh and McKeganey have produced a valuable article that shows that drug users do not have to hit 'rock bottom' when they decide to desist from taking drugs, but they may make a rational choice using their own free will.

Chapter 3

The history, legislative changes and key policy documents involved in the field of substance misuse

A C H I E V I N G   A   S O C I A L   W O R K   D E G R E E

This chapter will help you to develop the following capabilities, to the appropriate level, from the **Professional Capabilities Framework**.

- **Professionalism** – Identify and behave as a professional social worker, committed to professional development.
- **Values and ethics** – Apply social work ethical principles and values to guide professional practice.
- **Diversity** – Recognise diversity and apply anti-discriminatory and anti-oppressive principles in practice.
- **Knowledge** – Apply knowledge of social sciences, law and social work practice theory.
- **Interventions and skills** – Use judgement and authority to intervene with individuals, families and communities to promote independence, provide support and prevent harm, neglect and abuse.

See Appendix 1 for the Professional Capabilities Framework diagram.

This chapter will also introduce you to the following standards as set out in the 2008 social work subject benchmark statement.
5.1.1 Social work services, service users and carers.
5.1.2 The service delivery context.
5.1.5 The nature of social work practice.

Introduction

Although most public and political attention tends to focus on illegal drugs as a source of social problems, this should not overshadow the significance of problems associated with legal drugs... Undoubtedly... the Royal College of Psychiatrists... was correct to call alcohol 'Our Favourite Drug'. (South, 2002, p15)

This chapter is concerned with giving the reader an understanding of the genesis of drug taking over time and the measures that have been adopted to deal with this. It will concentrate on the illegalities of substance misuse but the reader should not forget the health problems associated with tobacco (nicotine intake is often an associated consequence of smoking cannabis as well) and the problems associated with excessive alcohol consumption.

There have been five key drug policy documents in recent years, in 1995, 1998, 2002, 2008 and 2010. These will be described and analysed in this chapter. The main legislation remains the Misuse of Drugs Act 1971, which will also feature here. For substance-misusing offenders the Drug Treatment and Testing Order (DTTO) from 1998 marked a major change in the way that offenders were dealt with in the criminal justice system. Social workers need to know how substance-misusing offenders are dealt with as they are likely to have clients who break the law and thus face a court disposal. It may be that the client is a partner or relative of the social worker's client and working holistically the social worker and probation officer may be working in partnership. There is a case discussion like this in the next chapter.

We will see that originally DTTOs were assessed in terms of number started (i.e. output driven), rather than in terms of successful completion (i.e. outcome driven). The 2003 Criminal Justice Act replaced the DTTO with a community sentence with a Drug Rehabilitation Requirement (DRR). The DRR is very similar to the DTTO and the success of this sanction will be assessed.

The Offender Management Act 2007 changed the structure of the probation service and current proposals make it likely that the supervision of low and medium risk offenders will be moved away from probation offender managers to the private and third sector organisations. This would affect who supervises many substance-misusing offenders and will be linked to payment by results.

Background

The key legislation in the arena of drugs is the Misuse of Drugs Act 1971 and this has been reinforced by the Drugs Act 2005. However, before discussing these in detail, I intend to start this chapter by going further back and examining how drugs policy has evolved over time. This will allow us to consider how views about drug taking have changed and we can consider what might be the most effective way to tackle the problems related to substance misuse. This approach must include helping individuals, their carers and families to access support across organisations in different fields, e.g. health, education, criminal justice, etc. Some professionals might not have had links with the criminal justice field and may well lack confidence, not least because the possibility of attending court might appear somewhat daunting.

Mott and Bean (1998) provide a useful history of the development of drug control in Britain. They comment that opium was readily obtainable in Britain in the nineteenth century and that control of dangerous drugs originated in the twentieth century. They add that regulation was more concerned with 'the development of the medical and pharmaceutical professional bodies than to concern about its use' (p31). This was reflected in the Pharmacy Act 1868 that was more concerned with poisons and did not concern itself with patent medicines that contained opium. Opium from British India was exported to China and came into Britain from Turkey.

In 1894 a seven-volume report of the Indian Hemp Commission was published that concluded:

Viewing the subject generally, it may be added that the moderate use of these drugs [opium and cannabis] is the rule, and the excessive use is comparatively exceptional. The moderate use practically produces no ill effects... The injury done by the excessive use is, however, confined almost exclusively to the consumer himself; the effect on society is rarely appreciable. (Working Party of the Royal College of Psychiatrists and the Royal College of Physicians, 2000, p31)

ACTIVITY 3.1

Think about the assumptions in the extract from the nineteenth-century report about the use of opium and cannabis. How would you go about trying to make the links between drug use and its effects? What are the main issues for you that the extract highlights?

COMMENT

This report is interesting and demonstrates an early discussion on the question of harm reduction or abstinence as a way of controlling drug use. There is an implication that drug users can limit how much they take and that there is not a 'slippery slope' that leads inexorably to excess. Furthermore, the warning that 'soft' drugs lead to 'hard' drugs is not assumed here. Finally, no link is being made between drugs and crime. Society is not seen as being endangered by the use of drugs; rather it is seen at worst as a self-harming activity. Can we make this distinction today and how does it fit with social work values?

The start of legislation on drug control

The Hague Opium Convention 1912, ratified by Britain in July 1914, was concerned with the suppression of opium, morphine and cocaine. The outbreak of the First World War heightened the need to control drug smuggling as there was evidence of involvement of British ships in this trade, leading to fears about cocaine use in the armed forces. Following on from this an Army Council Order in May 1916 forbade members of the armed forces from receiving cocaine or any other drugs unless it was on prescription. The Home Office and the police were seen as the most appropriate institutions to deal with this (Mott and Bean, 1998).

The Dangerous Drugs Act 1920 restricted the possession of drugs to those authorised, and ensured that records were kept for this purpose. Interestingly, there was no limit on self-prescribing by doctors because of opposition by the medical profession, and responsibility for dangerous drugs and its legislation was given to the Home Office rather than the Ministry of Health, created in 1919 (Mott and Bean, 1998).

ACTIVITY 3.2

The Home Office has retained the responsibility for the control of drugs until this day. What are the implications for this, as opposed to the responsibility shifting to the Department of Health?

COMMENT

As you will see from this and other chapters, there is a clear link between drug misuse and crime. Anecdotal evidence from discussions with DAT co-ordinators suggests that pathways into treatment are quicker for offenders as there is recognition for this link. However, National Treatment Agency reports give encouraging news that entry to treatment for all substance misusers has become quicker in more recent years. One further implication focuses on the awareness of social work practitioners about their clients. It is easy to make assumptions that if the area of practice is not directly linked to substance misuse this is not an area to be concerned about. The thesis of this book is that all practitioners need to be aware of and actively checking out with clients that substance misuse is not a problem. Locating responsibility in the Home Office might result in practitioners assuming that they do not have to think about substance misuse as their clients are law-abiding people and not offenders.

Moving to a treatment model

The Rolleston Committee Report in 1926 focused on whether individuals who were addicted to morphine and heroin should be treated and given supplies of the drug. It was seen as a disease rather than 'vicious indulgence' (Mott and Bean, 1998), but it concluded that there was very little opiate addiction in Britain. Furthermore, those using injectable morphine were middle-aged or elderly, professionals like doctors or pharmacists or those who had developed an addiction from earlier treatment (Working Party of the Royal College of Psychiatrists and Royal College of Physicians, 2000). The recommendations from the Rolleston Committee formed the basis for drug policy for the next 40 years (Bennett and Holloway, 2005). The absence of a perceived drug problem might have been because the Committee medicalised rather than criminalised users, a further consideration of Activity 3.2 above.

In 1958 the Brain Committee, set up by the Ministry of Health and led by Sir Russell Brain, maintained the belief in the medical model, but recommended that prescribing to addicts should become specialised in treatment centres. This can be seen therefore as the start of the restriction on prescribing and hence a move towards limiting medical dominance (Bennett and Holloway, 2005). The Brain Committee was reconvened in 1964 when there was evidence that private doctors in London were prescribing heroin to street addicts. Between 1955 and 1965, the number of addicts known to the Home Office trebled, and the age of new addicts declined. The use of cannabis also grew and the drug was no longer predominantly being used by artists and musicians, etc. Amphetamines ('pep pills') also became more prevalent. The recommendations of the Brain Committee in their report of 1965 were translated into the 1967 Dangerous Drugs Act, which set up new treatment centres and restricted the power of GPs to prescribe heroin or cocaine. The Drug Dependency Units opened in 1968 with the mandate to prescribe only sufficient drugs that the user could take on a daily basis, with stringent checks to stop them selling on to others.

In 1971 the Misuse of Drugs Act replaced the 1967 Dangerous Drugs Act and other Acts that had had the intention of reducing the level of drugs in the community. This

Act continues to be the key Act, with some changes, with drugs grouped into Classes A, B and C. Class A drugs include heroin, LSD, ecstasy, cocaine, etc.; Class B includes cannabis, amphetamines and barbiturates; and Class C ketamine. Each class has its own set of penalties for possession and supplying and the severity of these may well surprise drug takers, not least in how much of the drug has to be in their possession to attract a charge of supplying rather than possession for their own personal use. The penalties for supplying are much more severe than for possession. The Act allows the police to stop and detain people on 'reasonable suspicion' that they are in possession of a controlled drug. They can also be searched.

In 1985 the government published *Tackling drug misuse: a summary of the government's strategy.* Bennett and Holloway (2005) comment that this marked the end of the medicalisation and prominence being given to doctors. Instead misuse would be tackled by: reducing supplies from abroad; making enforcement more effective; maintaining effective deterrents and tight domestic controls; developing prevention; improving treatment and rehabilitation. It can be seen that social work practice arrives in the last of these five points. Clearly the major emphasis was on control rather than rehabilitation.

In 1995 the government published a White Paper *Tackling drugs together: a strategy for England 1995–1998.* This had three major aims:

- Crime – to reduce drug-related crime; to enforce the law against drug suppliers; to reduce the public's fear of drug-related crime; to reduce the level of drug misuse in prisons.

- Young people – to discourage drug taking by young people; to ensure that drug education took place in schools; raising awareness among all school staff; to provide services to young people.

- Public health – to protect communities from all risks associated with drugs; to discourage substance misuse; to ensure access to services, including advice, counselling, treatment and rehabilitation, etc.; to provide support to families of substance misusers.

Three years later, in 1998, a further White Paper on drugs was critical of this original strategy, although it highlighted some of the positive results:

- It focused on structures rather than results and did not engage the public (has this changed?).

- It treated drug misuse largely in isolation from other social and environmental factors (has this changed?).

- It advocated partnership without making sufficient structural and fiscal changes to support it.

- It was too short term and did not bring together common research, information and performance bases.

- There was a review of international drug activity, with the intention of lessening the flow of drugs into Britain.

- It strengthened links between national agencies.
- There was to be more collaboration of resources.
- It created and developed drug action teams.
- There were to be local initiatives, disseminated by the Drugs Prevention Initiative.

This White Paper, published a year after the change from a Conservative to a Labour government, was entitled *Tackling drugs to build a better Britain*. This was the government's Ten-Year Strategy for Tackling Drugs Misuse. It had the following aims:

- Young people – to help young people resist drug misuse in order to achieve their full potential in society.
- Communities – to protect our communities from drug-related anti-social and criminal behaviour.
- Treatment – to enable people with drug problems to overcome them and live healthy and crime-free lives.
- Availability – to stifle the availability of illegal drugs on our streets.

This was endorsed by the prime minister, who appointed Keith Hellawell, a former chief constable, as the first 'drugs tsar'. Drug action teams were to be established with partnerships at the centre to tackle the problem of drugs.

By March 1999 it was expected that:

- all agencies should realign their priorities, resources and operational focus in line with this White Paper and produce their forward plan;
- all agencies should develop corporate and individual performance targets and measures;
- national, local, private and voluntary-sector funding should be realigned in support of the plan;
- there should be an annual report and plan of action against drugs to be repeated annually.

In broad terms the message was that treatment worked and working in partnership was the vehicle to deliver it.

So how bad was and is the problem with drugs in society?

As can be seen from the above history of legislation and strategy documents the fight against drugs has developed and gained pace in the last 40 years. How does this link to actual drug usage and other related social problems?

Nigel South (2002) points out that fatalities linked to tobacco and alcohol greatly outweigh those connected to illegal drug use. As mentioned in the history, early misusers included medical professionals, the bohemian fringes of society as well as, for example, the opium pipe smokers in the East End of London. In the Second World War, the USA was a hub for painkiller opiates. Even in the 1950s the level of recorded addicts was only in the 3–4 hundreds. In the 1960s the numbers of recorded addicts began to rise slowly and in the anti-establishment atmosphere that prevailed in some areas and the counter-culture that was emerging there was a growth of cannabis use as well as of LSD and some working-class use of heroin and amphetamines.

In the latter part of the 1970s more heroin entered the country from South West Asia that could be taken in ways other than injecting. In the 1980s this was joined by cocaine, but not especially crack cocaine. The availability of illegal drugs changed during the 1980s, as did the distribution networks. Groups who previously had not been involved with drugs saw the potential for profits and began to become involved (Ruggiero and South, 1995). In the 1990s a poly drug culture developed, which means a mixture of drugs. Ecstasy was a drug taken by 'normal' youngsters intent on a night out clubbing and it became part of the popular culture.

Berridge (2002), writing on AIDS and British drug policy, mentions the reports that emerged from Edinburgh in late 1985 revealing 'a prevalence of HIV antibody sera-positivity among injecting drug misusers' (p93) and which led to a policy of harm minimisation as there was a risk that HIV would spread from infected drug misusers into the general population. This led to making sterile injecting equipment more available (needle exchanges) and to substitute-prescribing (this had been cut back, not least substituting methadone for injectable drugs).

The Probation Service and substance misuse in the 1990s

Whereas in the past the probation service relied on the Home Office to produce reports, in 1993 Her Majesty's Inspectorate of Probation (HMIP) produced *Offenders who misuse drugs. The probation service response*. The report commented that the traditional approach of the probation service, which was one of promoting abstinence, changed after the report in 1981, *Aids and drug misuse: Part 1*, to one of 'harm reduction'. The link between the exchange of needles between addicts and the growth of HIV had forced a change of approach on the service. However, many of the probation officers interviewed during the inspection felt ill-equipped from their training to deal with drug-related issues. The report described a useful survey undertaken by the Inner London Probation Service's Demonstration Unit that had revealed that they had 2,907 known offenders who took drugs – most commonly heroin, alcohol, cocaine, amphetamines and barbiturates. Of these, 72 per cent were white, 25 per cent black, 20 per cent women, and 60 per cent were known to other agencies relating to their drug abuse. The probation service was seen as likely to be the first agency to have contact with some of these users. It was seen that this work would make 'heavy demands on probation officers' assessment, observational, intuitive and engagement skills' (6.3).

What was interesting in terms of client self-determination and the later development of the Drug Treatment and Testing Order in the Crime and Disorder Act 1998, was an italicised extract from the 1991 Advisory Council Report: *'almost everyone who enters treatment for drug misuse does so under some form of pressure... those who are impelled to enter treatment by a court are not in a fundamentally different position'* (10.3). The implication was clear: although working with drug-taking offenders might require further knowledge and skills, it did not mean that this should imply that National Standards need not be adhered to. The consequence of this was that offenders with a substance misuse problem would still need to attend the probation office weekly or their court order or licence would be breached and they would be taken back to court for resentencing (if the breach was proved). The report made a number of sound recommendations in terms of treatment, support, liaison with specialist agencies and the setting up centrally of procedures for offenders to be referred for residential rehabilitative help (15.8).

In 1997 HMIP produced a second report entitled *Tackling drugs together*. This report started from the premise in the Foreword (by the Chief Inspector) that there are links between drug misuse and crime. The report coincided with the appointment of the 'drugs tsar' and the timetable set out in the government White Paper *Tackling drugs together: a strategy for England 1995–1998*, published in May 1995. This had stated that in 1995–96 each probation service would produce a drugs policy and strategy, following guidance from the Home Office and the Association of Chief Officers of Probation (ACOP); in 1996–97 the probation inspectorate would report on the implementation by the services of their drug strategies, and in 1997–98 the above report would be produced.

The report commented that probation officers and specialist workers were unaware of research which found that whether a person entered treatment voluntarily or under some form of coercion mattered less than the quality of the treatment. It appeared that the probation service was committed to inter-agency work and comment was made that:

> *In this inspection sample, drug misusing offenders posed no greater problem for the supervising POs in working to national standards than other offenders on areas' caseloads and did not bear out the view held by some probation staff and sentencers that drug misusing offenders were necessarily more difficult to supervise within the standards because of their chaotic lifestyles. As one Senior PO said: If they can keep their appointment with their drug dealer they can keep their appointment with their probation officer. (2.6)*

It was stated that there was some concern from health and voluntary agencies that 'drug misusing offenders [were] being sentenced to treatment' (2.9). It was worrying that as late as 1997 the report could say:

> *Probation services had little information on which to assess the particular needs of female and ethnic minority drug misusing offenders, nor were they able to evaluate the effectiveness of their responses to these offenders. The inspection findings, though limited, indicated that a broadly similar service was being provided for those arrangements as for white male drug misusers. (2.10)*

If this served to raise concern for good anti-discriminatory practice, the report also commented on the very high level of drug misuse in hostels. Data from November 1996 from 18 probation hostels indicated that 53 per cent of the 419 residents had a drugs charge or conviction, or were assessed as having a drug problem (2.11). In prisons also it was a problem that even if the prison probation officer was knowledgeable about drugs and treatment, it was difficult to be effective if the prison had no clear objectives (2.12).

When the Chief Inspector of Probation had been the Chief of the Inner London Probation Service, he had officially endorsed a policy of harm reduction. The report stated that at the time of the inspection the official government view 'was that abstinence from drugs must be the ultimate goal of services for drug misusers' (3.4). The Crime and Disorder Act 1998 included the provision for Drug Treatment and Testing Orders, implemented early in 2000, with abstinence as the goal.

CASE STUDY

Jane was convicted of driving over the limit and her pre-sentence report revealed that she had a long-term history of excessive alcohol consumption. She also used illicit drugs, particularly cannabis and occasionally cocaine. She was sentenced to community supervision with a requirement to attend two groupwork programmes. The probation service uses a predominantly cognitive behavioural approach and after meeting and having three sessions with her case manager Jane completed a 'drink-impaired driver' programme and a 'think first' programme, as she was assessed as having anger management problems.

Her probation officer asked Jane to keep a drink diary as she was not prepared to abstain from alcohol, although she realised that illicit drugs could get her into further trouble. Jane had had several troubled relationships and reported feeling abused in some of them, particularly recent ones. The probation officer worked with her on her financial management and to improve her irregular employment. There was a suspicion that the alcohol consumption was higher than Jane was prepared to admit and she expressed negative feelings about her self-worth. The community order ran its full course with Jane regularly attending. Her anger seemed to be under more control but the alcohol consumption periodically became a problem. The probation officer felt that while Jane had stabilised her life to some extent over the course of the community sentence, there was still more that could have been achieved, if she had been more willing to address her personal difficulties. The probation officer gave full details of the local drug action team to Jane, hoping that she would be willing to seek help if her drinking started to get out of control again. She wondered whether a more formalised testing of Jane might have imposed an external control on Jane.

Drug treatment and testing orders

The Drug Treatment and Testing Order (DTTO) was introduced in the Crime and Disorder Act 1998 so that offenders who 'have a propensity to misuse drugs' have the opportunity to tackle their drug problem, supported by specialist drug agencies in the community. The orders were intensive, being delivered in either day or residential settings. These orders were being piloted in three areas but they were rolled out nationally before the completion of their evaluation.

Supervisees on DTTOs were tested twice weekly for the first 13 weeks, for at least their drug of choice. For those offenders who do not comply with treatment or submit to testing, a decision may be taken to return the offender to court for breach of the DTTO. This decision is taken by the probation officer, in consultation with the treatment provider, and the Act envisaged that the probation service and treatment providers would work closely in partnership. The offender must return to court for at least one review after 28 days for the court to be satisfied that the offender is trying to change from their old substance-using habit. This makes the sentence unusual as it makes the court more central to the process of supervision.

The DTTO was amended by the Power of Criminal Courts (Sentencing) Act 2000. The Criminal Justice and Court Services Act 2000 also contained new powers to deal with drug users. It gave the courts the power to make a Drug Abstinence Order, which was backed up with mandatory testing. The DTTO built on concepts in *Tackling drugs together*, the national strategy for working with drug issues. The 10-year strategy *Tackling drugs to build a better Britain* set targets to halve the number of young people using illegal drugs, especially heroin and cocaine; halve the levels of re-offending by drug-misusing offenders; double the numbers of drug misusers in treatment; and halve the availability of drugs, especially heroin and cocaine, on the streets.

In preparation for the introduction of the DTTO it was decided to run three pilots of different models across England. The final report of the pilots by Turnball et al. (2000) indicated that there were issues around inter-agency working, referral procedures, assessment, managing the individual into treatment, interpretations, objectives, expectations of drug use in DTTOs, effectiveness of urine testing, continuity of sentencers at court reviews, streamlining breach procedures and how to monitor the order effectively. The government however decided to roll out nationally the DTTO in advance of the publication of the final report on the pilots.

Travis, writing in the *Guardian* at the end of 2002, pointed out that 'David Blunkett, the Home Secretary, has ditched these targets and replaced them with "vague promises" instead. The new policy described as "tough love" will target drug users to increase the numbers attending treatment programmes with a target of 55 per cent of problem drug users by 2004 and 100 per cent by 2008.' The result of this would be a doubling of the number of offenders sentenced to DTTOs. For Yates, these changes signify a downgrading of the role of the UK Anti-Drugs Co-ordinator, but more importantly 'a transfer of the levers of power to the Home Office' (Yates, 2002, p122). In policy terms, this is a linking of drug misuse with crime.

The introduction of the Criminal Justice Act 2003 replaced the DTTO with a community order that can include a drug treatment requirement similar to the old DTTO. As with other adult community orders, the courts will decide on the precise 'cocktail' of requirements that are appropriate for the offender. This means that the court can order a Drug Rehabilitation Requirement (DRR) that is appropriate for the type and level of drug being consumed. As the Community Order is so new, we will examine the impact of the DTTO, as reported in the research.

Factors influencing the introduction of DTTOs included the poor take-up of the addition of specialist treatment to probation orders (known as 1A6 orders), a growing awareness of the influence of drug use in offending and a wish to build on American models of practice where specialist drugs courts had been in operation for some time. It was recognised that there was a need for fast access to assessment and treatment for drug-abusing offenders. Thus the DTTO was instigated to replace for drug misusers (but not those with a propensity to misuse alcohol) the provisions of Section 1A6. Indeed, Buchanan and Young (2000) estimate that 85 per cent of the UK drugs budget has been spent on 'prevention, prohibition and punishment' rather than 'treatment, rehabilitation and social reintegration'. This is a planned intervention to target problematic drug users. Under the Criminal Justice Act 2003 the DTTO has been replaced by a generic community order that can include a condition to treat a drug problem. For the purpose of this section the term 'DTTO' will be used as shorthand for this condition.

The DTTO is an extremely restrictive sentence and should be reserved for the more serious offenders. Many practitioners may feel that it is appropriate that some attempt is made first to engage in a non-coercive way with treatment providers. DTTOs had a requirement that for a period of between six months and three years offenders received treatment at either a residential or non-residential facility. Because of an emphasis on sensitivity to local structures and provision there was no one model for the delivery of DTTOs, either across the country or within individual probation areas. This could mean in some instances that treatment was delivered 'in-house' by multi-disciplinary teams; or case managers within the Probation Service could arrange treatment with partnership providers. Research by Wild et al. (2001) indicates that while 'clients and counsellors' value the notion of self-determination in the treatment process, this view is not shared by the judiciary and the general public, revealing a difference of opinion on the efficacy of compulsory treatment. Drug policy has changed since this time to one that has abstinence as a major goal of policy, please see Chapter 6. We will have to see what impact this will have on the level of drug use and misuse.

One further innovation that practitioners need to be aware of is the use of conditional cautioning, introduced in the Criminal Justice Act 2004. For the first time it is possible to attach to a police caution a condition that enables drug-misusing offenders to enter treatment for the purpose of rehabilitation. However, if they do not meet the condition of the caution then they can be charged with the original offence (this was the way that probation orders operated until the Criminal Justice Act 1991). Thus the notion of voluntarism has a coercive element, as failure to comply can trigger a court appearance, but the reward for compliance is the avoidance of a criminal conviction.

Interestingly, the conditional caution is also available for restorative justice purposes and there is no reason why substance-using offenders should not be allowed to enter into this approach either, as many of them will regret their actions when they are forced to confront the consequences of their activities.

In restorative justice, the offender will try to make amends to the victim for the damage they have caused them. As acquisitive crime is linked to substance misuse, the offender will have an opportunity to put right the damage to the victim, and victim awareness is an important part of making the offender realise the consequences that their offending has on others.

The use of the conditional caution is to be greatly expanded across the country as an early intervention approach for substance misusers before their lifestyle becomes too entrenched and criminalised. What is clear is that drug testing and monitoring will become more common in pre-court and post-court sentencing.

The Drugs Act 2005 introduced Required Assessment for people testing positively for certain Class A drugs at the point of arrest or charge. The police can impose a requirement for assessment for treatment as there had been a low take-up rate of those testing positive at the point of arrest to go on to be assessed. Assessment and treatment can also be included as a condition of bail in some areas and is currently being evaluated prior to possible national roll-out. What this means is that the ability for offenders to choose whether or not to enter treatment has been curtailed by legislation and practice.

Evaluating DTTOs

The 'delivery and effectiveness' of seven of the 12 DTTOs across London has been evaluated by the National Addiction Centre (*Probation*, 2003, p3). Most offenders were using crack and heroin and were spending on average £724.70 per week on drugs, mainly financed through acquisitive crime. After three months, many that were still on the DTTO had reduced their frequency and amount of heroin and crack taken. Their level of crime had also reduced and there were improvements to their psychological and physical health. Young offenders and those on stimulants were more likely to drop out and the most successful 'were those with the longest and most serious histories of drug use and offending'. This is not surprising and accords with the research by McIntosh and McKeganey (2001) that drug users do not have to hit 'rock bottom' to decide to stop offending, but may do so after making a 'rational decision' using their own free will to decide to desist from drugs. Thus the decision to stop taking drugs need not be one of life or death but rather 'having a powerful desire to exit based on the unacceptable nature of what they have become' (McIntosh and McKeganey, 2001, p54).

There were variations between clusters in terms of frequency of testing and the service offered and the report stated that when stricter parameters were set there were larger falls in drug use and offending. Equally interesting was the variation in knowledge of and frequency of making DTTOs by Magistrates' and Crown Courts. There was an acknowledgement that the order was 'a good idea in principle' but was seen to need motivation by the offender.

The House of Commons Committee of Public Accounts took evidence from key staff, including the Chief Executives of the National Offender Management Service (then Martin Narey) and of the National Treatment Agency (Paul Hayes), and the Director General of the National Probation Service for England and Wales (Stephen Murphy). This produced some challenging exchanges between the MPs on the Committee and the three people above that are pertinent to how substance misusers are perceived by the nation's elected representatives.

> **Mr Narey** [answering question 48]: *We are giving people a great deal of support, we are not requiring abstinence, we are being pragmatic about the fact that they [substance-misusing offenders] are unlikely to turn away from taking drugs very quickly and they may relapse over and over again. We are not giving them financial support, but we are giving them a great deal of other support to try to wean them off drugs. The thing that I like about this order [DTTO] is that it is absolute realism about the nature of drug addiction.*

> **Q49 Mr Jenkins**: *But you see it is a continuing problem for our society and it is one which is not going to go away, so let us try to contain it.*

> **Mr Narey**: *I am rather more optimistic than that. There is some containing of this and as I mentioned earlier on, evidence suggests that re-offending for every day that you are on this programme is perhaps 75 per cent reduced. The eventual aim is to get people off drugs permanently and it may take a number of attempts, but eventually we can and will solve the drug problem, which is very nearly overwhelming, but I think it is a very pragmatic and practical approach to doing so.*

> **Mr Jenkins**: *I wish you well in this task.*

> **Mr Steinberg**: *Mr Narey, I like you a lot, I have known you a long time, but you should be a social worker and nothing to do with prisons, to be quite honest.*

> **Chairman**: *Was that a compliment or an insult?*

> **Q50 Mr Steinberg**: *It was a compliment. He is too nice to be in the Prison Service and that is probably the reason it is the way it is. I was asking Parliamentary Questions about this six months ago, as you are probably aware. I was talking to some solicitors and they were asking me to put some questions in the House about the Drug Treatment and Testing Orders because they felt they were a waste of time, a failure. They were spending more time now back in court than they were previously with all the offences which are being re-committed whilst they are on these Orders.*
> (House of Commons Committee of Public Accounts, 2005, pEv9)

ACTIVITY 3.3

What do you understand from the above exchange? What does it say about how effective practice with substance abusers is understood by politicians?

COMMENT

The reference to social work seems to imply that it is an activity that is 'nice' and therefore cannot apply to work with offenders, especially if they have a substance misuse problem. This seems to be a rather crude stereotype and may have been designed to put the National Offender Management Service (NOMS) chief executive on the defensive.

The report commented on the impact of the DTTO, which could run between six months and three years, the average being 12 months. Of the original sample in three pilot areas, 80 per cent had re-offended within two years of the start of their order. Only 28 per cent had reached full term or had been revoked early for good progress, 44 per cent of offenders had failed to keep to the terms of the order, 22 per cent had been convicted for a further offence and 6 per cent of orders failed to be completed due to problems of ill health or the person having died.

Completion rates varied between 8 per cent in Kent and 71 per cent in Dorset; however, this is not comparing like with like as in the latter area, orders tended to be for only six months and all on orders were placed in a hostel.

ACTIVITY 3.4

Are DTTOs cost-effective?

The report chose to aggregate the full costs of putting offenders on DTTOs and attributing this against only the offenders who were successful. The figures then appear as follows:

Cost per DTTO averages at £6,000
Cost of a prison place per year £30,000
Cost of successful completions (including the cost of failures) £21,000.

What do you think of assessing DTTOs in this way?

COMMENT

The report acknowledges that NOMS 'argued that this estimate failed to recognise that benefits from reduced drug use were often derived even though offenders did not complete the order' (House of Commons Committee of Public Accounts, 2005, p10).

The MPs had interviewed drug-misusing offenders and found that some had had problems getting their Job Seekers Allowance started, and had significant housing problems, either being homeless or finding it difficult to get away from their 'drug-misusing peer group'. Others needed further support after the order ended, as breaking a long-term drug habit was not a short-term proposition. (House of Commons Committee of Public Accounts, 2005, p15)

The Misuse of Drugs Act 1971 – 30 years on

In 2000 there was an independent report into the 1971 Misuse of Drugs Act, chaired by Lord Runciman, that found that in the period of almost 30 years since the Act it had not been possible to eradicate drug use. They thought that this was not achievable, was not a realistic, nor could it be, sensible goal of public policy. The report was 'forcibly struck' by the lack of research into drug use in the United Kingdom and the fact that the largest part of the drugs budget went into enforcement without knowing if this worked. Despite large seizures of drugs, the amount available was still substantial, no less pure and not more expensive. Choking off the supply side and not doing enough on the demand side was not working. They commented:

> Our overall conclusion is that demand will only be significantly reduced by education and treatment, not by the deterrent effect of the law ... harm [will not] be reduced by imprisoning those whose problematic drug use could, more effectively, be helped by treatment and rehabilitation in a setting where all the other problems almost always associated with such drug use can be tackled too. It is clear to us that tackling problem drug use must always also involve tackling social deprivation. (pp8–9)

ACTIVITY 3.5

How would you as a social worker seek to tackle social deprivation on an estate where you have young clients who are vulnerable to the temptation/threat of taking substances?

COMMENT

Dealing with issues of deprivation can lead to practitioners feeling impotent to create change. However, there are strategies for tackling deprivation and it is important to learn what strategic alliances can be formed with other professionals in the voluntary and statutory sectors. This is not a problem that can be solved by an agency working in isolation. It is worth making contact with the Crime Reduction Partnership and community safety team. With Sure Start, Children's Fund, Youth Inclusion Support Panels and many other initiatives potentially available, homework is essential. Local councillors and community groups can be mobilised and are probably already wanting to create change. Your task may be to persuade local people that effective work with disaffected youth would mean offering constructive alternatives to hanging around the estate and not 'pinning' them into their homes on anti-social behaviour orders.

In 2002 the government launched its Updated Drug Strategy (which is mentioned briefly in Chapter 2, along with the Crime and Disorder Act 1998 that introduced Drug Treatment and Testing Orders). This latest strategy envisages active partnership at government level between the Home Office, Department of Health, Department of Education and Skills, HM Customs and Excise, the Office of the Deputy Prime Minister and the Foreign and Commonwealth Office. At a local level the National Treatment Agency will work with the Drug Prevention Advisory

Service to support local organisations. Drug action teams and local agencies work together to deliver the services needed.

In particular, there are key targets, which the strategy states as follows:

- prevent young people from using drugs by maintaining prohibition which deters use and by providing education and support; targeting action on the most dangerous drugs and patterns of drug use and the most vulnerable young people;

- reduce the prevalence of drugs on our streets; tackling supply at all levels from international traffickers, to regional drug barons and street dealers, with an increased emphasis on intelligence sharing and effective policing and confiscating the proceeds of drug trafficking;

- reduce drug-related crime: providing support to drug misusers and communities most in danger of being destroyed by drugs; working together to create stable, secure, crime-free lives and neighbourhoods; and taking every opportunity within the criminal justice system and within the community to refer people into treatment; and

- reduce the demand for drugs by reducing the number of problematic drug users – those who already have serious drug problems: providing effective treatment and rehabilitation to break the cycle of addiction whilst minimising the harm drugs cause.

Working with families

The new environment

In 2008 HM Government launched the fourth drug strategy entitled *Drugs: Protecting families and communities 2008–11* (Home Office, 2008). The Home Secretary described the difference in the latest strategy as focusing more on families, addressing the needs of parents and children as individuals, as well as working with whole families. There was a commitment to working with communities but also to target the most prolific drug users.

What will be of particular interest to social workers is the stress given to working together with other professionals. However, there is a degree of conflation between social work and community issues that confuses the notion of joint work:

> *Ensuring that children's social services should know about drug-using parents where children are at risk as a result of their drug use, or local communities can work with the police and other agencies to disrupt and dismantle open street markets and close down cannabis factories and crack houses.* (Home Office, 2008, p5)

After reminding drug users that they had a responsibility to engage in treatment, in return for help and support, the new strategy continued by highlighting its determination to be strong on enforcement and then to the concept of treatment before discussing prevention and communications. The strategy discusses the importance of a whole family approach.

The question of prioritisation of substance-misusing individuals is an interesting one. Social work is concerned with the rights of the individual and the subject of coercion is a tricky one where the individuals are damaging themselves as well as upsetting their families. The new strategy prioritises those who cause most harm to communities and families with the intention of getting offenders and parents into treatment. Social workers are likely to be liaising with police, probation and other agencies that they may not be used to working with. It is envisaged that there will be more 'Family Intervention Projects' which are seen as already working with around 1,500 families engaged in anti-social behaviour (ASB). This is unfortunate as it links the need for family support for substance misuse to ASB but many families have a substance-misusing member who is not anti-social in outlook and this labelling is not helpful. This will be discussed further in the chapter.

On a positive note the strategy is more flexible than earlier versions in that effective treatment is acknowledged as including harm reduction methods as well as abstinence. Indeed this might include injectable heroin, methadone or drug replacement approaches. Evidence-based approaches are seen as the key to effectiveness. This should result in family/carer involvement in the planning process, and using budgets to help those who successfully complete treatment to access housing, employment, education and training. Substance misusers who are out-of-work will be offered specialist support with employment specialists to overcome barriers to work and ensure that there are links between drug partnerships and treatment providers and Jobcentre Plus.

Preventing harm

The report advocates prompt treatment for drug-misusing parents with a treatment need, which might require a package of interventions. Thus parents might need parenting skill support, young people drug education, family support that might include grandparent involvement, with financial support to carers of children classified as 'in need'. Children can be pushed into an inappropriate caring role and it is important that young people are given support and are not left to flounder and have their development impaired. There will be guidelines published *to improve the involvement of family and carers, including in the shaping and delivery of treatment/ support, and the development of family intervention skills of drug misuse workers* (Action Plan, Home Office, 2008, p12). Self-help family groups will be supported, and the 'third sector' and kin carers, such as grandparents who take on family responsibilities will be given more support, which could be financial (from local authorities).

Klee et al. (2002) conducted a parenting study documenting the experiences of 50 women drug users during pregnancy, through childbirth and into the early period of the child's life. There was a supplementary study of 49 social work and health care professionals. The differences in female and male patterns in substance misuse mirror the different roles and views present in society. Thus when it comes to pregnancy it is easy for those who do not have experience of working with substance misusers to adopt a judgemental attitude. Pregnancy can amplify this with the complication of the drugs adding to the low self-esteem of the women. Lewis (2002) (Chapter 3 in this book) makes the point that substance abuse does not stop a woman from being a good mother but the myth of the ideal mother may inhibit a woman who is taking substances from accessing services. Pregnancy is obviously a very emotional time for women and for those who take substances it is essential that the worker is non-judgemental and does not label the woman as deviant. It is vital that as wide a support network as is wanted is nurtured and facilitated.

In the sample of this study approximately three-quarters of the women had not planned their pregnancy and this added to their stress level. Some had not revealed the level of their drug taking to partners, friends or family, or might be in unstable relationships. There might also be a fear of informing health and social services in case they were seen as inadequate mothers. Indeed there was a fear that they might have their child taken into care. Social work contact could be a source of stress, although women who had been in care were more likely to acknowledge that they would benefit from support (Klee and Lewis, 2002). Klee, while acknowledging the limited sample size, made some interesting observations about the relationship between the pregnant client and the professional. In a chapter entitled 'overcoming the barriers' there was evidence that the professionals were becoming more aware of the particular needs of drug-using women. However, when understanding or sensitivity was missing the lack of trust that followed was long lasting. Fear of the child being taken into care resulted in a fear of social workers and indicates that social work intervention has to be sensitive and has to acknowledge and work on its image. One interesting finding was that the variation in parenting skills in non-substance-abusing women was as significant as between substance-abusing women. Social worker and other professionals need to work on their protocols for sharing information to make inter-professional work a reality. Interestingly the book also includes some impressive examples of good practice so suspicion and 'silo mentalities' do not have to be the rule.

As parents move in and out of stability Barnard (2007) comments that the needs of the children within the family can become secondary to the need to obtain and use drugs. This can lead to 'neglect and abuse'. Citing a number of studies from the US and the UK she makes a strong case that parental problem misuse of drugs and alcohol is one of the most likely causes for children being taken into care. Substance misuse can affect the emotional bonding between parent and child and lead to problems with attachment. Her book is a very penetrating study of how families struggle and cope with the knowledge and understanding of having a member who has a drug problem. The Scottish study drew on the experiences of families where substances were taken by parents or their children and gave a graphic demonstration of the impact of substance and alcohol misuse on the family. On occasion parents could become split on how to deal with their children who were taking drugs – in Barnard's words: *the family was at war with itself*. There was some evidence that mothers were more prepared to excuse and mediate the behaviour of the children whereas the fathers withdrew as a coping mechanism. This role could leave the mother isolated within the family.

Siblings

One strength of the Barnard study was to reveal a hidden group who often suffered in silence when a child took substances. This group is the siblings who appeared to be sidelined by the helping professionals. The siblings might be seen by social workers or specialist drug workers as potential supports but their distress often passed unnoticed. When parents were able to stabilise, they were usually able to see the impact of their drug taking on their children. However, when they were not stable this led to problematic behaviour that was not healthy for the child. It is worth quoting Barnard's views from her research:

> The prevalent operational presumption of the recent past *not to anticipate* problems with childrearing just because that parent has a drug problem runs counter to the conclusions reached by this research. We do not help parents, or indeed their children, if we fail fully to recognise, and address the potential for drug problems to compromise parental capacity. This is not an issue confined to agencies charged with social welfare for children and families, but for any agency dealing with problem drug users. Where someone has a drug problem and is a parent, their children have to be taken into consideration. (2007, pp78–9)

Kroll and Taylor (2003) citing a number of studies in the US and the UK found the evidence on links between substance misuse and child care contradictory. Indeed it might be the over-reaction of professionals that creates the link between these two concerns. They comment that it is necessary to understand why the substance use is occurring and whether it is in effect an intervening variable, used to ameliorate another problem. Is it a symptom or a cause of problems within the family? In Barnard's study the responsibility of taking on the children often fell to grandparents and other members of the extended family. The level of support of these extended family members and of the parents might explain why some siblings took to drugs when others didn't. The personality of the young person was also likely to be a significant factor. This is a complex area and does not lend itself to simplistic solutions.

The family

There is a danger that specialist research on alcohol does not engage with the wider literature on families (Velleman and Orford, 1999). Their research consisted of asking a number of 16–35-year-olds their recollections of being brought up in a household where a parent had a drinking problem. They cite research which found that such children recalled more family rows (Black et al., 1986), which were not necessarily focused on the drinking but might include issues such as gambling, infidelity, finances or behaviour (Wilson and Orford, 1978). Black et al. also found the children of alcoholics also reported more violence (from all family members) and there was an increased likelihood of sexual abuse. Weighing up the evidence on the links between parental drinking and the long-term impact on their children, Velleman and Orford are cautious in proffering possible explanations. They do not discount a possible genetic link (see also Phillips, 2007) and are more persuaded by a differential association explanation whereby young people are 'taught' this type of drinking behaviour, which they learn to model. A further model draws on a positivist explanation whereby the family environment is seen as the cause, with family stress and discord leading to role reversal between parent and child. The child has to cope with inconsistent parenting, which might include both loving and fear. They concluded that as children, the offspring of problem drinkers were at more risk of having problems themselves and of going on to have substance misuse problems in later life. What was encouraging about Velleman and Orford's research was the conclusion that:

> (T)he offspring of problem drinking parents, as a group, do not have much poorer adulthood outcomes than comparisons, and that in the case of many variables of interest differences are completely absent...(p230)

This research referred to the situation where the child remained with their parent(s). The situation becomes more complicated when the child moves to a foster carer or adoptive parent. Mather (2007) comments that it may not be possible to parent this situation in a sensitive manner without detailed knowledge of the child's history. The child might have witnessed the impact of drugs on their family. They may have been stigmatised because of their social network. Following on from this, when substitute carers become involved with children of substance misusers they can be given misleading advice. Consequently carers need to be given direct access to the child's medical records so that they understand the full medical history of both the child and the parent(s). Phillips (2007) gives an example of a very difficult case where a young man called Euan, with two parents who were heavy substance misusers, was adopted at the age of 11 (pp202–11). The case highlighted the extremely difficult situations that adoptive parents can find themselves in when there is continuing contact between the natural parents and their child, with their role being compromised by the unstable behaviour of the parents. Social services do not emerge with great credit in the story as practitioners failed to recognise that the adoptive parents would need support from time to time when situations became very unstable. Indeed they were accused of wanting financial support by a social worker when they requested skilled specialist support for the young man. The implication was that once the adoption had gone through they were expected to cope with whatever problems arose.

Fortunately this poor practice does not have to be the norm. Bell and Sim (2007) who are senior officers in the Families for Children Team, the fostering and adoption section in Glasgow social work services, give an impressive account of good practice. In July 2003 they estimated that 807 out of 1,100 accommodated children and young people were in 380 foster care households. They commented that chronic substance misuse was one of a number of factors that led to parents being unable to care for their children. Undertaking novel research it was found that in 395 cases (48 per cent) out of the 807 parental drug misuse was the reason for the need for accommodation or else a reason why the parent was unable to be rehabilitated. They felt that the 48 per cent figure was an underestimate if longer-term care was also included.

In Chapter 7 the 'wheel of change' model is described that highlights the likelihood of relapse. Bell and Sim (2007) comment that children in foster care are likely to be anxious about the health of their parent as they know how chaotic their parents' lifestyle is likely to be. Thus, missed contact appointments can be very worrying for the child. They described a 'growing belief' that very challenging young children needed a 'professional' family placement before they could move on to a permanent placement. Unlike the adoptive parents of Euan, they talk about support being available *beyond 5 pm and be available over weekends and holidays* (p283). They stress the need for partnership and openness and the need, in some cases, to sever the link between the most vulnerable young people and their chaotic substance-misusing parents.

This last study highlighted substance misuse, but what about families where alcohol is the major problem? Forrester and Harwin (2007) make the point that research has shown that parental substance misuse was a major factor in local authority interventions into families. In their research in four London local authorities 100 out of 290 families – 183 children – had substance misuse as an actual or alleged concern. Of these 100 families 41 had an alcohol problem, 32 drug misuse and 27 both alcohol and drugs. Issues of neglect were common to all groups with alcohol linked to domestic violence, and drug misuse a threat of harm to newborn babies. Alcohol was also linked to non-co-operation with social workers.

Children of drug- and alcohol-misusing parents clearly experienced inner conflicts as they had attachments whilst they suffered from deep neglect. This makes the task of the social worker difficult as they balance the desire of the child to maintain contact with their parent with the harm they experienced in doing so. Children may feel guilt about their parents' behaviour, possibly as they resent what they are forced to do to keep the household intact, when they would prefer to be doing the same as their peers. They may subjugate their own needs, start to offend, have other problems e.g. eating disorders (Kroll and Taylor, 2003).

Forrester and Harwin's (2007) study has very important implications for social work. First, they comment that many social workers were ill prepared to work with substance misuse, with little input on this in their training. Second, in alcohol cases (68 of the 100 cases) children were more likely to have experienced harm, which was often serious in nature. It would appear that in drug cases the social worker was more prepared to consider out-of-home placements than in alcohol cases. Despite the fact that home placements were more likely to break down in alcohol cases than in drug ones, this was the preferred outcome for social workers. Earlier research by Forrester found that social workers viewed drug cases as more serious than alcohol ones. This may be due to the illegality of the substances, perhaps related to criminal activity. The conclusion of Forrester and Harwin was that social workers tended to be over optimistic in cases where there was alcohol misuse in comparison to drug ones. There was a need to educate social workers about the nature and levels of drug and alcohol misuse, with an emphasis on alcohol issues.

The carers

Drug Action and Alcohol Teams (DAATs) offer a fast track service to substance misusers and get users into treatment very quickly. They also offer support to family members who are often the catalyst for change and also keep the family intact as a unit, at great emotional cost. The carer may have been struggling for a long time without support and be on the verge of breakdown. It is patently very stressful to see close family members abuse themselves and damage others by their inconsistent and unpredictable behaviour. The carer may be young – parenting the parent – their needs may be partially met by them having contact with other young people in a similar situation. When should this situation be allowed to continue and when will there need to be an intervention will have to be assessed by the social worker? As an example of what can be offered one London DAAT offers a nine-week structured programme/ support group to carers.

In week one the session looks at the 'ripple effect' on all areas of life and relationships; the impact on physical and emotional health, finances, children and the family. Week two examines the different substances and their impact as well as physical and psychological dependence. This will perhaps explain the behaviour of the user.

Week three is very important. By this stage the group is likely to have gelled and the members will be engaging in open dialogue about the pain and distress of living in a household where there is drug/alcohol use and misuse. Treatment methods, issues of motivation and the role of the carer would be covered. They may feel empowered to encourage the user to change or they may be empowered themselves to withdraw from offering care. The programme may have the effect on the carer of making them realise that they do not wish to continue in this role. Week four continues with a local carers' organisation explaining the support that can be offered.

Week five is an opportunity for carers to discuss the sorts of crises that can emerge and possible responses, Some crises will be more severe than others and may require different responses. Week six has some service users join, where carers can ask questions that they may feel inhibited from asking their own family members: what works and what doesn't.

Week seven looks at strategies for carers to manage their own stress. This might be techniques and/or alternative therapies. Week eight looks at the nature of families and the impact of substances on roles and relationships. Finally, week nine consolidates the learning, reviews the course and informs where further support can be sought.

The programme is one that draws on skills that social workers should be capable of fulfilling. There may be gaps in knowledge but this could be filled with appropriate reading and liaison with professionals who work in the field. Empowering carers may be the catalyst for change that can change the life of a substance misuser. Family therapy where there is substance misuse might be systemic in form, or psychodynamic or cognitive behavioural. Social workers may feel confident in working in this way and the family may well be the way to change the cycle. The family can be a source of great strength but with a need to 're-balance' and to tap into the resources present within it. The skill of the therapist is to search for solutions, be non-judgemental and to help the family to reach a successful outcome. Washton and Zweben (2006) in their chapter on assessment examine in detail what can be learnt from the assessment process and in offering therapeutic feedback to determine the nature and extent of the clients' drug-taking behaviour. It includes an assessment of the roles that family members may play in the substance taking.

The drug strategy (Home Office, 2008) emphasised a new approach of family support, more prevention, intervening earlier with families at risk, with what is described as a 'whole family approach'. This is described as:

> *(I)ntervening to meet the needs of the entire family, involving the family in the planning and process of treatment, extending family interventions and introducing better support for parents to access drug treatment.* (p24)

The Drug Strategy 2010 has three key themes: reducing demand, restricting supply and building recovery (see Chapter 6). This fits with the EU Drugs Strategy 2013–2020 published by the Council of Europe. This aims to protect human health and social stability and security. The intention is to reduce drug supply and demand for individual nations, within the EU and internationally. There is a recognition that the illicit drugs market exists beyond national boundaries and that there are trends in usage that also transcend these boundaries. In particular it recognises:

- an increasing trend towards poly-substance use, non-opioid drug use and new psychoactive substances;
- the need to provide access to prescribed controlled medications;
- the need to improve the quality and access of demand reduction services;
- the need to reduce the levels of blood-borne diseases such as hepatitis C and outbreaks of HIV infections;
- the high level of drug-related deaths in the EU;
- the need to provide an integrated health care approach;
- the intention to reduce psychiatric co-morbidity;
- the aim of reducing illicit drug markets and changing trafficking routes;
- the prevention of distribution of essential chemicals used in manufacturing illicit drugs and those used as cutting agents.

The strategy also encourages the dissemination of knowledge about drugs and recognises the contribution of Europol for policing matters and the EMCDDA for facilitating knowledge and evaluation. In turn, the EMCDDA has produced information on the strategy, which can be accessed at: http://emcdda.europa.eu/topics/pods/eu-drugs-strategy-2013-20

The EMCDDA helpfully summarises the strategy and highlights the growth of new psychoactive drugs, the challenge of users combining illicit drugs with alcohol and the phenomenon of 'legal highs'. In addition to the usual aims of reducing demand and supply it includes for the first time 'the reduction of the health and social risks and harms caused by drugs' as a key policy objective. Thus social reintegration and recovery becomes a core driver and this includes young people, older users and those in prison. This should result in quality standards and an evidence-based approach.

In order to meet the ambition of the 2010 Drug Strategy the then key organisation, the NTA, produced a document entitled *Medications in recovery. Re-orientating drug dependence treatment* (July 2012). This was directed at heroin users, the largest single group in treatment. While fewer younger people are presenting as dependent, there is an aging group for whom the prognosis is not good. Opioid substitution treatment (OST) has been offered to users but has often become an end in itself rather than a step in the change process. US studies indicate that over a 30-year period half of the users die, a fifth stop and the rest may cut back on their usage to some extent. The report was critical of practices that left people long term on OST; rather it advocated a more joined-up and holistic intervention with broad-ranging support for individuals and their families.

This fits with Kroll and Taylor (2003) who concluded that what is needed is a holistic approach that brings together specialists from both adults' and children's services to which I would add specialist drug and alcohol services. What is needed is a clear assessment of the life and pressures on the child/young person to protect and/or strengthen the support available to them. The needs of the child must be considered separately to the needs of the parent, although they may be heavily intertwined. This might require support to strengthen the family or a decision to separate them. It needs an active decision, not an outcome through 'happenstance'. We need to be aware of the impact of substances on individuals and not to minimise the impact of alcohol. Above all else, whilst adults have the right to make their own decisions, the state has a responsibility towards its young. There is no excuse for social workers to be ignorant about substances, their impact on families (Barnard, 2007), what can be done, and professional responsibilities.

ACTIVITY 3.6

Reading the last paragraph do you think that there is potential for professionals to over-react when substance use is present in clients with children? Why might this be the case and how can the social worker avoid this?

COMMENT

Social work is strongly committed to anti-discriminatory practice and the concept of client empowerment. If social workers are knowledgeable about alcohol, drugs, their impact and the concept of harm reduction, then the danger of making ill-informed decisions will be reduced. Is the client motivated to change? Are they co-operating with professionals? Are young people in the family safe and being seen as the primary focus for concern, i.e. child protection issues are not being downplayed? The 2008 Drug Strategy is based on the notion of early intervention. In what is described as 'Our new approach' it comments:

The five major initiatives on drugs are reproduced in tabular form below for easy reference:

1995	1998	2001	2002	2008	2010
Tackling drugs together: a strategy for England 1995–8	**Tackling drugs together to build a better Britain: the government's 10-year strategy for tackling drug misuse**		**Updated drug strategy**	**Drugs: protecting families and communities**	**Reducing demand, restricting supply, building recovery. Supporting people to live a drug free life.**
The White Paper had three major objectives for the newly formed drug action teams. *Crime* – to reduce drug-related crime; to enforce the law against drug suppliers; to reduce the public's fear of drug-related crime; to reduce the level of drug misuse in prisons. *Young people* – to discourage drug taking by young people; to ensure that drug education took place in schools; raising awareness amongst all school staff; to provide services to young people. *Public health* – to protect communities from all risks associated with drugs; to discourage substance misuse; to ensure access to services, including advice, counselling, treatment and rehabilitation etc.; to provide support to families of substance misusers.	*Young people* – to help young people resist drug misuse in order to achieve their full potential in society *Communities* – to protect our communities from drug related anti-social and criminal behaviour *Treatment* – to enable people with drug problems to overcome them and live healthy and crime-free lives *Availability* – to stifle the availability of illegal drugs on our streets Drug treatment and testing orders are contained in the Crime and Disorder Act 1998, as a major sanction to be used with offending substance misusers	June – the post of anti-drugs co-ordinator abolished (the drugs tsar). Government strategy moved from the Cabinet Office to the Home Office. The National Treatment Agency (NTA) launched in England, with other arrangements in place in the rest of the United Kingdom. The NTA commissions and co-ordinates treatment for drug misusers.	*Prevent* young people from using drugs by maintaining prohibition, by providing education and support; targeting action on the most dangerous drugs and patterns of drug use and the most vulnerable young people; *Reduce the prevalence of drugs*; tackling supply at all levels, with emphasis on intelligence sharing and effective policing, confiscating proceeds of drug trafficking; *Reduce drug-related crime*: providing support to drug misusers and communities most in danger of being destroyed by drugs; working together to create secure, crime free neighbourhoods; taking every opportunity within the criminal justice system and within the community to refer people into treatment; *Reduce the demand for drugs* by reducing the number of problematic drug users: providing effective treatment and rehabilitation to break the cycle of addiction whilst minimising the harm drugs cause. In addition, models of care for substance misuse treatment was launched.	*Protecting* communities through robust enforcement to tackle drug supply, drug-related crime and antisocial behaviour. *Preventing* harm to children, young people and families affected by drug misuse. *Delivering* new approaches to drug treatment and social re-integration. *Public* information campaigns, communications and community engagement. There will be a concentration on supporting communities and families. Local areas will have greater autonomy and flexibility to respond to the local needs and to the priorities of local communities. Focus to remain on the drugs that cause the greatest harms to communities, families and individuals. Local areas will have more flexibility to determine their response to the drugs which are causing the greatest harm to their communities. For young people, all substances should be addressed, including alcohol and volatile substances such as gases, glues and solvents.	*Reducing demand* – helping those who haven't tried drugs before to remain drug free and helping users to come off drugs. *Restricting supply.* *Building recovery* in communities.

(W)e must place a sharper focus on effective prevention and on intervening before problems become entrenched. Our new approach will emphasise family support, intervening earlier with families at risk, such as those where children may experience harm as a result of parental substance misuse, providing targeted youth support for vulnerable young people in all areas and providing effective treatment for those who do develop problems. We will take a whole-family approach, intervening to meet the needs of the entire family, involving the family in the planning and process of treatment, extending family interventions and introducing better support for parents to access drug treatment. (pp23–4)

This quotation fits very well with good social work practice and implicitly includes the need for a thorough assessment of the family, a task that draws on social-work knowledge, skills and judgement. The voluntary aspects inherent in this might not be seen as problematic. However social workers might not be comfortable with the notion of compulsion in treatment, but as we will see in Chapter 5 when we examine the work of Trotter (1999), constructive work can be achieved if we are clear, honest and transparent about our role. In truth all social work should uphold these values and often they are unspoken. So the final point about effective treatment, which as mentioned is the theme of Chapter 5, is the point where we use our knowledge, values and skills to bring about change in the client. Working with substance-misusing clients is a great challenge and there are ground rules to observe, like not trying to work with a client when they are under the influence of drugs and being very clear about the role that you have to follow.

CHAPTER SUMMARY

This chapter has looked at the history of drug legislation and policy and then examined the way that Drug Treatment and Testing Orders have been used with substance-misusing offenders. The evidence suggests considerable variation in how these orders were implemented in England and Wales, also that unless the offender has support on a number of social problems the risk of re-offending is high. Change is a slow process and offenders were breached for non-compliance twice as often as they actually re-offended. Social work is about seeing the totality of the client's life and empowering them to work towards change. Sims sums up the problem for correctional agencies, echoing the words of Martin Narey in his exchange with the MPs on the Committee of Public Accounts:

[T]here is a need for correctional treatment providers and criminal justice personnel to recognise that recovery from substance abuse is not perfectly linear In institutional- or community-based corrections, and more often than not, the realisation that recovery from substance abuse is a step-up/step-down/step-up process is critical yet is difficult to accept given the requirements of institutional rules or probation/parole conditions of supervision. (Sims, 2005, p23)

Social work is now catching up with the need to engage with clients with drug and alcohol problems (Kendrick, 1999). The 2008 Drugs Strategy should put social work centre stage in this respect.

Bennett, T and Holloway, K (2005) *Understanding drugs, alcohol and crime.* Buckingham: Open University.
Bennett and Holloway give a comprehensive overview of the links between drugs, alcohol and crime. They also cover drug policy.

Sims, B (ed.) (2005*) Substance abuse treatment with correctional clients. Practical implications for institutional and community settings.* New York: The Haworth Press.
This is an American textbook that examines compulsory intervention with substance-misusing clients.

South, N (2002) Drugs, alcohol and crime, in Maguire, M, Morgan, R and Reiner, R (eds) *The Oxford handbook of criminology* 3rd edition. Oxford: Oxford University Press.

Nigel South's chapter reviews trends in drug and alcohol use and examines issues such as decriminalisation versus prohibition.

Working Party of the Royal College of Psychiatrists and the Royal College of Physicians (2000) *Drugs. Dilemmas and choices.* London: Gaskell.

This book gives a history of the growth of drug taking, discusses why people take drugs, the consequences of this and what treatment can and can't achieve.

www.homeoffice.gov.uk/drugs/
Home Office: drugs resource.

http://emcdda.europa.eu/topics/pods/eu-drugs-strategy-2013-20
The EMCDDA website: Commentary on the 2013–20 EU drug strategy.

Chapter 4

What is known about drug misusers and drug offenders and the drugs commonly used?

Introduction

In this chapter you will consider what is known about substance misusers and drug offenders from the research, as well as implications for their needs. We will discuss what types of drugs are commonly used and what they do. How can you recognise whether your client is likely to be or is actually taking drugs? There is a practice example with a family, where the knowledge of substance misuse is put to good effect and abstinence and harm-reduction issues are important in the outcome of the social work intervention.

We will consider the problem of dual diagnosis, when a client might be taking substances while suffering from a mental health problem. There will be activities for you to work through to enhance your knowledge of drugs and effective interventions with clients.

What types of drugs are commonly used and what do they do?

In the 2005 document produced by the Home Office entitled *Tackling drugs – changing lives. Delivering the difference*, which is available online, the point is made that 'controlled drugs are dangerous and no-one should take them' (p4). It would be naïve in the extreme to believe that clients can be persuaded to change their substance-taking behaviour by providing insights, warnings or threatening them with the consequence of their actions. It should be remembered that clients can have access to prescription drugs, like barbiturates, that can be dangerous if the recommended dosage is exceeded. They may also be in surroundings where drugs like ecstasy are taken recreationally and they may not see this as a problem. This is discussed later in the chapter.

Barton (2003) believes that young people make conscious decisions as to what drugs they are going to take, with cannabis the most common drug followed by 'dance drugs' like ecstasy. This has led to young people becoming more 'drug wise'. Large numbers of young people experiment at some point in their lives and to some extent will regard this as 'normalised behaviour' (Parker et al., 1998). What is therefore important is that any discussion with the public, whether young or old, has to be realistic. Attempts to scare people into not taking drugs will not work when they see friends and strangers indulging and enjoying the experience. The hedonistic pleasure obtained from drugs makes it difficult to counter for some people who may need some time to acknowledge that there are negatives to taking substances. They may not be aware of the long-term dangers and potential effects on their mood and behaviour.

We will discuss in Chapter 7 what works and what doesn't work when social workers have contact with substance misusers. For example, use of labels, confrontation, scare tactics or trying to impose one's own goals, rather than working with the client, are very unlikely to succeed (McMurran and Hollin, 1993).

Social workers must start by understanding what drugs are commonly used and what they do. How do you recognise if your client might be taking substances, when if you don't ask and challenge you may never know if they are or not? In the past probation officers ignored this area and the level of awareness about substance misuse by offenders was low. It is now recognised as a major problem area to be checked out as part of the assessment process.

ACTIVITY 4.1

Before you start to learn about substances, let us start by examining the level of knowledge you bring with you. How would you list drugs that people take? You will then be able to test your starting knowledge against what would be useful to know.

Continued

Can you list common drugs that are often taken by substance misusers? Can you then list the symptoms that indicate their use?

Did you find this a difficult exercise to complete? Illegal drugs are categorised as being either Class A, B or C. Can you say what are the classes of drugs that you have thought of? Finally, what are the legal consequences if caught using or supplying them?

COMMENT

There is no reason why a social worker should have a strong knowledge of drugs but this can be resolved easily as there are plenty of sources available on the internet as well as in books. We cannot be experts in all aspects of human habits and behaviour but what social workers are good at (among other things) is their ability to network, to find out what they need to know and to reflect on learnt experiences. Sadly it is inevitable that some of your clients, whatever area of social work you practise in, will use and abuse substances and there is a need to be aware of the consequences and not to assume the worst possible outcomes because of this. Clients can be worked with effectively if they use substances but within limits. You cannot work with a person if they are 'under the influence' even if at other times you enjoy a good relationship with them. Fortunately, there is an excellent resource available to clients and professionals that provides much useful information, namely 'Ask Frank', which can be found at **www.talktofrank.com/**

Firstly, let us consider drugs in the context of Activity 4.1. All the following information below was obtained from the Ask Frank website and books by Gossop (2000) and the Working Party of the Royal College of Psychiatrists and the Royal College of Physicians (WPRCPRCP) (2000).

Drugs that reach the cells of the central nervous system are known as psychoactive. Psychoactive drugs are typically classified as stimulants, depressants and hallucinogens. Stimulants include amphetamines, cocaine, crack cocaine, ecstasy and also caffeine and tobacco. Depressants include cannabis, opiates, inhalants and alcohol. Finally, hallucinogens include LSD and 'magic mushrooms'. These drugs can be taken in a number of ways: orally, anally, snorted, smoked and/or injected. Many people take more than one drug at a time, which is usually referred to as poly-substance use. Use of drugs does not imply addiction and may be simply a facet of the individual's enjoyment of the effects of these substances. Others may take drugs recreationally as there is a social scene attached to them. It becomes misuse when the drugs involve a level of dependency that is unhealthy, when the person cannot control their use and it leads to problematic behaviour. Illegal drugs are put into three categories known as Class A, B and C. The maximum sentences for possession and supplying are given in the table below.

	Class A	Class B	Class C
Example of drug	Heroin, cocaine, LSD, ecstasy	Amphetamines (like speed), cannabis	Ketamine
Maximum penalty for possession	Seven years' imprisonment	Five years' imprisonment	Two years' imprisonment
Maximum penalty for supplying	Life imprisonment and an unlimited fine	14 years' imprisonment and an unlimited fine	14 years' imprisonment and an unlimited fine

Cannabis is a Class B drug and growing one's own can also be considered as dealing, which many people do not realise. This also includes selling to friends. Although it is possible that adults might not be prosecuted for possessing small amounts of cannabis for personal use, publicly smoking the drug can lead to arrest and being charged. This is likely if it is used near where children and young people go. Cannabis is a commonly taken illegal drug. Illicit drugs have a variety of different names and social workers may not know all of these and which drug they refer to. For example, with cannabis, when it is home grown it is often called skunk and may be twice as strong as imported 'herbal' cannabis. However, potency can deteriorate if the drug is stored for some time and the strong odour emanating from skunk when smoked is not a guide to its potency.

If you want to know about drugs then 'talk to Frank'

For professionals and clients the National Treatment Agency has produced an excellent website, the details of which are given again at the end of the chapter (it was given at the end of the Introduction).

Cannabis

'Ask Frank' covers much useful ground: the appearance of both cannabis and skunk; their cost, purity, their short-term and long-term effects; the chances of getting hooked; the risks, and most importantly the law. It warns that while cannabis *per se* is not physically addictive, people do get hooked on tobacco. Addiction is a difficult concept. Even when there is not a physical dependence on the drug, the person may feel that they need to take it for psychological reasons as they think that it helps them to keep troubling thoughts or pressures out of their consciousness. There is evidence that cannabis can have acute effects on the user, including anxiety, respiratory illness linked to the use of tobacco when taking cannabis, the increased risk of psychotic illness and the possibility of depreciation of memory and attention even after abstinence.

Cannabis is the most heavily used illicit drug in the world. It is available either as a resin or a herbal preparation. It can be cultivated in this country, in addition to being imported, and the former type can be significantly more potent. The issue of potency, measured by the level of the chemical THC, is an area according to Hunt et al. (2006) that is unclear in terms of the consequences of taking higher-potency cannabis. Increases in THC potency have been reported in the United States, Canada and the Netherlands. Cannabis may be smoked, vaporised or eaten. It is not injected. The link between cannabis and mental health is discussed later under 'Dual diagnosis'.

When people take cannabis they may feel happy and 'chilled out', they may get the giggles and feel happy, and get hungry. It will affect co-ordination, making driving and other operations hazardous. Users can become psychologically dependent and need to use the drug very often. This can lead to problems in other areas of the client's life, which can include relationship problems, numerous attempts to stop taking the drug, needing more of the drug to get the usual effect, spending more time obtaining the drug and less time on other activities. In short, life revolves around the drug and it ceases to be a leisuretime activity.

Cocaine

Cocaine is a Class A stimulant drug that can be sniffed (usually in a line), smoked or injected. It is an expensive habit to maintain. It has a quick effect on the user, creating a feeling of euphoria and extreme well-being. One problem that the user may face is not knowing what other chemicals may have been mixed in with it as it may well not be sold in a pure form. Physiologically the heart will beat faster and the person's body will become hotter. Users are likely to have a strong craving for more when the (short-term) effects wear off. Psychological dependence is likely to be strong also.

Clients using cocaine or crack may become very anxious or panicky and physically are at risk of developing serious health problems, including heart and/or respiratory problems, damage to veins (if injecting), ulcers, etc. Users may not be aware of the damage that they are doing to themselves as the drug acts to deaden pain. For social workers who are aware of a client who is both pregnant and a regular cocaine user there is a concern to investigate that the baby may be born with abnormalities and possibly suffer from withdrawal syndrome. There is a danger that the mother might miscarry or go into premature labour.

Ecstasy

Many young people, possibly up to half a million at weekends according to Drug-Scope, take ecstasy at weekends for the feelings of energy and well-being that it engenders. Emotions might become more intense and the young people dance for many hours at a time. There are concerns that the drug can be adulterated with other substances and the user might overdose after taking more of the drug while they wait for the effects to kick in. The drug has caused over 200 deaths in the past decade, often caused by the body overheating and dehydrating. Drinking excessive amounts of water can cause the body's salt level to change as the chemical prevents the production of urine. The immune system can also be affected. People who have various other conditions like heart problems are especially vulnerable.

Ketamine

This drug is a powerful hallucinogenic drug that has become more popular in recent years. It acts as an anaesthetic with a consequent loss of bodily sensation and possible inability to move. Mixing this drug with others is very dangerous.

Alcohol

Alcohol has been described as 'one of the more powerful, addictive and destructive drugs that is used on a large scale' (Gossop, 2000, p70). It has an anaesthetic effect and acts on the central nervous system. In small doses it is a depressant but in large doses it can kill. It is not a stimulant, despite the fact that alcohol can 'loosen the tongue' if drunk beyond moderation, which will vary between people. It would appear that small amounts of alcohol might protect against coronary disease and what con-stitutes a safe level is controversial (WPRCPRCP, 2000).

Alcohol impairs judgement, slows reflexes and can change people's behaviour, mak-ing them aggressive and violent. Many car accidents are a direct consequence of alcohol consumption and domestic violence can result from (typically) men coming home having drunk excessively. It is possible to build up a tolerance so that it appears that the person is not as incapacitated as they actually are. Alcohol causes liver damage (cirrhosis) and can cause liver cancer. As it is a toxic drug its effect can be found in a wide range of tissue problems throughout the body. Mothers who con-sume alcohol heavily in the early stages of their pregnancy can produce a baby with 'foetal alcohol syndrome'.

A report published by the Centre for Public Health on 4 August 2006 disclosed that in England around 217,900 men and 147,000 women were admitted to hospital in 2004–05 for alcohol-related conditions. The areas of greatest deprivation experience the greatest pressure on the health service, with areas like Liverpool, Manchester and Middlesbrough having 1,400 men per 100,000 of the population admitted to hospital, a rate 70 per cent higher than the average for England. The average loss of life expec-tancy due to alcohol is almost 10 months for men and five months for women. In Blackpool these rise to 23 months and 13 months respectively (that is, the women's rate here is higher than the national rate for men). What is also very dangerous and high is the level of binge drinking, where people drink twice as much in a single day as the recommended level. This is recorded per week, i.e. has the person binged on at least one occasion in the previous week, and the average level in England is 18.2 per cent. However, this increases to over 27 per cent in northern areas like Newcastle upon Tyne, Liverpool and Durham.

This is relevant for a number of reasons, including the link between alcohol and violence (including domestic violence). In 2005–06 there were 367,000 violent offences attributed to alcohol, according to the report. Thus for social workers there is a need to know what excessive consumption of alcohol can do to the client, their family and their ability to function in both the short- and longer-term.

The All Party Parliamentary Group on Alcohol Misuse published a report on the future of alcohol treatment services in May 2009. It recommended that the government needs cross-departmental leadership to tackle the growing alcohol problem. Heavy drinking among all age groups needs to be targeted as well as alcohol-related crime and hospital-related admissions. All PCTs need to have effective alcohol services that are accessible to local communities. The report revealed inconsistencies in the level of funding that had been directed towards alcohol services and in some cases it recorded that a harm reduction approach had been driven by a crime and disorder strategy rather than 'health considerations'. While members of the public might expect services to be developed in this area this was not 'a simple exercise'. Mental health services in some areas refused to treat clients who were dependent on alcohol.

The effects of alcohol can be devastating and clients need to be aware that they should seek support rather than try to abruptly stop drinking (cold turkey), which can be dangerous. About.com (an American website) highlights the physical impact of excessive alcohol: the destruction of brain cells, cirrhosis of the liver, infection, chronic inflammation, malnutrition, cardiovascular problems, sexual problems, increased risk of cancer and diabetes, etc. If not medically treated withdrawal can be dangerous. Mild symptoms could be the shakes, sweats, nausea, increased blood pressure but some might experience delirium tremens (DTs), the symptoms of which are disorientation, hallucinations and cardiovascular problems. DTs cannot be treated and can lead to heart attacks and/or strokes. The important message to give to clients is that mostly clients can be treated at home but some will need hospitalisation. It is very difficult for a regular drinker to stop without support. Alcohol is discussed further in Chapter 6.

The following table, which draws together the information on the different types of drugs, gives an indication of their effects and some of the risks in taking them.

Type	Stimulants	Hallucinogens	Depressants
Common name	Amphetamines, cocaine, crack, ecstasy, caffeine, tobacco (nicotine), khat	LSD, magic mushrooms, cannabis (a mild hallucinogen), ketamine	Cannabis, opiates including heroin, morphine, inhalants, alcohol, GHB, solvents
Effect	Can cause excitement, sense of well-being, feelings of relaxation, alertness	A 'trip' can last for a number of hours, affecting the mood of the user who may experience a different sense of movement, sounds, colour, etc. – illusions and delusions	Relaxation, lowering of inhibitions, euphoria, social pastime
Risks	Anxiety, tiredness, possible hallucinations and panic attacks, health problems possibly related to the heart, sharing of equipment can lead to hepatitis B or C and HIV/AIDS. Prolonged use may lead to extreme depression and lethargy	Bad trips can be terrifying, panic attacks, flashbacks can occur a long time after the drug has been taken, for those with a mental health difficulty this can be exacerbated. Users may become nauseous, anxious, depressed and totally disoriented	Opiates affect breathing, the heart, and all parts of the body. Pregnant women run the risk of miscarriage and the baby can be born addicted. Babies may die while being withdrawn. Death (for adults) can occur from suffocation caused by inhaling vomit when unconscious, damage to vital organs, irreversible brain damage. Some drugs are highly addictive. Health problems possibly related to the heart, sharing of equipment can lead to hepatitis B or C and HIV/AIDS

It should also be remembered that some users mix their drugs and this greatly adds to the danger of health problems, both mental and physical. Many drug fatalities are as a result of poly-drug use.

What is known about substance misusers and implications for their needs?

The EMCDDA situation summary report for the UK published in 2012 states that drug-related expenditure, including indirect consequences of drug abuse, remained broadly stable in percentage terms between 2005–10 (between 0.07 and 0.08 per cent of GDP). The UK drug strategies do not have a specific budget attached to them, with annual budget allocations given to those charged with providing services. Services for funding treatment have remained unchanged in cash terms but other budgets, for example counter-narcotics work in Afghanistan, has declined (**emcdda.europa.eu/ publications/country-overviews/uk**).

The 2004 National Report to the European Monitoring Centre for Drugs and Drug Addiction (EMCDDA) on the United Kingdom (Reitox, 2004) commented that we gain our knowledge about the level of drug use from household surveys that are under-taken in England and Wales (UK), Scotland and Northern Ireland. British Crime Surveys are carried out annually in England and Wales but less often in the rest of the United Kingdom. Various surveys are also undertaken among school-age children, again annually for children aged 11–15 in England and Wales but less often in the rest of the UK. The government spent £1,244 million in 2003/04 on direct expenditure for tackling drugs, with £149 million on protecting young people, £212 million on safe-guarding communities, £503 million on drug treatment and £380 million on reducing supply.

In England and Wales, where drug use is the highest, it is estimated that a third of the adult population have used a Class A drug and 50 per cent of the population will try an illicit drug at some point in their lifetime. It is young adults under the age of 30 that are most likely to use illicit drugs and the good news is that there is a gradual decline in use by 16–24 year olds (Reitox, 2004, p7). What is of concern, however, is the increased consumption by young people of crack, cocaine and ecstasy.

The 2008/9 British Crime Survey estimated that around two in five young people have never used illicit drugs, nearly one in four had used one or more drugs in the last year and about one in eight in the last month (Hoare, 2009). This type of information has now been discontinued. The Crime Survey for England and Wales (CSEW) in 2011/12 conducted among people aged 16–59 found that 36.5 per cent of respondents had tried drugs at least once in their lives, more specifically there was a lifetime prevalence of 31 per cent for trying cannabis, 11.5 per cent amphetamines, 9.6 per cent ecstasy, and 5.3 per cent LSD. The use of cannabis has declined steadily, since 2003/4; cocaine use increased from 1996 until 2003 and although there is some decrease it is still the second most frequently used drug.

Cannabis is the most commonly taken drug among all drug users throughout the UK for adults and those in school surveys. In younger people there was a difference in that in England among 11-year-olds use of volatile substances was more common than cannabis.

Having discussed different drugs let us now consider a case study where a number of substances, including alcohol and heroin, are being taken by a husband and wife where they have dependent children.

CASE STUDY

Phase one

Ted and Jo were in their late 20s and had three children, aged between four and eight years. Both parents had a history of drug and alcohol use. There had been several incidents of domestic violence, which took place while one or both of them were under the influence of whatever they had been taking at the time. (As time went on, it became apparent that the older two children had witnessed some of the violence.) They lived in an inner-city area of local authority housing, where unemployment, substance misuse, domestic violence and theft are commonplace. The area was frequently visited by the police. Ted and Jo's main parental figure was Jo's maternal grandmother, who was in her early seventies.

Ted had already served a prison sentence for drug- and alcohol-related offences and was again in prison serving a two-year sentence. This meant he would be in custody for one year and would be released to the supervision of the probation service. Jo found it extremely difficult to cope with the children without him. During the time Ted was in prison, the older two children reached school age. Jo, who had her own dependency problems to deal with, was unable to enrol the children into schools. They therefore missed their early educational experiences. Her grandmother helped her with the day-to-day management of the children, and always ensured that the children had enough to eat.

As the children did not attend school, services were not alerted at first to the difficulties Jo was experiencing. During this time, she also failed to attend medical and developmental check-ups for all of them, and as within the area there was a high turnover of PCT health visiting staff, they were not initially followed up.

A new health visitor picked up the children and alerted social services to the family. They were immediately visited by the initial contact team, and an assessment of the family's needs was made. This led to an initial case conference.

ACTIVITY 4.2

What would the initial assessment of the family have included? As the parents both had a history of substance misuse, but had no known history of social services involvement before this referral was made, how would the social worker have started to gather the cumulative information needed about the children?

In what ways could the impact of the parents' substance misuse on the children be assessed? Taking into account environmental aspects, do you consider that the area in which the family were living has an impact on Jo's ability to cope with her children?

COMMENT

This family have a number of presenting problems and the potential for a number of agencies to be involved with them. They have had police involvement, and it is possible that if they had been a social nuisance the local housing department might have an open file on them. The education department and education welfare service would see them as problematic and the health visitor too, although this needed following up. The social worker would thus join the number of organisations already involved. The family appear to be relying on the grandmother to keep the family unit going but is this realistically a long-term prospect?

Jo has a history of substance misuse; the social worker could refer her to the local Drug Action Team for an assessment and to see whether there was a need for immediate support in this aspect of her life.

CASE STUDY

Phase two
Following an initial case conference the family was allocated a social worker. From this, Jo was encouraged to take the children to their routine check-ups and immunisations. Jo was encouraged to register the two older children (who had missed early learning experiences) at their local primary school, and to place the third child's name on the waiting list for nursery. As she was already four and a half by this time, the social worker also helped Jo to put her name down for a Reception class place. She found out that this list was already full, and so had to register her son at a neighbouring school, where there were still places. This posed another difficulty for Jo, as while Ted was still in prison, she would have to get her children to different schools at the same time, before 9.00 a.m.

Immediately, the children's attendance suffered, becoming increasingly erratic as they went down with the childhood illnesses which many children contract when first starting school. Despite the regular support from her grandmother, Jo had difficulties motivating herself to do everything that she needed to do to manage everything the children, and the services working with her, required. She retreated into herself. This resulted in both the school and the education welfare service becoming more closely involved with Jo and her children.

ACTIVITY 4.3

Consider the number of agencies who were becoming involved with this family, and look at the ways in which they could work in a joined-up way. Think of the experiences the children had already encountered, and what support social workers could offer them to cope with what they had seen, heard, missed, etc.

COMMENT

Jo was trying to cope as a single parent with young children and a low income. She had a history of substance misuse and while it was important to focus on the needs of the children to ensure that they are not at risk, it was also important to work with the mother. A link to the local drug action team (DAT) could be very important, so what could this offer? The DAT might have a daily drop-in centre where Jo would get support with her drug and alcohol problems. They would offer her immediate triage to assess her health. She might benefit from Alcoholics Anonymous/Narcotics Anonymous meetings or if she is starting to become unstable in her use of substances she might be offered a maintenance script. The essential element here is to get her stable. A key worker from the DAT would be able to liaise with the other professionals who are involved. What is important is that all the professionals work together and this requires consistency. The social worker would have a key role here and the separation of roles ensures that the children and the mother have their needs met in a way that the welfare of the children is paramount and there is no role confusion as to who is responsible for the child and who is supporting the mother.

Helping to get Jo's children into school and the youngest one into nursery can help but there have been problems and the level of support may need to be increased. The important point here is to work with Jo and to recognise that being the sole parent is having a stressful and depressing effect on her. The issue of substance misuse should not be forgotten and the danger of her relapsing should be discussed openly and strategies discussed in how to deal with the danger symptoms that might trigger push her back towards taking substances. The issues related to relapse will be discussed further in Chapter 7. Jo might gain strength from support groups with fellow parents and this might be available through social services. Parenting support might also be effected by introducing a family aid worker into the family. Whatever assistance is given should be decided in discussion with Jo.

Looking at the above points, they are mostly what social work good practice is typically all about but with the important addition that the substance-misuse aspect has been factored in and appropriate extra assessment/resources put in place. This is not an optional extra but essential good practice. Adding a further professional organisation, in this case the DAT, means that the lines of communication must be clear and open.

CASE STUDY

Phase three
In the meantime, Ted finished his prison sentence. He returned home, to the same area, friendships, pressures and temptations as before. He had a probation officer too, with whom he had regular contact.

Within a short period, his former contacts offered to pay him for collecting and delivering illicit supplies of drugs. He was aware that, if caught, he would go straight back to prison, but he felt initially that having been absent from the family
Continued

CASE STUDY *continued*

for so long, he had a responsibility to make up his absence to them, by making some money. He was very open about this activity to the family's social worker. He saw his probation officer at the probation office and the social worker in the family home as there were regular visits when the social worker met with Jo, Ted and the children.

ACTIVITY 4.4

How does the social worker work with Ted, and with which other agencies, in order to enable Ted to reflect upon the effect his activities are having on his family?

COMMENT

This is a worrying development and implies that there is a huge risk that Ted will return to his substance misuse. Furthermore, there is a danger that the social worker will be compromised if given information of illegal activity and this is not shared with fellow professionals. While Ted was in prison he should have been given support for his substance misuse. Ideally this through-care should have continued into after-care. The social worker and the probation officer need to liaise as Ted will be seeing the probation officer weekly. It can be very difficult on discharge for an ex-prisoner to rejoin a family where their role has been taken over by the other parent. A period of readjustment is often required. Furthermore, a person who has taken illicit substances will need support not to rejoin their peers who may encourage them to go back into their old habits. Thus staying off substances requires a major break from previous contacts and their old way of life.

This is a family where parental relationships have been strained in the past and both partners have misused substances, so the professionals involved need to be vigilant in the period after Ted is discharged. In this case the social worker talked to Ted about the effect a further offence would have on the family and that short-term solutions would not help the family to stay together in the long term. The probation officer discussed relapse and motivating Ted to change his lifestyle away from illicit substances (discussed in Chapter 7).

CASE STUDY

Phase four
Soon after Ted returned home there were further pressures on Jo and Ted. Jo became pregnant with their fourth child. She had started drinking alcohol again and it appeared that this had started a little while before Ted was discharged. Their third child aged four had an accident, falling down a flight of stairs in the block of flats where they lived, resulting in an emergency trip to casualty. This rang many alarm bells for the professional services, although after investigation no

Continued

blame was attached to the parents for this. Ted found that while managing to stay off substances as much as possible, he was drawn back in, using heroin again.

The final 'cry for help' was an incident witnessed by school staff, pupils and parents. At home time one day, Ted collected the children from school, and was seen to be verbally abusive in the street to his oldest child, who was distressed. The following day, the head teacher called him in to discuss the incident, and informed him that he had referred Ted to social services (during the period he was in prison, the children had remained on the child protection register). The children's social worker arrived at the school to discuss the developments.

ACTIVITY 4.5

What do you think was discussed at this meeting? What could have been set up to support Ted, Jo and their family during this difficult period of readjustment for all of them?

COMMENT

The professionals looked at the factors that had triggered the serious concerns about the children. Jo and Ted were not exercising their responsibilities as parents and this was seen to be linked to their consumption of substances, although they were not taking these regularly.

It was decided that the social worker would work closely with the local drug action team, who were now to see both Jo and Ted. With the children's welfare in mind, the school's Learning Mentor was asked to work closely with the social worker to visit the family at home, and to work on trust building.

The social worker was honest with both parents about the need to protect the children and it was clear from the conversations that both Jo and Ted wanted to keep the family unit together. They appreciated that if Jo drank this could affect the unborn child and the reasons why Jo drank were fully explored. These were connected to how she dealt with stress and the fact that she had initially experienced Ted's release as a stress rather than as support. The social worker therefore worked with the couple to be honest with each other and to realise that there were concerns about the children. The situation was to be kept under careful review and both parents were aware of this. Jo stopped drinking and attended the drop-in daily at the DAT where she was monitored. This was seen by her as a support, much like Alcoholics Anonymous; she took her life one day at a time and found the drop-in enabled her to show to others that she was able to keep to her contract with the social worker.

CASE STUDY

Phase five

During Jo's pregnancy, which was not straightforward, Ted took on the responsibility of getting the two school-age children to school and once the third child had recovered from the accident, he helped her to settle into the nursery. To do this, Ted brought the children into school each morning. He began to report their sickness whenever they were absent. He stayed each afternoon and settled his smallest daughter into nursery. He began to stay and work with other children in the nursery. He met his children at the end of their day with a smile. He was genuinely pleased to see them. He also worked more closely with his probation officer, who by this time had encouraged him to discuss his dependency with the drug action team. Ted was prescribed methadone, a heroin substitute that could be taken orally and legally. He realised that he could not stay off substances at this point in his life and would be more stable if he had a (lawful) script. The local pharmacist, at this same time, proved to be extremely helpful and encouraging. Ted looked forward to his daily visit to the pharmacy. Rehabilitation for the family took a very long time, and there were setbacks and occasional lapses, but after many months there were signs of a turnaround in the way in which the family managed.

The children became increasingly settled. The new baby was born, and Jo kept in touch with the health visitor regularly. Ted began to volunteer his help to the school. They were very pleased, as there were no other dads who helped, and they felt that Ted could become a positive male role model not only for his own children, but for many other children who had no positive male role models.

Throughout this time, the children remained as a central focus for the social worker. They had a change of social worker, but the parents tried very hard, as they were helped to see that they had the potential to be very effective parents. The children are all delightful, and continue attending school regularly and achieving well. They have parents who are proud of them.

COMMENT

This case study raises many questions. Child protection is often linked to substance misuse but the inclusion of drugs into a family does not mean that the children have to be removed from the family home. What is required is honesty by the professionals in their relationship with the clients. Effective partnership between the different agencies is vital in cases where substances are involved and the drug action teams are likely to have close links with the child protection and the children and families team. In this case both parents were prepared to work with the professionals and for Jo it meant abstinence and for Ted, harm reduction. Because the parents had substance misuse problems it does not follow that the children will necessarily exhibit behavioural or emotional problems (Cleaver et al., 1999).

The knowledge, values and skills of good social work practice are what are needed in cases where substances are involved. The drug action team will have access to extra resources that are needed to get drug habits under control and we will discuss further in Chapter 7 how to work with clients to motivate them to acknowledge and work on their substance misuse, then to deal with the problem of relapse.

Pike et al. (2006) examined the relationship of 346 children in 173 families where there were at least two children aged between four and eight. Whether families were one or two parent did not affect the relationship between the mothers and their children. In our example the mother was in transition and had to make room for the children's father. Mothers who were more emotionally volatile experienced poorer relationships with their children compared to those who were more even in their temperament. By contrast, fathers' relationships with their children were dependent on the nature of what was described as the 'family climate'. Finally, sibling relation-ships were better when they lived in 'well-organised homes with parents who enjoyed a good relationship together'. Substance misuse can trigger instability within the family. It can lead to neglect and poor relationships between the parents. It is a further factor to consider when working with families.

Offending behaviour: the impact of drugs and alcohol

The links between drugs and crime are difficult to quantify. It can be seen as a 'chicken and egg' syndrome – that is, what comes first? Walker and Logan (2005) comment that there are no easy explanations but they put forward five possible causations:

- Drug use leads to crime, in that there is a need to fund the habit, which in itself is illegal when the drugs taken are illicit.

- Crime leads to drug use, as people who mix in the criminal culture get exposed to and socialised into drug use.

- Criminal personality traits predispose some individuals into drug use; which might be seen as controversial. What is meant is that if a person is socialised from an early age into impulsive and risk-taking behaviour, then drugs can be part of a lifestyle characterised by short-term goals and anti-social behaviour.

- Mental health and emotional problems result in drug use, as the person uses drugs to 'blot out' painful emotional problems or depression and anxiety. Some people go to their doctor for anti-depressants but others may take illegal substances in addition or as an alternative to these. It can be seen as a form of self-medication.

- Poverty and lifestyle cause drug use: life on an inner city estate, for example, with limited job prospects could be relentlessly depressing and unfulfilling, and taking and dealing in drugs provides money, status, and a reason to be.

Adult offenders often have a cluster of problems. The London Probation Service ana-lysed a sample of pre-sentence reports and found that of the offenders: 48 per cent were unemployed, compared to 7.2 per cent of the London population; 8 per cent had mental health difficulties; 22 per cent had severe financial problems; 25 per cent did not have secure accommodation; and 43 per cent had severe problems with alcohol or drugs (Probation in London, 2006).

Given this level of substance misuse in adults there is an interesting question: whether for younger people substance misuse with soft drugs (cannabis for example) led on to hard drugs (opiates like heroin and crack cocaine). This was investigated by Pudney (2002), who analysed a sample of 4,000 young people aged between 12 and 30 from the 1998/9 youth lifestyles survey in England and Wales. Pudney was very cautious of making a firm link between soft drugs and the later use of hard drugs. Instead he concluded in a way that highlights where social work intervention has an important role to play:

> Social, economic and family circumstances seem to be the dominant influences on young people's risk of becoming involved in crime and drug use. Indirect policies, aimed at problems of local deprivation and family breakdown may offer at least as much hope as more direct anti-drug and anti-crime policies. (Pudney, 2002, p28).

The issue of substance misuse and offending is taken very seriously by the Youth Justice Board, who are conscious that many young offenders have used illicit drugs. They have taken steps to counter this and have written about the problem in *Youth Justice Board News* (April 2004, p7). Every Young Offender Institution or Secure Training Centre or Local Authority Secure Children's Home should now have a substance misuse manager with an Integrated Substance Misuse Programme. The new programme will contain five main elements:

- prevention and education activities (including improving custodial provision);
- screening and assessment – ensuring screening requirements are of a consistent standard;
- support and programmes – again developing young person specific programmes;
- detoxification and clinical treatment – ensuring consistent services across the estate;
- through-care – so that support is in place before young people leave custody and linking this to wider resettlement work.

This might be useful when one considers that the recent HM Inspector of Prisons: Juveniles in Custody report found that a quarter of young people in their sample had not received a visit while inside and of those over 16 who were to be released in the next two months, half said that they still needed help with resettlement issues. A major concern was that 83 per cent of boys and 65 per cent of girls had been excluded from school, affecting their literacy and rendering future employability problematic. A third of all young people felt unsafe at some stage. Should we be placing so much emphasis within the custodial institutions? Does it enhance this sentencing option and make it more attractive to sentencers?

In addition to this the YJB has developed a target for youth offending teams (YOTs) from April 2004. I quote:

All young people are to be screened for substance misuse, those with identified needs to receive appropriate specialist assessment within five working days and, following assessment, to access the early intervention and treatment services within ten working days.

This will be a joint delivery by the National Treatment Agency (now Public Health England) and the YOTs. The Criminal Justice Act 2003, activated on 4 April 2005, brought into the ambit of young offenders some of the sanctions that were already in existence for adults; in particular, treatment and testing could be made initially as components of Action Plan Orders and Supervision Orders and now as part of Youth Rehabilitation Orders. There can be a Drug Treatment Requirement, a Drug Testing Requirement and/or a Intoxicating Substance Misuse Requirement. With the new powers, those aged 14 and above can be tested for Class A drugs at a number of key stages: on arrest, pre-sentence, as part of treatment and testing components of Action Plan Orders and Supervision Orders and on release from custody. These testing provision points will be tested in pilot projects.

The change in approach for younger people was partially recommended in the report issued by the Home Office Drugs Prevention Advisory Service (DPAS, 1999 – the web link for this is given at the end of the chapter). The report comments on interventions that 'Effective intervention programmes should be based on a professional assessment of need, followed by a rapid response to the identified needs'. It also spelt out an important caveat that is worth stating in full:

All responses with young people should be undertaken in accordance with the guiding principle of the Children Act 1989, that the welfare of the child is paramount. In addition we recommend that parents, or those with parental responsibilities, should be involved in the planning and delivery of drug interventions for their children.

Programmes of help should follow from individual assessment of needs, embracing drug education, prevention and treatment as appropriate. Interventions and services for young people should be appropriate, taking account of their age, developmental stage and life circumstances. Adult services and approaches may not be appropriate. **(p4)**

In its response to *Every child matters* the British Association of Social Workers (BASW) expressed concern that a schism was opening between the principle of child welfare and what happened to children who committed offences:

The proposed developments mapped out in 'Youth Justice, the Next Steps' will only succeed in driving the concepts of youth justice and child welfare further and further apart. If the sole purpose of the youth justice system is the prevention of offending, then it will lose all engagement with welfare concerns unless there is a very strong message broadcast at the political level, and repeated frequently, that prevention must include investigating the possibility in every case that the roots of offending, and/or the maintenance of antisocial behaviour, may lie in abuse, deprivation, or neglect. (BASW, 2003)

This obviously has implications for young substance misusers, many of whom also become offenders. Preventing substance misuse by young people is integral to the Updated Drug Strategy. Nationally there are 22 custody suites that are piloting drug testing for 14–17 year olds, after charge, to identify those who may be at risk of developing a drug and offending problem. Early intervention is central to this and a child or young person may be required to enter into treatment tailored to their needs. Unlike treatment for adults, the approach will be holistic and child- or young person-centred. This means that it will not rely on the young person's willingness to engage with the treatment; rather the service has to be able to work with them. Furthermore, it will need to engage with the young person's parents/carers and families.

The DPAS report (1999) described the findings of a Drugs Prevention Initiative demonstration project in Sandwell, Derby, and St Helens and the key characteristics were as follows:

- the majority were between 15 and 17 years of age, the youngest being 13;
- levels of drug taking were high, including poly-drug and intravenous drug use;
- the average age of onset of drug taking was low (10 years of age);
- they had previously committed a broad range of offences, although few had convictions for drug offences. Most started offending relatively early (9–12 years of age);
- few had ever had their involvement with drugs addressed;
- young offenders often have a number of interlinked problems which may include, or in some cases be exacerbated by, their involvement in drugs;
- young offenders may view both offending and drugs as exciting;
- young offenders will often not see drugs as a problem;
- young offenders who have the most problematic and chaotic offending histories are more likely than their contemporaries to engage in chaotic or problematic drug use.

While the emphasis on getting young offenders into treatment seems very positive, the success rates for DTTOs for adults is currently running at 28 per cent, with a target to raise this to 35 per cent. Is it likely to be higher for young people?

Dual diagnosis

Kothari, Marsden and Strang (2002) express some concern about the partnership between the health and criminal justice systems as probation staff have the 'right to override any recommendations given' (2002, p415). This is despite the fact that successful programmes are those that enjoy inter-professional partnership (Turnbull et al., 2000). They also point out that drug users who also have psychiatric conditions 'are increasingly appearing before the courts' (2002, p424). Many of these individuals 'self-medicate' with illegal drugs and the use of 'chronic psychostimulants' may induce psychotic disorder. Frischer and Akram (2001), in their preliminary analysis of a large

UK general practice database over the period 1993–97, found that where patients had experienced co-morbidity (diagnoses of mental illness and drug abuse at any time during the period under analysis but not necessarily simultaneously) it was mostly for neurosis. In gender terms, 65 per cent of those diagnosed with drug abuse were male, with the reverse for mental illness, 34 per cent. The findings showed that those regarded as non-drug dependent were little different in mental health terms from those classed as addicted or dependent on drugs. It was estimated that nationally there were likely to be 60,000 people with mental illness and drug abuse problems.

Ann Hagell wrote a report for the Mental Health Foundation in 2002 that demon-strated from her review of a number of studies that problematic drug misuse was very high in the population of offenders. This can be direct as possessing or supplying drugs is illegal or because many offences are committed to feed a drug habit. In terms of young offenders she cited a study by Milin et al. of:

> *111 young offenders referred from court for possible alcohol and drug problems [...] 91 per cent were shown to also have conduct disorder, 58 per cent oppositional disorder, 33 per cent aggressive conduct disorder, 32 per cent depression and 23 per cent attention deficit disorder... Those abusing both alcohol and drugs were not only worse off, but also had a different pattern of substance abuse to the others in the sample... in this study the possibility is raised that at least some of the psychiatric symptoms may be the result of the substance abuse. However, they also hypothesise that some of the substance misuse may be an attempt on the part of the adolescents to self-medicate for pre-existing psychiatric problems, particularly attention problems and depression. Riggs et al. assessed levels of depression in a sample of 90 young offenders (13–19 years) who had both conduct disorders... and substance use disorders. The authors concluded that depressed young offenders were more likely to abuse substance, had behaviour problems that started earlier, had more anxiety and more trauma events than non-depressed young offenders.*

According to Hunt et al. (2006), citing research conducted by Hunt et al. (2001), the relationship between cannabis and mental disorder may be due to four possible reasons. After highlighting these, there will be an exercise to examine what role social work has in responding to these different causations.

Firstly, there may be 'sociodemographic, economic or genetic factors'. Secondly, can-nabis and/or other drugs may be used as a form of self-medication to block out the symptoms and problems from the mental illness. Thirdly, the cannabis itself may cause the mental illness, and fourthly, for some people who may be more susceptible to mental illness the use of cannabis may trigger the risk of the onset of the illness. This fourth possible explanation was contentious in the past but has gained greater accep-tance in more recent years. Anecdotally the author has experience of clients who developed psychotic symptoms after heavy and prolonged use of the stronger forms of cannabis. The study by Hunt et al. is very illuminating and provides convin-cing evidence of studies that show that people with schizophrenia used cannabis much more than the general population and, conversely, regular cannabis use increased the chances of developing schizophrenia or schizophrenia-like psychotic illness two- or three-fold. The note of caution that has to be made is that despite the level of cannabis taking increasing over the past 30 years the level of psychotic illness has not matched this.

Cannabis use also raises the risk of psychotic relapse. However, links between cannabis and depression are much less clear cut and may only have a moderate effect. The other main result in mental health terms is related to anxiety and panic attacks. Clearly, although liberal attitudes to cannabis intake may have been related to its widespread use by university students it is becoming clearer that it is a damaging and illegal drug. The role of the social worker therefore is not to condone its use but to inform the client that it is still illegal and that it can affect the long-term health of the user.

ACTIVITY 4.6

How would you establish the reasons why a person might take drugs? Which area would you seek to work on first?

COMMENT

Establishing why a person takes drugs is not a quick activity. You will need to gain their trust and carry out a structured assessment. What is important is to keep in your mind that the use of substances might be linked to their mental health. Can you think of ways to discuss health issues without being confrontational?

You can suggest to the client that they keep a substance diary to establish when and why they take them. Is it for example when they are under stress or to block out feelings of depression? How aware is the client of the effects of the substance – are they in denial? We will discuss this further in Chapter 7.

The 2008 Drugs Strategy (Home Office, 2008) had the goal of targeting those at greatest risk of developing substance misuse problems, which includes young people in families at risk (where parents and/or siblings have already developed a habit); where young people are from a vulnerable group (including looked after children, those excluded from school or who are truanting, or are involved in anti-social behaviour); during transitional times (moving from primary to secondary school, leaving school) and those where there are particular risk factors present (where substance misuse is normalised in the locality, or drugs are readily available in the locality). The 2010 drugs strategy makes abstinence a high priority and it places more responsibility on individuals to seek help, it is intended to be more holistic and to listen to the needs of local communities, who are meant to have more power and accountability to tackle drugs and the harm they cause. See Chapter 6.

What social workers need to know about the links between drugs, drug policy and likely related risk factors

The Updated Drugs Strategy was launched in 2002 by then Home Secretary David Blunkett and this links problematic drug use with other problems:

- other substances like alcohol and tobacco;
- youth offending;
- truancy and school exclusion;
- family problems and living in crime-ridden, deprived communities.

(Home Office, 2002, p4)

The emphasis, as in youth justice, was to be on prevention programmes targeted at 'the most vulnerable young people and those who develop drug problems will be identified and supported early before problems escalate'.

The 2008 Drugs Strategy (Home Office, 2008) had the goal of targeting those at greatest risk of developing substance misuse problems, which includes young people in families at risk (where parents and/or siblings have already developed a habit); where young people are from a vulnerable group (including looked after children, those excluded from school or who are truanting, or are involved in anti-social behaviour); during transitional times (moving from primary to secondary school, leaving school) and those where there are particular risk factors present (where substance misuse is normalised in the locality, or drugs are readily available in the locality).

Cusick, Martin and May (2003) refer to 'trapping factors' that make the possibility to exit from prostitution difficult. In particular:

- involvement in prostitution and/or 'hard drug' use before the age of 18;
- sex work 'outdoors' or as an 'independent drifter';
- experience of at least one additional vulnerability indicator such as being 'looked after' in local authority care or being homeless.

The most vulnerable girls in their study were exposed to all three trapping factors:

- the mean age of first prostitution for this group was 13.8 years;
- they were problematic drug users – once addicted, they continued to be involved in prostitution to fund their habits;
- they were girls;
- they were likely to have been 'looked after', 78 per cent by their local authorities;
- they had supported at least one boyfriend's problematic drug use.

The two most important factors cited for exiting were the separation of private and commercial sex and not having drug use as the principal reason for sex work.

The updated drug strategy commented that studies had shown little difference in drug use between boys and girls and the proportion of 16–24 year olds using Class A drugs had remained stable at 8 per cent. Unlike earlier strategies, it did not attempt to set future reducing targets for drug intake; rather it was to increase the numbers in treatment.

The figures reveal that the known population is predominantly young, white and male. Why should this be so? Patel, in his research on drug taking in the South Asian community, found that this:

> *community in Britain are prone to a range of physical, emotional, sociological and psychological problems caused by racism, deprivation, poverty and class*

> discrimination . . . all the necessary ingredients for a young Asian person to
> become involved in the problematic use of drugs . . . the 'whiteness' of
> Britain's heroin epidemic was so much taken for granted that social
> researchers, almost invariably, did not bother to use any system of ethnic
> monitoring. (Patel, 2000, p43)

Fountain et al. (2003) found that there was a lack of knowledge about the nature and extent of drug use by black and ethnic minority groups, and much of the literature was described as 'grey', meaning qualitative and without academic rigour, producing 'snapshots' of information. Certain groups had not figured in these pieces of research. This is despite the fact that the Race Relations (Amendment) Act 2000 places a general obligation on all public authorities to promote racial equality.

Risk factors centred on social exclusion and deprivation. Many communities were less likely to use illicit drugs than whites but prevalence was growing, as it is in the white population. Cannabis is the most widely used drug among younger people, but heroin and crack use is reported; injecting is less common but is not exceptional. There is a barrier to accessing services due to discriminatory policies, lack of acknowledgement of the problems within the communities, lack of knowledge of the services, fears of breaches of confidentiality, lack of minority ethnic staff, etc.

European comparisons show that prevalence of drug taking is broadly similar in most European countries (EMCDDA, 2000), although amphetamines are used much more in the UK (EMCDDA, 2000). Most European countries target younger drug users, agree that imprisonment is not the answer and that methadone and drug-free treatment can reduce recidivism. In terms of the effectiveness of drug testing, as envisaged initially in the DTTO, it is necessary to examine the experience of the United States. Here the evidence is somewhat equivocal, and may depend on the integrity of the programme and be expensive, not least in terms of court time (Cullen et al., 1996). This is echoed by other research where intensive supervision programmes (ISPs) led to an increase in technical violations and a subsequent increase of offenders going to prison: 'In no instance did the drug ISP reduce officially recorded recidivism' (Turner et al., 1994, p245). Community orders with a drug treatment component will therefore have to be demonstrated to be successful, cost effective and more appropriate than other ways of working with drug users.

ACTIVITY 4.7

What are the implications of all this on young drug-taking offenders?

COMMENT

Graham and Bowling (1995) identified four key factors that made young people more likely to commit crime:

- low parental supervision;
- truancy and exclusion from school;
- having friends and siblings who were in trouble with the police;
- poor family attachment.

Once young people start to offend, the roles of the family and school start to fade. Peer influences remain strong, especially for males. Girls tend to grow out of crime, leave home and enter stable relationships, young men do not. For them, avoidance or extrication from delinquent lifestyle, including heavy drinking and drugs, are key to desistence.

Hammersley et al. (2003) interviewed a number of young offenders who used substances. Two key characteristics were that many had been excluded or had dropped out of school before the age of 16, leaving without any qualifications. A high proportion were neither in education nor employment. Mostly the young people lived with their mother only, a greater proportion than in the general population. Many young people suffered from low self-esteem, especially the females. Nearly a quarter had been a victim of crime in the previous two years. Over a half had experienced at least one of:

- social exclusion;
- parental divorce/separation;
- a family member with a criminal record;
- bereavement.

The drugs of choice were mostly alcohol, cannabis and tobacco. However, there was no evidence that the age of first trying drugs had dropped or that heroin or cocaine were commonplace in the under-16-year-olds. The authors make the interesting point that:

> Despite the sophistication of drug services, many are less experienced with younger clients and available packaged interventions may not match contemporary needs. (p70)

They concluded that drug use has become normalised among young offenders and they use too much, with uncertain long-term implications.

RESEARCH SUMMARY

Ward et al. (2003), researching on drug use and care leavers, found high levels of self-reported drug use compared with the general population of the young. In particular:

- *73 per cent had smoked cannabis, 52 per cent in the previous month and 34 per cent daily;*
- *10 per cent has used cocaine in the previous month;*
- *15 per cent had used ecstasy in the previous month;*
- *10 per cent had tried heroin and/or cocaine.*

Having tried and used more drugs, 'maturing out' of drugs occurred at an earlier age than that found in the general population. The study confirmed a lack of specialist services for young people with drug problems. However, this was only a small part of the challenges that these young people faced as care leavers.

RESEARCH SUMMARY *continued*

Wincup et al. (2003), researching on youth homelessness and drug use, found, not surprisingly, high lifetime, last-year and last-month prevalence rates for illegal drug use, especially cannabis, amphetamines and ecstasy. Many had used heroin and crack cocaine. Many had first become homeless at an early age, over half following episodes of running away. There were many reasons for this beside drug taking; also family conflict and experiences of abuse were cited.

The strong message from the research is the need for dedicated and appropriate provision for young people, which addresses their substance use within the context of the many problems that they face.

CASE STUDY

Tom, aged 15, is very withdrawn from everyday life and the school is concerned about him as his attendance is becoming erratic and his performance is deteriorating. He admits to his form teacher that he is unhappy and that he has been experimenting with a variety of drugs. How would you approach meeting with him if you have pastoral responsibilities within the school? How will you approach your meeting with Tom? What is it that you would like to find out? Should you involve his parents?

COMMENT

It is important to engage with Tom and in a way that is not intimidating. Do your homework first and find out what services are available to help him. There are a number of useful sources that can be accessed and you should be ready to discuss these with him. He can access them himself and do this without needing to tell his family, although it is possible that they are worried about him. They may be users themselves, so do not make any assumptions about either Tom or his family. They may be the cause of his change in emotions.

Taking substances may be purely a personal choice or the result of peer pressure. The buzz of the drug may have been the initial factor and this might have worn off, to be replaced by symptoms related to the after-effects of taking them. His friends might be able to control their consumption better than he can and he may not be willing to admit that he has a problem. Remember that threats and warnings are unlikely to succeed in helping him address his substance-misusing behaviour.

CHAPTER SUMMARY

This chapter started with a discussion of whether for some young people taking drugs had become part of what might be described as 'normalised' behaviour. The point is that many young people experiment with substances at some point in their development. There was then an examination of the different types of drugs and their classification under the Misuse of Drugs Act 1971.

Continued

81

CHAPTER SUMMARY *continued*

We then moved on to consider a complex case study that had a theme of substance misuse in an adult couple with children. The case raised a number of important issues. The local drug action team is a resource and is a gateway for a number of client-centred services. Just because substances are involved does not mean that children have to be taken immediately into care even if it is an additional cause for concern.

People can change and get their substance misuse under control. In the case study the mother abstained – important as she was pregnant and we know that alcohol misuse can cause permanent damage to the unborn child – and the father stabilised on a harm reduction programme using a maintenance script. The case highlighted the multi-agency approach and the need to draw on different professionals' knowledge and skills and access to resources.

We considered the links between drugs and crime. Research shows that many offenders have substance misuse as well as other difficulties in terms of housing, accommodation and other practical issues that can make rehabilitation problematic. In this respect the complexity of dual diagnosis was discussed (the link between mental health and substance misuse). This can be for a number of reasons and research shows that co-morbidity does exist. Reasons why individuals decide to take drugs are complex. However, social workers have the ability to work with clients with substance-misuse issues, to conduct assessments, to refer on as necessary and to work in collaboration with specialist teams for the benefit of the client.

FURTHER READING

Cleaver, H, Unell, I and Aldgate, J (1999) *Children's needs – parenting capacity. The impact of parental mental illness, problem alcohol and drug use, and domestic violence on children's development.* London: The Stationery Office.

Cleaver et al. highlight the child protection aspects of working with substance misusers and is therefore essential reading.

DPAS (1999) *Drugs and young offenders. Guidance for drug action teams and youth offending teams.* London: Home Office.

The DPAS report highlights good practice in working with young offenders who take drugs. This guidance is equally helpful when thinking about all young people who are at risk of misusing substances.

Hunt, N, Lenton, S and Wilton, J (2006) *Cannabis and mental health: responses to the emerging evidence.* London: International Drug Policy Consortium.

Hunt et al. highlight the complexity of the relationship between cannabis and mental illness, which has become more apparent in recent years.

Reitox National Focal Point (2004) *National report to the European monitoring centre for drugs and drug addiction* (EMCDDA). **www.emcdda.eu.int/**

The Reitox National Focal Point gives a European perspective on the use of drugs.

WEBSITES

www.emcdda.europa.eu/publications/country-overviews/uk
The EMCDDA website has details of the up to-date summary of the national drug situation in the UK.

Chapter 5

Policy changes and substance misuse

Introduction

So long as there are drug takers there will be drug casualties. No form of drug taking is without its dangers, but the quest to eliminate drug taking has proved to be the search for a chimera. Drug taking is here to stay and one way or another we must learn to live with drugs. (Gossop, 2000, p218)

In this chapter we will continue to gain knowledge about the nature and extent of substance misuse in more recent years. The above quotation by Gossop highlights the incongruity at the heart of drug policy: do we attempt to coerce substance misusers to abstain from taking drugs or do we attempt to minimise their harm? We will examine a number of studies to expand our knowledge of effective interventions and practice. If we examine recorded drug crime, the figures look encouraging. The 105,570 drug offences recorded in England and Wales in 2004 represented a 21 per cent drop from the previous year, although this included a 2 per cent rise in Class A drug offences. The most common disposal was a caution for possession offences (44 per cent) whereas for dealing it was prison (61 per cent). In terms of gender, 12 per cent of drug offenders are female (Mwenda, 2005). MacGregor (2005) aggregates official figures to estimate that 4 million people have tried an illicit drug and 1 million had tried a

Class A drug in the previous year. This was a fivefold to eightfold increase over the last 30 years in Britain.

MacGregor described a total of 14 studies that had been commissioned under the Drugs Misuse Research Initiative (DMRI) for a cost of some £2.4 million. These varied from randomised control trials to secondary analysis of large-scale data sets and other methods. Experts emphasised the link between recreational use and problematic drug use, the concepts of risk and protective factors and finally research linked to the pre-vention of injecting and reduction in the consumption of drugs. In terms of treatment there was a need for more research on treatment and care, implementation and pro-cesses involved, improving practice, shared care and finally contracting and funding of services. In terms of vulnerable groups the following were identified: people of Asian origin and women with child care responsibilities, children of injecting drug misusers, those with early damaging childhood experiences and the prison population.

ACTIVITY 5.1

What do you think of the above priorities for the DMRI as commissioned by the Department of Health? Would you have added other areas and why?

COMMENT

What will become apparent in this chapter is that government policy is both a 'carrot' and a 'stick' approach. What is meant by this is that while substance misusers are encouraged to undertake treatment there is also the threat for those whose drug habit has got them into trouble with the law, and who do not wish to take advantage of the increased resources being put into drug rehabilitation, that they run the risk of being targeted and prosecuted if they maintain their habit. Substance misuse is seen by government to be strongly linked to offending and the intention is to challenge this by intervening as early as possible, even at the point of arrest. By taking drugs, individuals who may not see themselves as offenders per se are likely to get drawn into the criminal justice system and social workers need to be aware of the implica-tions of this, not least in terms of child care and other areas of practice.

The report *Every child matters: change for children: young people and drugs* (Home Office, 2004b) details that there will be a key performance indicator on substance misuse among looked after children and the target is to increase the participation of young problem drug users (under the age of 18) in treatment between 2004 and 2008. Furthermore, each year 20,000 young people become adult problem drug users.

What about alcohol?

Let us start with some definitions. It can be instructive to think honestly about our own levels of alcohol consumption, particularly in relation to weekly consumption and the occasional special event when inhibitions to drink are lowered. Mostly, people who do not permanently abstain will have an overuse on occasion but it is easy to deny regular excess. The relationship between alcohol and behaviour is often understated and excused. We normally refer to drinking alcohol in terms of units but this refers to specific measures and not the generous ones in large glasses that we might pour for ourselves. A unit of beer is half a pint but, again, ordinary bitter and not the very strong types freely available in pubs and supermarkets.

Alcohol Concern has a very useful website and specific reports on men, women, young people and other groups, and alcohol. It alerts us to recent publications, for example, the Health and Social Care Information Centre published on 30 May 2013 *Statistics on Alcohol: England 2013,* which highlighted that hospital admissions for alcohol related conditions rose by over 50 per cent over the past 10 years. Alcohol Concern estimated that only one in 16 people with alcohol problems was receiving specialist help. The recommended level was 21 units per week for men and 14 units for women but the government report *Sensible drinking* in 1995 changed this to 3–4 units for men and 2–3 units for women per day. 'Binge drinking' is defined as twice these amounts per day. Drummond et al. (2004) define 'hazardous drinking' as being between 22–50 units per week for men and 15–35 units per week for women. 'Harmful' is in excess of 50 units for men and 35 for women per week. Why men and women indulge in excessive drinking has been discussed in the Alcohol Concern reports mentioned above. For men it may be related to tendencies to indulge in risk-taking behaviour, also the disinhibiting effect of alcohol leading to behaviour that is normally suppressed. Consideration of gender roles and expectations might also play a part. Figures indicate that drinking is spread across social class but problem drinking is twice as common in the poorest socioeconomic groups. Illnesses linked to excessive drinking are chronic and often irreversible. Over half of prisoners were hazardous drinkers in the year prior to entering prison. When alcohol is combined with mental health or behavioural problems, there is a serious risk of social exclusion and for younger people from education. Again, alcohol can be linked to sexual activity and certainly to crime (see Matthews et al., 2006).

For adult women (over 16), in studies cited by Alcohol Concern, 22 per cent of adults in 2002 (3.2 million) reported drinking on at least five days per week, with 3 per cent (over half a million) drinking at harmful levels. Twenty-two per cent exceeded the daily safe benchmark. Young women tend to binge drink and the level for women is increasing although it still lags behind men. This level of consumption may be linked to the pressure of juggling work and domestic responsibilities, coping with life's stresses and low self-esteem. Women are increasingly targeted by the advertising industry and the strong 'lads' image portrayed in advertisements may have been joined by a 'sophisticated glamour' image for women. Women who drink to excess face dangers of sexual attack and unsafe sex. For both sexes alcohol may be used to hide painful events from the past, including physical and sexual abuse. For social workers working with these clients abstinence may lead to the client facing up to these horrors from the past. Finally for children, the picture is somewhat changeable. Alcohol Concern show that while the proportion of young people drinking in the previous week has dropped in the past six years, the average consumption had doubled to 10 units per week from the early 1990s until 2004. Of interest here is the sale of alcopops, which are not targeted at young people but are popular with them. These drinks are strong but this is not always realised by young people.

The Alcohol Harm Reduction Strategy for England (Prime Minister's Strategy Unit, 2004) identified a high level of alcohol misuse and related harm to people. It aimed to reduce the level of alcohol-related crime and anti-social behaviour. Matthews et al. (2006) reported that over half of 10–17-year-olds reported having had an alcoholic drink in the past 12 months. This was not related to gender and more worryingly, a third of the 10–17-year-olds who said that they were drinking once a month or more also reported being very drunk once a month or more in the previous year. Almost half got drink from their parents but those getting drunk used a variety of sources other than their parents. The 2012 Alcohol Strategy is discussed in Chapter 6. Drummond et al. (2004) conducted the first alcohol needs assessment in England and found a high level of need across the population, with 38 per cent of men and 16 per cent of women having an alcohol use disorder. The overall figure of 26 per cent equates to approximately 8.2 million people in England. Twenty-one per cent of men and 9 per cent of women are described as binge drinkers.

There are significant regional variations, with black and minority ethnic groups having a significantly lower prevalence for harmful and hazardous drinking, although they have similar levels of alcohol dependence as the white population. GPs do not tend to formally identify, treat or refer on patients with alcohol problems and in particular underidentify young people with alcohol use disorders. Referrals to alcohol treatment agencies are more likely to be by the client themselves (36 per cent) than by GPs (24 per cent) and assessment waiting times varied between 3.3 weeks to 6.5 weeks, with an average of 4.6 weeks.

It is important that social workers routinely check out with their clients their level of alcohol consumption in a non-threatening manner. If the client is not sure how much they are consuming then they can be encouraged to keep a drinks diary, although a relationship with the client will help to encourage them to be honest with themselves. From this it will be possible to see if drinking is triggered by particular stressful situations or circumstances. Strategies can be rehearsed to help the client deal with these times without having to drink more than they should. It should be remembered that *Models of care* (NTA, 2002) does not provide specific guidance on the commissioning and implementation of alcohol treatment. The drug action team is still an essential source of information for the social worker.

Recent policy and practice

In Chapter 2 it was mentioned that the *Updated drug strategy* (Home Office, 2002) had the four-track strategy of preventing young people from using drugs, reducing the prevalence of drugs, reducing drug-related crime, and reducing the demand for drugs. In 2004 the Home Office published a cross-government report *Tackling drugs – changing lives*, which was a progress report and blueprint for what was intended to be achieved by 2008. It commented that there were strategies in place also in Wales, Scotland and Northern Ireland. These included action to reduce the supply of drugs, international co-operation to target criminals, targeting drug dealing by closing crack houses, seizing assets of those convicted and tackling anti-social behaviour. The Police Reform Act 2002 (from 1 April 2003) placed a statutory duty on local authorities, police, police authorities, fire authorities (and health authorities in Wales) to both formulate and implement a strategy to reduce crime and disorder as well as a strategy to combat the use of drugs. Crime and disorder reduction partnerships (CDRPs) were to work closer with drug action teams (DATs) or to merge with them. In unitary/ metropolitan authorities they were to operate as a single partnership; integration was more likely in two-tier authorities. The primary care trusts in England (PCTs) were already subject to an order to start these responsibilities from April 2004.

For young people, the website 'Frank' was launched, receiving over 3.5 million visits from May 2003 and over 657,000 phone calls. Positive Futures was a preventative programme started in 2000, aimed at young people, and this had had more than 50,000 young people participating in its programmes. The report commented that more support was available for young people at risk, including more specialist drug workers in the youth justice system, and £18 million was to be made available for the year 2004–05 to drug action teams specifically for young people's drug treatment. Clients receiving treatment has risen by 54 per cent over the past six years and the waiting time of two to four weeks to start treatment had dropped from 6–12 weeks from 2001. It was recognised that many of those who were hard to engage had mental health problems. With a strong emphasis on illegal drugs, the report had a criminal justice theme permeating its proposals but this should not mean that the issue of substance misuse could be ignored by non-offender agencies.

Indeed, looking to the future the report highlighted:

- improved identification and assessment of children and young people's substance-misuse-related needs;
- increased services to vulnerable young people at risk;
- support to schools in the most disadvantaged areas;
- more information to young people and their parents;
- extra support in the areas of greatest need.

The 2008 Drug Strategy highlights that the Department for Children, Schools and Families (now the Department for Education) will have a lead role on preventing substance misuse among young people. It postulates that the way forward is to strengthen and to support families to build up young people's strengths and resilience. This will be achieved by giving more information, involving families in young people's treatment and developing additional support for families at risk.

When parents are misusing substances, there is a need for prompt treatment and assessments that take account of family needs. In terms of child protection there needs to be increased communication between children's and adult services, but not ignoring pre-natal concerns where dialogue might be between maternity and treatment services. There is a need to develop new interventions with families, which might be intensive, and grandparents may be asked to take on child care responsibilities.

For social workers it highlighted the young client group that professionals were likely to engage with, namely looked-after children, truants, school excludes, young offenders and the children of substance misusing adults. Professionals were expected to gain the skills to identify drug problems, as well as other risk factors during their training.

The report by McGrath et al. (2006) examined 290 unpublished studies on drug prevention and the young, of which 128 were rejected for not being sufficiently rigorous. These types of studies had the advantage over conventional studies in that they often include details on process, implementation (and difficulties in this aspect) and can be more practice focused. With these important provisos the report highlighted a number of important issues that are helpful to our understanding of young people and drugs.

Primary and secondary school-based drug education intervention programmes, with police input, appear to increase knowledge of drugs, at least in the short term. Drama is also helpful in this respect. These approaches do need to be built into the curriculum to have longer-term benefits. What was disappointing were the results of a multi-component programme that was longer term and which was not effective in preventing drug use. The type of drug becomes important when linking usage to life skills training. Here desistance is linked to the taking of legal substances and the effect on illicit drugs is small. In terms of ethnicity, drug prevention programmes that are effective on young white people also work with black and ethnic minority people; however, the programme should include material that increases cultural and religious sensitivity and understanding.

ACTIVITY 5.2

As can be seen from the above and the various drug strategies, there is a strong emphasis on young people and drugs. Why do you think young people might experiment with substances? Think of some risk factors. Is there a danger of labelling young people if we undertake this type of exercise?

COMMENT

The report by McGrath et al. (2006) cited evidence that in a national survey 10 per cent of young people aged 11–15 had tried an illicit drug in the previous month, rising to 18 per cent in the previous year. This was mostly cannabis (11 per cent) followed by glue/solvents (6 per cent). Boys and girls report similar usage until the age of 14, when boys use drugs more frequently. Offers to take drugs are as high as 50 per cent. Thus social workers working with young people are likely to have the potential of working with a young person who is experimenting with drugs. The 2003 Crime Justice Survey, cited in the report, indicated that more than half of the Class A drug users aged 10–24 belonged to a vulnerable group (defined as those who had ever been homeless, truants, school excludes, and young offenders). This was for a sample of less than a third of the sampled population. Members of more than one vulnerable group had higher levels of Class A drugs.

The difficulty of this analysis is two-fold. There are many young people who fit the higher-risk category who do not go on to take illicit substances and many who are not in a high-risk category that do. How does this fit with social work? Firstly, we should not make stereotypical assumptions about people who are likely to be taking substances. Secondly, we must not assume that they are not taking them either, because they seem settled or from a 'respectable' or 'stable' family background. Social work includes the ability to formulate a risk assessment based on evidence, not hearsay. We do have our antennae up when we speak to clients who seem to be more at risk, but that needs to be tested out in discussion, necessitating an open dialogue with the client.

RESEARCH SUMMARY

Wanigaratne et al. (2005) examined the effectiveness of psychological therapies on drug-misusing clients and found that 'there is a good evidence base for the effectiveness of psychological treatments for substance misuse' (p3). This means a process whereby there is a relationship between therapist and client, with the intention 'to increase the client's self-understanding and/or make changes in their cognition, emotion or behaviour'. It is suggested that working with substance-misusing clients has two distinct and clear aims: firstly the client has to change their behaviour towards substances and, secondly, to address co-existing mental health problems. The first approach might well employ motivational interviewing and relapse preventative techniques and this is dealt with extensively in Chapter 6. The approach favoured very strongly in the criminal justice field is to use cognitive behavioural therapy techniques. This is an evidence-based approach that draws on a well-defined set of underlying principles. The second part, according to Wanigaratne et al., is to address underlying issues such as anxiety, depression, post-traumatic stress disorder, childhood sexual abuse and other factors that may pre-date the onset of their substance misuse.

The evidence suggests that psychological treatment linked to substitute prescribing is more effective than either of these two options used alone, especially for users of opiates, tranquillisers and alcohol.

Michael Gossop has written extensively on drugs and his books are highly commended. He has conducted research on reconvictions following treatment, and Gossop et al. (2006) reported on the latest findings from the National Treatment Outcome Research Study (NTORS), which evaluated a cohort of drug misusers admitted to addiction treatment services starting in 1995. It examined pre-treatment behaviour and subsequent behaviour on discharge. Results are very encouraging, with a reduction for all offences of 24 per cent after one year, 29 per cent after two years and 50 per cent after five years. The overall number of offences also dropped. In particular, acquisitive offences dropped 22 per cent, 60 per cent and 77 per cent after the same time periods. The figures for drug offences were 9 per cent, 16 per cent and 58 per cent respectively. However, as the NTORS

Continued

programme was for drug-dependent patients who entered clinical treatment, the authors could not say that their positive findings could be generalised to drug misusers who entered treatment via the criminal justice system, or to treatment provided through the criminal justice system. There are a number of treatment services available in the community and the NTORS results could not be assumed to work for these disposals either. Clearly there is a role for social work practitioners within the inter-disciplinary team in the clinical setting.

Of interest to social workers who have substance-misusing clients who have not broken the law are Gossop's findings about the large numbers of users seeking treatment who are law-abiding (Gossop, 2005). In this report, while he acknowledges the complex relationship between drugs and crime, he commented that:

> crime and addiction do not inevitably go together. Half the NTORS clients reported committing no acquisitive crimes and more than two-thirds reported committing no drug offences during the period before admission [to treatment]. *(p2)*

It is worth adding that the report does show impressive and sustained long-term reductions in offending and this would enable the person to stay out of prison and stabilise their lifestyle. However, this is for clients who were seeking treatment purely voluntarily, not because they were facing a court appearance. A long-term study in the USA of heroin addicts put on to a treatment programme had a poor outcome. In this country there is a trend by policy-makers to provide treatment principally within the criminal justice context and this may well affect treatment outcomes.

Two further points relate to gender and the issue of abstinence and harm minimisation. Firstly, the gender difference in crime showed that women did not reduce their offending as much as men. This might be due to them having less ability to adapt to alternative lifestyles. As Gossop surmised, for those women on low incomes, particularly if they have dependent children, shoplifting might represent a tempting way of obtaining goods and money. Secondly, he found that less crime was committed by patients on methadone maintenance than by those addicts out of treatment that were comparable in other aspects. This is important as drug policy is predominantly one of abstinence and this could create a tension between law enforcers, treatment providers and the clients themselves. Here Gossop makes an important point that is worth quoting at some length:

> outcomes are influenced by an interaction between treatment intervention and the psychological and social context in which it occurs. Effective treatment requires more than just exposure to treatment. It requires client engagement in the processes of change and sufficient exposure to treatment to facilitate change. Studies of a range of treatment modalities in different countries have shown that the impact of treatment on drug use and other outcomes, including crime, is affected not merely by admission to treatment but by retaining clients

Continued

RESEARCH SUMMARY *continued*

in treatment programmes for sufficient periods of time to permit treatment processes to have an effect. Minimum retention thresholds for effective treatment have often been defined as 90 days for residential and outpatient care, and a year for methadone treatment programmes. *(2005, p5)*

The report by the Advisory Council on the Misuse of Drugs (June 2003) focused on a number of areas relevant to social work. In terms of child protection it was concerned that poly-drug use, often using injections, could be linked to socioeconomic deprivation, chaotic lifestyles and unpredictable behaviour. It warned that this could compromise the health and development of the child from conception onwards. It could also affect children's overall development. Maternal drug injecting could transmit HIV and viral hepatitis to the baby and other drugs carry other risks.

As well as poverty, there might be abuse in all its many forms, neglect – benign or malign – bond disruption, inadequate supervision and general care, proximity to toxic substances, isolation and disrupted education and underachievement. The knock-on effect on the child can easily be imagined. Again, it should not be assumed that this has to be the case and each situation should be assessed on its own particular circumstances.

CASE STUDY

The youth inclusion support panel in a local authority, financed through the Children's Fund, was made up of a multi-disciplinary panel. They brought examples to the panel of cases where children aged 8–13 were causing them concern. A project worker who worked on the panel contacted the family and offered them support, possibly leading to a family group conference where all concerned would get together to discuss what was going wrong. This was not with blame attached but was meant to empower the family to examine and suggest what could be done to change their circumstances. In this example, the children in the age group were failing to attend school and were running riot on their estate. What happened next?

COMMENT

The project worker engaged with the family and what emerged was that the mother has a serious alcohol problem. She agreed to go initially for inpatient treatment and then continue with counselling support. Support was also given to the children, who had witnessed their mothers' incapacitation. The emphasis was on empowerment and working with the whole family. The long-term prognosis was very encouraging and the mother commented that she had felt included in the decision-making when she had been able to acknowledge that firstly she had had to 'let go' and have a period of inpatient treatment for her alcohol problem. Here was a situation where the family were becoming known to many different agencies and the mother could have been seen as failing to look after her children, who could have been taken into care. By adopting a non-blaming and holistic approach the mother's difficulties were sympathetically approached and she felt able to work on them. Her time in a residential rehabilitation facility was not seen as a failure to keep the family together and in a later interview she commented positively on her relationship with the project worker. She was empowered to change her situation and the relationship with her children improved. She was able to cope with the responsibilities of bringing up her children once her dependency on alcohol had been broken. It is easy to imagine that the scenario would have had a different outcome had she been prosecuted over the poor attendance of her children and their bad behaviour could have resulted in the family being evicted from the family home.

A national perspective

The Advisory Council on the Misuse of Drugs (2003) report contained a survey that they had carried out when questionnaires were sent to all maternity units and social work services in the UK in early 2002. They commented that they received a response rate of 55 per cent and it was likely that those who did not respond generally had less service provision. From the responses there was an average of 2,000 new cases of children in need, and 143 on the Child Protection Register. Of these, substance misuse figured in a quarter of the cases. Only 43 per cent reported providing specific services for these families and liaison with general practitioners was relatively infrequent. Clearly we still have a long way to go before we can say that we are able to provide a full service to families where substance misuse is an issue and as the report commented, the Laming Report did not address the issue of parental problem drug use.

In terms of social services departments it recommended that in their work with the children of problem drug users:

- there should be an integrated approach, based on a common assessment framework, used by all frontline professionals;
- staffing should be adequate for the assessed need;
- children and family services staff should be trained appropriately to deal with problems relating to drug and alcohol use;
- there should be a co-ordinated range of resources available to support families with drug problems as well as protecting and helping their children;
- foster care and respite care should be available for these children when necessary;
- residential care should be available when necessary and also adoption if necessary;
- the new social care councils throughout the UK need to ensure that all social care staff receive pre-qualification and in-service training on the potential harm to children of parental substance misuse.

This raises the question as to how joined up are the services available to drug users. The Audit Commission report *Drug use 2004* shows that we still have some way to go. It pointed out that little information is held nationally on how many drug users have a care plan. The fact that the government wants to increase the numbers in treatment does not imply examining the quality of that treatment. They added that local surveys report that the experience of drug users is that care planning is done 'to them' and not 'with them'. They gave the following as good practice:

- a common, clear process shared between client and worker;
- understanding of confidentiality and consent information sharing; and
- single assessment and multi-disciplinary review where possible. (p27)

Drug users do not seem to be getting the integrated care as laid out in *Models of care* (NTA, 2002). Yet the above three points seem to underpin good tenets of social work practice. We also need to ensure that the families of carers receive the support they need to help drug users to stay focused and change. Again this is good social work enabling practice and is in line with the Carers (Recognition and Services) Act 1995. The Audit Commission report was less positive about the time needed to get a detox, especially for non-offender clients. More information is also needed as to why the drop-out rate from treatment is so high: 52 per cent discharged in 2003–04 remained in treatment for 12 weeks and for community-based treatments the figure is 54 per cent.

The Audit Commission report recommended that a system was needed to incorporate the views of drug users and their carers, national and regional structures should involve users and carers in their planning and management and there should be easy access to community advice and peer support. Up-to-date information should be available for the drug users, carers and frontline staff. All users should have a care plan, including follow-on services like housing, education, training or family support. Younger people should be prioritised for help and strategies should be in place for this.

Government policy on drugs

The government strategy on tackling drugs was originally known as the Criminal Justice Interventions Programme (CJIP), which highlights the link between drug policy and crime without specifically mentioning drugs. It started in April 2003 but in September 2004 it was changed to the Drugs Intervention Programme (DIP). The aim of this programme is to try to get the offending client into treatment from the time of arrest to post-sentence (Frischer and Beckett, 2006). In the same month the government launched the Prolific and other Priority Offender Programme (PPO) linked to each crime and disorder reduction partnership area. The aim is that each scheme deals with a minimum of 15 offenders via multi-agency teams of police, probation and prison staff. It is intended that the Home Office and the Department of Health will establish joint protocols in order that information is exchanged between these departments. It has been estimated that 85 per cent of offenders targeted under the PPO arrangements have significant drug problems. The ethos of these schemes is officially described as 'a "carrot and stick" case management approach, which offers the offender access to rehabilitative services but, where this is not taken up, criminal behaviour will be addressed swiftly' (DIP E-bulletin, 2006, p7).

How does this notion of carrot and stick accord with social work values and practice?

COMMENT

At first appearance it may appear that this approach has no overlap with social work, but what is at the heart of this approach? As the name suggests, we are talking about prolific offenders who, it is alleged, commit a very large percentage of crime. They are very likely to go to prison if they do not change their behaviour. Drug testing at the point of charge is also being piloted in ten areas for 14–17-year-olds. Does the age alter your views on the PPO scheme?

The Criminal Justice Act 2004 introduced conditional cautioning. This is a condition conducive to restorative justice or rehabilitation, so the offender can either be required to make amends for the damage caused by the offence or undergo treatment for their drug problem. Failure to comply can lead to the offender being charged with the original offence. The idea is to try and break the offending cycle while it is still in its early stages.

The DIP programme has been rolled out extremely fast, including drug testing at the point of arrest in DIP intensive areas and restriction on bail across all of England, whereby any individual with a positive drug test at the point of arrest can be made the subject of restrictive conditions (DIP E-bulletin, 2006). Drug-misusing offenders can avail themselves of support while in prison through a service entitled Counselling, assessment, referral, advice and through-care service (CARATS). This support is available in all prisons and includes initial assessment, advice on substance misuse problems, liaison with health care in the prison and in the community, a care plan assessment, counselling and group work support and links with community drug treatment services.

Other innovations (not national) are 24-hour helplines to maximise engagement, offering rent deposit support for offenders leaving prison and/or residential treatment who would not be considered as being in priority housing need, providing support in education, training and employment (ETE), and peer-led support.

The Drugs Act 2005 contains the provision that individuals testing positively for a Class A drug at the point of arrest in relation to certain 'trigger offences' will be subject to what is known as a 'required assessment' of their drug misuse. Failure to attend or remain for the whole period of the assessment (without good cause) is a criminal offence. The intention is to try to break the cycle and relation between serious drug use and offending. Government policy is target driven and the goal of getting 2,000 substance-misusing offenders into treatment in a single month was achieved on October 2005. This concept of assertive attempts to push clients towards accepting treatment might seem alien to traditional social work practice; however, research does show that this can be effective with drug-misusing clients (see Frischer and Beckett, 2006). The irony, as Gossop (2000) pointed out, is that we can eat, drink and smoke ourselves to death but there are laws banning the use of certain drugs which may be less dangerous. We can recall that the attempt of the American government in the 1930s to ban alcohol, the era of prohibition, ultimately failed. Furthermore, Gossop added that he has known individuals who have maintained a heroin habit for more than 40 years, while maintaining reasonable physical and mental health. In the complex area of drug use and misuse, simplistic statements on what drugs do to users do not help.

In this respect there is potential for conflict between criminal justice and medical professionals over treatment outcomes. In terms of achievable results it may be more realistic to have a harm reduction goal, rather than one of complete abstinence. This may create conflict between the 'strict and punitive methods normally used [in criminal justice]' (Kothari et al., 2002, p426). Kothari et al. favoured educating criminal justice staff in effective methods of rehabilitating drug-using offenders, rather than having an ethos of administering punishment. This is even more important when research has shown that prisoners with drug problems have a greater risk of having other problems in their lives, including conduct disorders, previous psychiatric treatments and mood disorders than others in prison (p424). They concluded that:

> treatment needs to be in place for as long as the offender needs help, not simply for the duration of the sentence. More effective throughcare arrangements are required to ensure the money and time invested in treatment does not go to waste after release with the user relapsing and re-entering the avoidable cyclical process of drugs and crime. (Kothari et al., 2002, p428)

We will discuss the concept of lapse and relapse in Chapter 7 when we examine effective practice with substance misusers. In social policy terms the most serious drug problem areas have been concentrated in neighbourhoods suffering from a number of social problems and economic difficulties. However, this does not explain why some people choose to take drugs while others do not, when they both originate from the same area and face the same problems. Seddon (2006), examining the literature on drug users, commented that in the 1980s the new heroin users were almost entirely white. However, this may well have been because researchers did not find users from the minority ethnic population. It was at this time that the use of illegal drugs began to be linked with 'deprived' areas. It is difficult to apply causality to the link between unemployment and drug taking, especially heroin at this time as this phenomenon coincided with the availability of high-quality heroin from Iran and Pakistan. In other words, the supply side coincidentally became available, which researchers like Howard Parker linked to an explosion in acquisitive crime.

The impact on the wider community

Geoffrey Pearson identified three factors linking heroin, crime and socioeconomic deprivation. Firstly, that the privatisation of the housing markets at this time led to decline in housing estates, concentrating drug users and criminals. Secondly, with limited legitimate avenues to progress, drug dealing became an alternative economy alongside stolen goods; and thirdly, this made life without legitimate hope more bearable. In more recent times as traditional minority ethnic cultural constraints have become less strong, there is evidence that young Asians have been using heroin more extensively. In addition, the greater involvement of men in comparison to women in drugs may also be changing (Seddon, 2006).

What is occurring in local areas was researched by May et al. (2005), when they examined four local communities. They found that the relationship between the drug markets and the local communities was sometimes 'symbiotic' and sometimes 'parasitic'. The strong sense of community could actually facilitate the emergence of the drug market and many of the sellers came from the community where they sold drugs. Worryingly, although the participation of young people varied across the markets, in every case it was increasing. Drugs brought in money and cheap goods to the areas and it brought mixed reactions from the residents. It brought a negative reputation, a fear of violence and reprisals and a view that this could not be solved by the police on their own. It needed the wider involvement of the community itself.

ACTIVITY 5.4

Think about the above changes in our knowledge of substance misuse and think about the implications for social work practice.

COMMENT

Social work operates for the good of both individuals and the community. When people do not feel safe and there is pressure to engage in anti-social activity, the community, voluntary and statutory agencies need to work together to bring about change. The government have an agenda for this and have developed anti-social behaviour orders and the introduction of community safety teams to oversee these challenges. The local authority together with the police have formulated community safety audits and plans to tackle anti-social behaviour and crime, which are seen as closely interlinked. Social workers have a role to play here and will be represented, possibly at a senior level, in community forums and other committees. They will be able to provide knowledge of local issues and concerns and can bring influence to bear in this area. As May et al. (2005) concluded, prison was not a deterrent to drug sellers, some sellers mentioned family support, but what was needed was an alternative career to enable them to change. What did not appeal was what was currently on offer, namely anger management courses. Social workers, while not employment consultants, can help 'sellers' to reappraise their lives, and can act as 'brokers' to facilitate change.

Treatment

Philip Bean (2004) cited research from the biggest study of drug treatment undertaken in Britain by Gossop and colleagues, the National Treatment Outcome Research Study (NTORS), which found that there were considerable benefits in getting substance misusers into treatment. The study followed 1,100 misusers and found that there was no simple answer to the question of treatment and prevention. There were two parts to their conclusion. Firstly, that drug treatment 'that embraces social care and support as well as clinical intervention, can be effective in reducing drug-related harm' and, secondly, that 'most substance misusers require several attempts at treatment before noticeable success occurs' (Bean, 2004, p86).

Social work is holistic in nature and is committed to equal opportunities. Treatment is often seen in physiological terms, which may seem marginal to social work practice. However, the conclusion by Buchanan (2006, p57) highlighted why working with substance misusers is a social work activity:

> Many problem drug users have endured a difficult and disadvantaged childhood, have been immersed in a dehumanising drug centred lifestyle for most of their adult life, and have been subject to considerable prejudice and discrimination... There is an urgent need to develop services that are able to advocate on behalf of recovering drug users, tackle discrimination and begin understanding and addressing the underlying causes that cultivate, foster and sustain problem drug use.

As Buchanan further pointed out, the Drugs Act 2005 allows for further deterrent measures including powers to allow intimate body searches, X-rays and ultrasound scans, compulsory drug assessments for those found to have taken a Class A drug and a new civil order with drug counselling conditions. The agenda is of prohibition with relatively little spent on rehabilitation and treatment compared to what is spent on drug law enforcement. Despite this, Holloway et al. (2005) found using meta-analysis that the men allocated to treatment programmes they studied were twice as likely to reduce their offending compared with those not given any treatment or alternative treatments. There were no differences for the females in the study. In terms of after-care, what they described as 'maximum' after-care reduced crime by 90 per cent compared to 'minimum' after-care that had a 57 per cent decrease. Interventions with juveniles were more significant than for adults, although both were effective. Probation and parole supervision were particularly successful with the younger age group. What was also interesting was that the studies did not by and large examine the issue of causality. Thus if we find that a programme that gives clients methadone (synthetic heroin) is successful it is helpful to postulate and test out why this is the case. In Britain we do not attempt controlled trials with comparison groups, unlike the USA.

Finally, in terms of 'what works', the National Treatment Agency report *Retaining clients in drug treatment* (2005) contains useful practical advice. The personal touch has been shown to work so that personal letters to clients are likely to get them to return to treatment. Personal approaches, even using handwritten letters and phone calls, have improved attendance on individual/group programmes. Giving clear messages to clarify what will happen in the treatment and the expectations on the client will reassure them. It was found that just by spending 15 minutes clarifying client expectations from outpatient treatment increased clients' returns in one study by 40 per cent. We should remember that we are often dealing with clients with low self-esteem and we need to show them that they matter. Minimising the time to get into treatment is important and can ensure that the client starts to attend, but of course it does not follow that retention will follow. This requires continuing dialogue with the client and support, possibly using volunteers. The building itself should be as welcoming as possible. Here reception staff have an important responsibility to reassure the client and make them feel welcome. In gender terms, some women may feel anxious that if they report a substance misuse problem their child may be taken away from them and this needs to be on an open agenda. If they are to successfully engage with treatment then child care arrangements may need to be made to free them up to do so. Studies have shown that women may enter treatment earlier than men (NTA, 2005) and have more involvement with drug-using partners. The ratio of men to women as problem drug users has remained at approximately 3:1. The reasons why women use drugs may be different from those of men.

The Home Office Development and Practice Report *The substance misuse needs of minority prisoner groups: women, young offenders and ethnic minorities* (2003) found that in the women in the study there was a link between drug dependence and mental health problems. In ethnic terms, the white women were likely to be dependent on opiates whereas black and mixed-parentage women were more likely to be dependent on crack. For the women there was a need for treatment services and for ongoing support after the initial assessment and detox. Many of the clients in the survey combined poly-drug use with alcohol, which required a well-planned response. For the young offender group the levels of alcohol used in addition to drugs was described as harmful and many had deep psychological and emotional problems. The men from ethnic minority groups often used crack combined with alcohol and this could be associated with psychotic or manic episodes. Many of the men did not get rehabilitation from the specialist agencies.

The women's drug taking seemed to be associated with previous exposure to violence and abuse. They suffered from low self-esteem and mental health problems. These factors could result in them having contact with social workers but it appears that they were less likely to seek help. Clearly there is a service delivery gap here.

With the younger offenders there was a worryingly high level of injecting and a subsequent need for harm-minimisation strategies to be implemented. Alcohol was a serious issue too. It was commented upon that they did not know what to ask for and in general their knowledge of drugs was not strong. For all groups there was a need for good through-care that should lead to after-care. The issue of dual diagnosis was important and many clients needed to have access to mental health services.

Work with offenders has tried to incorporate the need to be sensitive to substance misuse. Practitioners may find that their clients are drawn into the criminal justice system through their substance use and misuse and therefore need to understand what the implications of this are. Integrated Offender Management (IOM) is an approach to do this among other goals, incorporating local Prolific and other Priority Offender (PPO) and Drug Intervention Programmes (DIP). In 2011 a survey by the Home Office of 493 respondents found that substantial progress had been made (**www.gov.uk/government/uploads/system/uploads/attachment_data/file/97804/ IOM-Survey-Exec-Summary.pdf**).

DIP was introduced in 2003 and as part of IOM is aimed at drug misusing offenders to promote recovery and reduce reoffending. Half the police services in England and Wales have drug testing on arrest in the custody suite. In February 2010 the DIP Operational Handbook was published with a framework for delivering DIP. Feedback on the DIP Operational Handbook and the DIP Self-Assessment tool was positive and would be useful to practitioners. Further details are given at the end of the chapter.

CHAPTER SUMMARY

The therapeutic alliance between the social worker and the client is one of the key factors in retaining the client in treatment and this needs to be established early on. In social work terms this requires honesty, respect and empathy – in short, good social work practice. In this chapter we have examined the issues around the prevalence of alcohol and drugs and examined this in relation to gender, ethnicity and age. In all aspects there is a social work role and this is a responsibility for all of us in our practice and not a task to be passed on to 'experts'. There is a policy issue about how resources are allocated between substance misusers who are also offenders and those who are not.

What is clear is that there are facilities that need to be available for non-offending substance misusers and they need to get into treatment as quickly as their offender peers. Whichever branch of social work we are operating in we are likely to encounter substance misuse. We need to be ready and knowledge-able about treatment and to be ready to engage, positively challenge and encourage our clients to change their behaviour, and this is the theme of the next chapter.

FURTHER READING

Michael Gossop's work is very helpful in developing our understanding of what is effective in working with substance misusers. The two references below follow from the national treatment outcome research that he and colleagues undertook following a cohort of drug misusers starting in 1995.

Gossop, M (2005) *Drug misuse treatment and reductions in crime: findings from national treatment outcome research study.* Research Briefing 8. London: National Treatment Agency for Substance Misuse.

Gossop, M, Trakada, K, Stewart, D and Witton, J (2006) *Levels of conviction following drug treatment – linking data from the national treatment outcome research study and the offenders index.* Findings 275. London: Home Office.

www.revolving-doors.org.uk/home/
The Revolving Doors Agency seeks to work with people with multiple problems in the criminal justice system.

www.homeoffice.gov.uk/crime/reducing-reoffending
Existing tools can be accessed on the Reducing Reoffending website.

Chapter 6

Developments since the change to a coalition government and the problems of alcohol

A C H I E V I N G   A   S O C I A L   W O R K   D E G R E E

This chapter will help you to develop the following capabilities, to the appropriate level, from the **Professional Capabilities Framework**.

- **Professionalism** – Identify and behave as a professional social worker, committed to professional development.
- **Values and ethics** – Apply social work ethical principles and values to guide professional practice.
- **Diversity** – Recognise diversity and apply anti-discriminatory and anti-oppressive principles in practice.
- **Rights, justice and economic wellbeing** – Advance human rights and promote social justice and economic wellbeing.
- **Knowledge** – Apply knowledge of social sciences, law and social work practice theory.

See Appendix 1 for the Professional Capabilities Framework diagram.

This chapter will also introduce you to the following standards as set out in the 2008 social work subject benchmark statement.

5.1.2 The service delivery context.
5.1.3 Values and ethics.
5.1.4 Social work theory.
5.1.5 The nature of social work practice.

Introduction

In May 2010 David Cameron formed a coalition government and published their programme for government. In a section entitled 'Public health' the programme stated that local communities would be given greater control over public health budgets, with payment by the outcomes achieved in the health of local residents. There were to be more incentives for GPs to tackle public health problems, an investigation into ways of improving access to preventative healthcare in disadvantaged areas and giving greater access to talking therapies, seen as reducing long-term costs for the NHS.

History of alcohol treatment

Considering alcoholism as a disease that can be treated is a nineteenth-century concept (Thom, 1999). This coincided with the growth of the medical profession and attempts to deal with habitual drunkards. Thom traces the fascinating history of interventions directed towards alcoholics with the Habitual Drunkards Act 1879 being a major development as it established state funding for residential treatment in inebriate reformatories. It is still contentious whether alcoholism should be considered as a 'disease'. Further, whether abstinence has to be the goal of treatment or if minimisation of consumption is more realistic. The Temperance Movement was very powerful in the US, with some one and a half million signatories by 1835 (Heather and Robertson, 1997, p12). In earlier times beer was safer than polluted water and drunkenness was not a major social problem. Why this changed is interesting, and can be linked to working-class aspiration to middle-class respectability. The embodiment of this was: 'the moral qualities of self-control, industriousness, and thrift, qualities prized as accompaniments of prosperity' (Heather and Robertson, 1997, p14). It is difficult to apply this to present-day notions of class and respectability.

Thom identifies changes in the conceptualisation of alcohol misuse between 1948 and 1990. The first change she describes as a shift away from a 'moral' model, which can be characterised as a deficit in willpower, to a disease model requiring medical treatment. The second paradigm shift removed the disease label, instead defining 'the problem in epidemiological and public health terms' (Thom, 1999, p15). These different conceptualisations continue to coexist. The starting point for treatment in the 1950s would appear to have been almost 'accidental' in nature, when Max Glatt, a psychiatrist, set up a treatment programme at Warlingham Park mental hospital in Surrey, as the patients with alcohol problems did not fit with the other patients. He developed links with the local Alcoholics Anonymous (AA) group, which produced promising results and for Glatt to press for specialist treatment centres (Thom, 1999, p37).

AA started with a chance meeting in 1935 between a stockbroker William Wilson and a physician Robert Holbrook Smith, both of whom had serious alcohol problems. Wilson had undergone an epiphany and was convinced that 'he could keep sober admitting himself to God that he was powerless to control his drinking and helping others to reach the same insight' (Heather and Robertson, 1999, p31). They were the founders of AA, which has become the best-known source of support for alcoholics. The message from AA, from the 1950s as it became embedded into the treatment of alcoholics in this country, and accepted by the government, was that it was the disease of alcohol that was the problem not alcohol itself (Raistrick et al., 1999).

AA has been evaluated for its effectiveness and this is considered by Heather and Robertson. Their conclusion is that AA's own figures, which are self-reported, are difficult to assess independently. It would appear that the figures might be over optimistic. Rather, it might be more helpful to consider that this approach works for some people in some circumstances; possibly those people who are more susceptible to group processes and/or who are more authoritarian in outlook and who see matters in black-and-white terms (Heather and Robertson, 1999, p34). Other self-help groups have grown in the US which have not subscribed to the religiosity of AA, or other aspects of it, including attitudes to women.

Addenbrooke (2011) in her book entitled *Survivors of Addiction* uses personal narrative to explore how and why people become addicted as well as long-term outcomes. Her analysis of an alcoholic would fit with the typology of Heather and Robertson, with the story of a chronic alcoholic who benefited from AA. This person used alcohol to counter his mental health problems, in an emotionally unsupportive family who did not tolerate alcohol. He liked the opportunity to take centre stage at AA meetings where previously he had been devious in hospital-based therapy sessions. In AA meetings he was accepted and he could be dramatic and influential, something he had lost due to his behaviour and drinking.

Thom highlights the issue of women and drink, which she links with nineteenth-century concern with having a healthy working class. Women were seen as vulnerable and also liable to 'misery drinking as a consequence of poverty and [the] joylessness of their lives' (Thom, 1999, p155). This stereotypical picture was rediscovered in the 1970s, perhaps because of the growth of the feminist perspective which was concerned to provide explanations of women's lives that did not patronise or pathologise, but instead critiqued policies, attitudes and resources available to women. US literature stated there was little research on women with drug and alcohol concerns there until the 1990s as men and women had been seen as having identical needs. Hence studies were based on male samples or with small numbers of women in mixed samples. Later awareness has highlighted the 'heightened vulnerability among women to the adverse medical and social consequences of substance misuse' (Brady et al., 2009). The contributions to this book are clinical in nature and demonstrate that there are biological differences between the sexes to substances, for example in the activity of many drug metabolising enzymes. This will have implications for both harm minimisation advice and treatment.

Whether the individual subscribes to the disease model or to some form of harm minimisation, whether the user decides to stop fully or gain control and maintain some continuation of use, it is possible to regain control of their life. As Addenbrooke commented: 'addiction is not necessarily a death sentence nor a lifelong sentence' (2011, p178). Self-awareness and insight can prevent relapse as individuals contemplate their lives and their future. People will still need help and support but the future does not need to be pessimistic. Working with individuals with alcohol problems does not imply that there is an increased risk of violence, but the practitioner needs to be sensible. There should be other people in the building when the client is seen, but this should be true for all client contact. Velleman (2011) describes his policy of ensuring that the client knows the boundaries of what is acceptable; he is clear that he will not see a client who is intoxicated but will see one who has alcohol on their breath, but is able to participate in a session. It is possible that the client can be talked to and not ejected from the building. The key word here is pragmatism, appreciating that the client is likely to have experienced rejection in their lives. The history of alcohol counselling has ranged from compulsory detention of inebriates, to the growth of alcohol dependency movements. In more recent years, treatment methods have recognised that clients may relapse, may not want to become abstinent, and most importantly, that social workers' skills are appropriate for working with drug and alcohol using clients.

The alcohol strategy

In March 2012 'The Government's Alcohol Strategy' was published and in the introduction the changes in alcohol consumption in the UK were spelt out. Most notably, the last 50 years has seen the UK change from having one of the lowest consumption levels to a cultural shift leading to binge drinking in private and public arenas. Citing a number of sources it paints a disturbing picture of almost a million alcohol-related violent crimes in statistics published 2010/11, 1.2 million alcohol-related admissions and binge drinking among 15–16 year olds, comparing poorly with other European countries. It placed alcohol third in terms of lifestyle risk factors for disease and death in the UK after smoking and obesity, with an estimated cost to society of £21 billion annually. It is interesting to note that this top three are all legal ways of life. The drinks industry is challenged to be more responsible in how it produces, markets and promotes alcohol through a Responsibility Deal. While Norway has introduced a complete ban on alcohol advertising and France on television advertising, it is not part of the Strategy to ban advertising in England and Wales. There is a self-regulated agreement, the Portman Code, which covers areas like marketing, sponsorship and packaging.

The Strategy has a priority of tackling irresponsible drinking, using a number of different approaches. These include ending cheap alcohol, giving areas the power to restrict alcohol sales and controlling late opening through Early Morning Restriction Orders. Whilst the Strategy stated that a minimum price per unit of alcohol was to be set, the government then had a change of mind and it no longer appears that this will happen. In 2010, £42.1 billion was spent on alcohol in England and Wales. Late night traders might have to pay a levy to offset the cost of policing with support for A&E hospital areas affected by drunken anti-social behaviour (up to a third of alcohol related A&E attendances are for under-18 year olds). The profits that can be made from the sale of alcohol have encouraged an increase in alcohol duty fraud and links to organised crime.

The evidential threshold has been reduced to reduce or revoke the selling of alcohol in licensed premises. It is encouraging that problems with alcohol are becoming formalised and not given secondary importance after illegal drugs. Since the Licensing Act 2003 it is an offence to serve alcohol to a person who is known to be drunk but the use of this power to date has been negligible. Sobriety schemes are to be piloted for people whose offending is linked to excessive alcohol consumption. In this respect the Strategy cited (p3) Barton and Husk (forthcoming) that two-thirds of 17–30 year olds arrested in a city in England had been drinking before going out, and Hughes et al. (2008) found that 'pre-loaders' were two and a half times more likely to be involved in acts of violence than other drinkers. For practitioners, these new measures are an opportunity to use their knowledge of local practices to inform authorities of breaches in practice. If outlets selling alcohol to underage children are known then this should be formally reported. The maximum fine for persistent selling of alcohol to those under 18 has been raised to £20,000. For young people, police can seize their alcohol and persistent users can be prosecuted for possessing alcohol in a public place. Professionals may have a view on this criminalisation, but they need to know what are the possible effects of drinking by young people: legal, health and social, etc.

The Chief Medical Officer's guidance (2009) states that children under 15 should not drink alcohol at all as early drinkers are likely to drink more frequently and more than those that start later. The government links the money that has been allocated to working with 'troubled families' – £448 million to work with 120,000 families – to multiple problems including alcohol misuse. Monitoring of Family Intervention Projects (FIPs) indicates that approximately 31,000 (one-third) of adults being treated for alcohol problems had childcare responsibilities. The Strategy includes a number of worrying statistics that indicate the refusal of people to recognise and deal with their alcohol problems. Eighty-three per cent of those who regularly drink above the guidelines do not think this is putting their long-term health at risk and only 18 per cent want to change their drinking habits. The statistics for the prevalence of foetal alcohol spectrum disorders (FASD) are not definitive but are preventable. Children with FASD have a wide range of problems including: lower IQ, memory attention, speech and language disorders; visual and hearing defects; epilepsy and heart defects. Advice on what constitutes a safe level of drinking during pregnancy has changed over time.

Between 2001 and 2009 there has been a 25 per cent increase in liver disease, with 37 per cent of all liver disease deaths being alcohol related, a very disturbing statistic (NHS End of Life Care, 2012). From April 2013, upper tier and unitary local authorities will receive a ring fenced public health grant, which includes funding for alcohol services. Public Health England, which will absorb the National Treatment Agency, will support this. Health and Wellbeing Boards will integrate the work of councils, NHS and local communities through the Joint Strategic Needs Assessment and develop a Health and Wellbeing Strategy. All this sounds very promising in policy terms and professionals will need to be fully involved to ensure that practice reflects this joined-up thinking. The new Police and Crime Commissioners have a role to play in cutting crime and anti-social behaviour. They will be budget holders and have commissioning powers, to include partnership work.

Social workers are almost certain to encounter clients with drink problems and many will be at risk of getting into trouble as a result. Social work practice traditionally encourages client self-determination, but in the political climate there is less tolerance for this. The Strategy is very specific on this point:

> We will end the notion that drinking is an unqualified right without any associated sense of responsibility. We will run innovative trials of enforced sobriety schemes making use of existing powers as part of Conditional Cautions and community sentence orders, for people convicted of alcohol-related crimes. (p14)

Alcohol Treatment Requirements can be made more flexible and there is the potential to use civil orders if the individual has indulged in anti-social activities.

Social and health workers need to be aware of alcohol consumption in their clients, and be ready to support them to change. Identification and Brief Advice (IBA) is a method recommended in the Strategy (see http://onlinelibrary.wiley.com/doi/10.1002/14651858.CD004148.pub3/full). The National Institute for Health and Clinical Excellence (NICE) recommends routine alcohol screening. Do social workers also undertake this? Alcohol dependency problems can also be associated with mental illness, with the complications of dual diagnosis. The difficulty is in ascertaining whether alcohol puts an individual's mental health at risk or vice versa. This can make treatment more complicated and difficult to obtain.

The report *Over the Limit* (October 2012), published by 4Children, contains results from a survey carried out on their behalf by ComRes (July 2012) extrapolated from their data (575 parents) to estimate that 280,000 babies are exposed to potential harm each year (17 per cent stating that they had increased their alcohol consumption after the birth of their first child). It found that 17 per cent of parents maintained their level of alcohol consumption on discovering they were pregnant, 35,000 women extrapolating from ONS figures. It also found that: '62% of parents did not think that their drinking behaviour had an effect on their family' (4Children, 2012, p3). Their concern was that families needed to be added to the revised government strategy that examined how problem drinking affected young people and communities.

The government responded to the House of Commons Select Committee on the Strategy agreeing that Public Health England is an important new organisation. Social workers should familiarise themselves with the notices that will emanate from here, which will encompass both drugs and alcohol. Much of this report confirms the usefulness of the Strategy in minimum price fixing and working with the drinks industry. The new Department of Health-funded Alcohol Learning Centre is a one-stop shop where commissioners can find guidance, data, tools and training resources. This will be essential support. Public Health England will be a valuable source of information for local authorities in the future for an evidence-based approach to service provision and intervention to address alcohol harm in order that each locality does not have to reinvent the wheel but can learn from each other.

ACTIVITY 6.1

'Hospital staff are taking a dismissive attitude towards patients with alcohol related liver disease, and lives could be lost, a review of patient deaths has reported' (Meikle, 2013). Would this intolerance towards what might be considered a self-inflicted illness be likely to be present in other areas like social services? What evidence do you have for and against this?

COMMENT

The review, cited by Meikle, was by the National Confidential Enquiry into Patient Outcome and Death (NCEPOD). He cited the chair of NCEPOD, who had commented that very ill patients were admitted by doctors who did not have specialist knowledge of alcohol-related illnesses and were not transferred to those who did. The report recommended multi-disciplinary alcohol care teams. With increasing pressure on resources it can be tempting to blame clients who exhibit self-destructive behaviour and working with clients who are addicted to alcohol can be very frustrating if and when they relapse.

The review noted that despite most hospitals having 'alcohol liaison services', in over a third of the cases patients were not referred for support. It is essential that social workers are aware of the appropriate procedures for referral and that they acquaint themselves with what to do when they encounter alcohol dependent clients.

The drug strategy

The latest drug strategy was also produced in 2010 and was reviewed in 2012. Both reports will be considered here. The report commented that many users also used alcohol and hence the need to consider drugs and alcohol together. It specifically rejected the idea of liberalisation and decriminalisation but considered it essential in its rhetoric for an holistic and individualistic response to each user. The main thrust of the report is contained in the following extract:

> *our ultimate goal is to enable individuals to become free from their dependence; something we know is the aim of the vast majority of people entering drug treatment. Supporting people to live a drug-free life is at the heart of our recovery ambition.* (Home Office, 2010, p18)

This is clearly a move towards abstinence approach, in contrast to harm minimisation. It continued by recognising that many people were on long-term maintenance scripts. While many of these people 'have jobs, positive family lives and are no longer taking illegal drugs or committing crime' (ibid, p18) it still wanted them to come off drugs. The way to do this was to build up social, physical, human and cultural capital; concepts familiar to social workers who recognise the need to anchor clients into supportive environments and also to strengthen the skills, values and beliefs of individuals.

The strategy has much in common with the alcohol strategy, already mentioned, although there is a major difference in the illegality of possessing the drugs. There are three key themes:

Reducing demand – helping those who haven't tried drugs to remain drug free and helping users to come off drugs.

Restricting supply – drugs cost the UK £15.4 billion each year.

Building recovery in communities – making recovery a major target for interventions.

The costing for users on benefits is spelt out. 'Approximately 400,000 benefit claimants (around 8% of all working age benefit claimants) in England are dependent on drugs or alcohol and generate benefit expenditure costs of approximately £1.6 billion per year' (ibid, pp3–4).

This strategy has two overarching aims to:

- reduce illicit and other harmful drug use; and
- increase the numbers recovering from their dependence.

The intention is to adopt what is described as a whole life approach, with the following objectives:

- break inter-generational paths to dependency by supporting vulnerable families;
- provide good quality education and advice so that young people and their parents are provided with credible information to actively resist substance misuse;
- use the creation of Public Health England (PHE) to encourage individuals to take responsibility for their own health;
- intervene early with young people and young adults;
- consistently enforce effective criminal sanctions to deter drug use; and
- support people to recover... (ibid, p9)

The intention to intervene early with young people and families will be facilitated by the creation of a single Early Intervention Grant, worth around £2 billion by 2014–15. This will integrate a range of funding streams and work alongside the public health grant.

The emphasis on restricting the supply side remains, with an expectation that the new Police and Crime Commissioners will have a significant role. The jury will be out on this one. The new generation of legal high psychoactive substances is given a high priority in order that there be a fast response to changing patterns. The rhetoric of the Strategy is positive, with ideas that may be useful, for example the idea of Recovery Champions:

i) Strategic recovery champions – leaders such as Drug and Alcohol Commissioners and Directors of Public Health who promote the recovery orientated system;
ii) Therapeutic recovery champions – those delivering services who are successful early adopters of a recovery approach; and
iii) Community recovery champions – people who are already in recovery, who will be encouraged to mentor and support their peers and contribute to prevention in communities and schools.

One difference between the alcohol and drug strategies is the emphasis in the drugs one on payment by results. This is a contentious area and, in the opinion of this writer, still unproven. A recent visit to a rehabilitation project exacerbated concerns in that the short time period (10 weeks) was not sufficient, I was told, to turn around users with long-established substance misuse problems. The project operated a 'payments by results' ethos and, consequently, either clients with less problematic lives were worked with, or there were 'economies' with the actual changes achieved. The notion of 'cherry picking' means that the most vulnerable clients are too risky to work with. Not because they can't be but because it makes payment risky, affecting the future of the organisation. Not a good result. The first annual review of the strategy in May

2012 confirmed the drive towards abstinence, the high priority to responding to the changes in legal highs, and piloting of payment by results. It is a work in progress.

Is alcohol dependency a disease?

Heather and Robertson (1997) differentiate between the consequences of drinking, that in excess damages many vital organs, and he notion that drinking behaviour per se is a disease. While expressing sympathy for problem drinkers they are emphatic in saying that the latter is not the case. Furthermore, this does not mean that the alcoholic should be blamed for their drinking behaviour. They do not accept that there is a genetic disposition to drink.

It is possible to give a very straightforward definition for problem drinking: 'if someone's drinking causes problems for him or her, or someone else, in any part of their lives, then that drinking is problematic' (Velleman, 2011, p5). Definitions of what is acceptable drinking can be complex, the notion of a social drinker is problematic in that others who drink socially may also indulge in excess of healthy guidelines which have been reduced over time. Indeed, the concept of a healthy daily amount has been replaced with the notion that vital organs need some time each week to recover through abstinence.

Velleman makes other useful points that differentiate working with substance misusers from other clients likely to be seen by a social worker. Some offices have a strict policy that no person who is under the influence of drink or drugs will be seen. However, the client may have taken sufficient to give them the confidence to be able to attend. What constitutes too much is subjective. This is a difficult area and other factors may be important such as the mechanisms for the personal safety of staff. I worked in an office that saw homeless and rootless offenders that had been made safer in that there were panic buttons in the interview rooms, a link between reception and the local police and a procedure that colleagues would all attend quickly if the alarm sounded. I would not have been so willing to see clients smelling of alcohol in different surroundings. Even well-known clients who are deemed safe can behave very differently under the influence.

Alcohol policy in practice

In recent years the damage that alcohol causes has become more prominent, perhaps encapsulated in the alcohol strategy. However, there appears to be a crisis of will when it comes to the implementation of the strategy, in particular the issue of minimum pricing. While the Prime Minister appeared to have a commitment to a proposed minimum unit price of 45p for alcohol, this was not shared by a number of ministers notably the Home Secretary, the Education Secretary and the former Health Secretary.

In the Foreword to an important report published by the University of Stirling (March 2013) entitled *Health first. An alcohol-based strategy for the UK*, Sir Ian Gilmore, Chair Alcohol Health Alliance UK commented that the time had come to acknowledge the scale of harm caused by alcohol in the UK. It challenged the marketing mix used by alcohol producers and retailers, namely the 'four Ps': price, product, promotion and place; stating that these could be used to reduce, in the words of the report, 'alcohol sales, consumption and harm'. It argued for a minimum price of 50p per unit of alcohol to counteract the deep discounting by retailers.

The report detailed the 'thousands of deaths' and 'millions of hospitals admissions' linked to drinking and the changing pattern of drinking whereby people 'pre-load' their alcohol level prior to going out. Clearly cheap alcohol for home consumption is appealing to many people and the report deplores the marketing of this. It recommended the banning of all adverts, sponsorships and particular products focused on the young. It wanted legislation to control the availability of alcohol products with at least a third of labels used to highlight the dangers of alcohol, drawing on evidence-based knowledge of the dangers to health.

Such is the appeal of alcohol that many people will interpret the recommendations as heralding the intrusion of the state into the individual right to a social drink; however, the evidence is persuasive that for many, cheap alcohol can lead to personal tragedy through ill health, financial ruin and destroyed relationships. The first chapter of the report is entitled 'Safer, healthier, happier'; it promotes what it calls the four Ps: pricing, products, promotion and place. Pricing, which is seen as central to the reduction of alcohol-related harm; products meaning changes in design again to reduce harm (alcopops is an example of a product that appeals to younger people); promotion, the potential for the alcohol industry to police itself is doubted; and place, the outlets where alcohol is sold need more regulation if they are also to exert control on drinkers. These four Ps are described as the framework used by the alcohol industry to expand and maximise sales.

The disagreement is sharply etched in the climb-down by the Prime Minister over minimum alcohol unit pricing. Wintour (2013) commented that Theresa May, Home Secretary, led a cabinet revolt against the coalition's plan to introduce a minimum unit price of 45p. This was supported by the head of the Wine and Spirit Association who is quoted as saying that minimum unit pricing would penalise responsible drinkers. This of course is true: it brings to mind the words of a classical philosopher from the age of Enlightenment, Cesare Beccaria, who talked about the need to move beyond self-interest, instead acting in such a way as to promote the concept of utilitarianism, promoting the greatest happiness for the greatest number. If the increased price of alcohol can be considered as a punishment on excess, another important philosopher from this era, Jeremy Bentham, had views that can be extrapolated to alcohol pricing. Bentham believed that prevention was the goal of punishment, thus the increased pricing could only be justified if it led to more 'good' than 'evil'. Should the role of the state include limiting legal behaviour?

The report makes a compelling case that it should. It does this by citing the statistics on the impact of alcohol consumption on health. Globally, it cites evidence from the World Health Organisation to show that more people die from alcohol (over two million every year) than from HIV/AIDS and tuberculosis. The Office for National Statistics (ONS) in March 2013 published a report on the 2011 General Household Survey with a chapter on drinking behaviour and recent trends over time. It commented that the Department of Health estimated that 'the harmful use of alcohol costs the

National Health Service £2.7 billion a year and 7% of hospital admissions are alcohol related' (OND, 2013, Chapter 2). It pointed out that there are over 40 medical conditions that can ensue from abusing alcohol, 'including cancer, stroke, hypertension, liver disease and heart disease' (OND, 2013, Chapter 2). This report also comments that medical guidelines have now been changed from advice on what constitutes safe drinking on a weekly basis. Earlier guidelines had suggested that 21 units for men and 14 units for women should be the maximum consumed. The current advice is that it is more advisable to set daily benchmarks of no more than between 3–4 units of alcohol per day for men and 2–3 units of alcohol for women. This followed on from an examination of the evidence of the risk of 'haemorrhagic stroke, hypertension and some types of cancer' (OND, 2013, Chapter 2).

ACTIVITY 6.2

Jim, when he is not working as a social worker, is fond of going to his local market. A man, Andrew, in his early 30s, takes up a regular spot begging outside the supermarket. He is polite and tells Jim over several occasions that he is shortly getting a flat after being a rough sleeper for several years. He had a serious drug and alcohol problem as had his partner, now dead. He appears to be sober. Would you give him money?

COMMENT

It is not uncommon to see people begging in the street and this situation might be seen as different in that there is the recognition that Andrew is trying and they recognise each other now. Giving money to an alcoholic might be seen as feeding their habit but, in the circumstances, it might be better to buy him food and drink from the market. Is this patronising or realism? It might be a way of helping him avoid temptation.

ACTIVITY 6.2 *continued*

Andrew's sobriety is not long lasting and he continues to beg but is clearly drinking very heavily. Do you continue to give him food and tea, not money?

COMMENT

This gets more difficult. You are not his social worker and is there an issue of role confusion? Does this come down to humanitarian concern and the ethics of keeping a person safe and with nutrition? It raises a number of issues of what do you do with a client who is self-destructive? Do individuals have the right to drink themselves to death? This is what can make the professional task difficult. Here, Andrew is not a client but we may know people like neighbours, relatives, work colleagues and friends who drink excessively and we are placed in the difficult position of knowing what to do with the knowledge of alcoholism. If you are in a position of authority with a client or colleague, you cannot ignore the knowledge you have and must act on it. Get advice if you are unsure what to do.

Andrew is seen buying alcoholic drinks for under-age young people. You tackle him about this and he admits what he has done but doesn't see it as a problem. They pay him to do this and he says if he didn't do it somebody else would. This may be true of course, but should you inform the police? Do you inform the shop? Do you ignore it? What do you say to Andrew?

COMMENT

This raises the stakes. You might feel that it is so serious that the police should be informed. You might warn the supermarket and you could tell Andrew that his actions have affected what you are willing to offer him. When people are determined to get drink and/or drugs they can resort to stealing from people they know and be a 'different' person. Andrew had exhausted his credibility and it would be important to let him know the consequences of his behaviour. Does he know where he can go for help and support? As an adult he has choices and relapse is not uncommon. He has lost his partner and a sober life may be a daunting prospect.

Ethnicity and alcohol

Drinking patterns amongst ethnic minority groups has been examined by Hurcombe at al. (July 2010). This report, a literature review covering a period of 15 years, contains much useful information. Most minority groups drink less than the British population and those from white backgrounds but there are exceptions. Irish people are less likely to abstain compared to the general population and the gender gap in this group may be closing. Scottish men and women are over-represented for alcohol-related mortality. People from mixed ethnic backgrounds are less likely to abstain than non-white minority groups, and also report heavier drinking rates compared with other non-white ethnicities. The report details findings for different ethnic groups, also how patterns of drinking have changed over time. Thus Sikh men have high rates of drinking and are over-represented for liver cirrhosis. Second-generation male Sikhs are less likely to drink as heavily as first-generation male Sikhs. Hindus are less likely to drink if they declare that religion is important to them and heavy drinking has not increased between the generations. Black Caribbean people have lower levels of drinking compared to those of white backgrounds but higher than people from South Asian and Chinese ethnicities. Knowledge of these drinking patterns is useful and helps break down ignorance and unhelpful assumptions about levels of drinking. The report postulates that drinking rates may be changing as minority ethnic groups settle into the new country and adapt to prevailing cultures. This can cause inter-generational tensions, with low tolerance towards those who drink, especially if it is forbidden by religion or is not seen as acceptable behaviour by women. Alcohol services must be culturally sensitive, flexible and targeted towards those who may feel insecure in obtaining treatment.

Research carried out in a high density Asian populated area in London found that 'Friends' drinking and friends' approval of drinking [in young people] was significantly associated with an increased likelihood of having ever drunk and higher rates of frequent, recent and binge drinking' (Goodman et al., May 2011, p6). The report also suggested that non-drinkers sought out other non-drinkers as friends, and may try to moderate heavy-drinking friends to consume less. Young people from minority ethnic backgrounds and religious backgrounds often cited health reasons as being important in their decision not to drink and this has implications for government campaigns to deter drinking among the young as these groups start from a more reticent position. Young drinkers who do not conform to cultural and religious expectations may find it difficult to access treatment services, and the role of peer mentors may well be helpful to young drinkers. Peer support programmes within schools may offer Muslim young people a place to discuss alcohol use if they feel unable to approach teachers and other people in authority.

Green and Ross (June 2010) also found that white young people who were not religious were more likely to drink and to indulge more frequently. A further finding that has high potential for later difficulties in life was that there was a strong link between being bullied at school and frequent drinking. Some schools might have a drinking culture: this was more likely when there was a high proportion of white students or those who did not receive free school meals. Without being able to ascribe causality the report found relationships between smoking, trying cannabis and alcohol consumption, all of which could be described as risky behaviours. It also 'found that drinking was associated with a number of negative outcomes such as the likelihood of not being in employment, education or training' (Green and Ross, June 2010, p2).

Heavy drinking

The concern on binge drinking was picked up by the government response to the House of Commons Health Select Committee, which had commented:

> *Despite some perceptions that binge drinking is largely a public order issue, the evidence presented to us suggests that it does contribute to some of the long-term health harms that have concerned us. We conclude that these health problems need to be addressed no less urgently than problems with public order and anti-social behaviour.* (House of Commons Health Select Committee, September 2012, p3)

The government response was that the advice from the Chief Medical Officer would consider what better advice to offer on this. It also confirmed its intention to legislate on the minimum unit price of alcohol, to consult on multi-price promotions, and to take action on the average strength of alcoholic drinks, a step beyond what the Health Select Committee had asked for. Whether this rhetoric will be turned into reality remains unclear.

Should we be concerned at the level of heavy drinking? The evidence suggests we certainly should, but this does not apply only to adults. A systematic review of published reviews of alcohol consumption by young people (Newbury-Birch et al., 2009) reported that some 35,472 young people, aged between 16–24, were hospitalised in 2005 with alcohol-related conditions. The problem is most acute in areas of high social deprivation. The amount consumed by the young who drank increased per week from 6.4 units in 1994 to 12.7 units in 2007. The largest increase was in 14 year olds (non-gender specific) where consumption rose from 6.1 units per week to 9.9 units per week. What is particularly worrying is that the report identified high levels of binge drinking, but young people did not understand the implications of this behaviour.

Social workers and other professionals need to understand and not minimise the problems associated with alcohol use and abuse. The legality of this substance and its everyday use, highly visible in the media in all of its manifestations, has a tendency to normalise its use with devastating effects on too many of the population. It could be described as a 'ticking bomb' in the havoc it can wreak to many people, rich and poor.

CHAPTER SUMMARY

This chapter has concentrated on alcohol use and misuse and has discussed the two substance strategies of the coalition government on drugs and alcohol. It has provided information on how diverse groups are affected by alcohol and the theme that alcohol use is not necessarily unchangeable. The government is particularly keen to promote abstinence as a goal, having acknowledged the immense damage to health caused by drink. It can be seen as a 'ticking bomb' ready to explode, with many individuals not appreciating the health problems they will encounter as they get older, and not in old age, but much earlier than this.

The thrust of the alcohol strategy is on tackling irresponsible drinking and a major theme is to raise the unit price of alcohol. However, since the strategy was published the government seems to have rolled back on this and the lack of legislation implies that it won't happen during the lifetime of the coalition government.

RTHER ADING

Goodman, A, Hurcombe, R, Healy, J, Goodman, S and Ball, E (May 2011) *Teenage drinking and interethnic friendships.* York: Joseph Rowntree Foundation.

Green, R and Ross, A (June 2010) *Young people's alcohol consumption and its relationship to other outcomes and behaviour.* Research Report DFE-RR005. London: Department for Education.

House of Commons (2012) *Government Response to the House of Commons Health Select Committee Report of Session 2012–13: Government's Alcohol Strategy.* London: The Stationery Office. (**www.wp.dh.gov.uk/publications/files/2012/09/Cm-8439-Accessible.pdf** accessed 5.2.2013)

Hurcombe, R, Bayley, M and Goodman, A (July 2010) *Ethnicity and alcohol. A review of the UK literature.* York: Joseph Rowntree Foundation.

Velleman, R (2011) *Counselling for alcohol problems.* 3rd edition. London: Sage.

Alcohol Concern **www.alcoholconcern.org.uk/**

BSITES

Alcohol Concern toolkit for families **www.alcoholandfamilies.org.uk/toolkits.htm**

Mentor International
http://preventionhub.org/prevention-update/search/tags/alcohol

Chapter 7

Professional practice issues and approaches

Introduction

> *Unless one understands the dynamics of ambivalence, a person's responses can seem counterintuitive and puzzling.* (Miller and Rollnick, 2002, p17)

This chapter introduces you to good practice interventions with drug and substance misusers. Many social work practitioners lack confidence in this area of practice, not least because many clients with substance misuse issues appear to lack serious motivation to change. There are additional skills and understanding needed to engage with reluctant clients, especially when they can appear to sabotage attempts to change and invite rejection.

In this chapter you will be acquainted with models of effective practice with clients who may be either difficult to engage or who seem to co-operate with the social worker, only to fail when they seem to be on the verge of successful change. Indeed their behaviour could be described as self-destructive. Emotions such as frustration, anger and/or ambivalence in the practitioner may produce uneasy feelings of being de-skilled. By presenting models that make sense of this behaviour, the social worker will have more insight into the area of practice and the confidence to work effectively.

What social workers need to know to work effectively with clients who take drugs

Social workers have the necessary skills to engage with drug and substance misusers as long as they are equipped with some further knowledge of what is effective. This chapter will include a discussion of the 'wheel of change' model of Prochaska and DiClemente (1994), motivational interviewing (Miller and Rollnick, 2002) and pro-social modelling, what works and does not work with clients (Trotter,1999).

Clients who have been using and misusing substances may have tried to cut back and stop. They may have achieved this for short periods of time but have then reverted to their habit. In time they may indeed persuade themselves that they cannot change. Such self-defeating behaviour may make the client seem unattractive to work with and the drugs mask the real character of the person who may lie, use charm, child-ishness and other ploys to avoid taking responsibility for certain aspects of their life. This stereotype will certainly not describe all individuals who take drugs. Others may be able to hold down jobs and maintain their child care responsibilities, with only occasional lapses. However, the key attribute of empathy between practitioner and client needs to be worked on and developed in the context of work that encourages the client to recognise that they have a problem that they need to solve. It will not be easy and they will need to change their thinking and behaviour in dealing with life's everyday problems.

- The prospect for people to change and stop taking substances will vary according to their lifestyles and opportunities but there are definite techniques that can be employed to encourage and promote change. The psychological causations leading to the need to take drugs is complex. Gossop (2000) gives the example of the Vietnam War, when cannabis was estimated to be used by more than three-quarters of the troops and 20 per cent had a serious addiction to opiates. Terrible events like the My Lai massacre occurred and may have been linked to drug taking. However, when the men returned to America, they ceased their addiction and only some 7 per cent continued to use opiates. Less than 1 per cent considered that they were addicted to drugs after their return. This is a very surprising result, not least when one considers the impact of post-traumatic stress disorder from which many continued to suffer. It highlights the need to consider the social, situational and emotional context the user is living in and not to make any assumptions that consumption of drugs must make the person an addict.

The scale of the problem

According to the European Association for the Treatment of Addiction report (EATA, 2003), there are approximately four million people in the UK who are using at least one illicit drug each year. Of these about a million are taking a Class A drug like heroin or crack cocaine. There are about a quarter of a million people in this total who will go on to develop a serious problem, harming themselves and those around them, dama-ging their communities in the process.

The cost of these drug habits is estimated to be anything from £10 billion to £18 billion and in response the government estimated that it would spend £537 million in 2005 on treatment services. The scale of the problem in human tragedy terms is difficult to imagine. What is clear from the figures is that social workers are almost certain to encounter clients who have dabbled in drugs or who have developed a major dependency problem – both physical and psychological.

The report makes an interesting observation that the perceived delay before treatment can be obtained is used as an argument for not engaging with treatment at all. In fact, there are drop-in centres that can be accessed immediately and specialised treatment can be obtained in three weeks. In the meantime, families struggle to cope with loved ones in crisis without knowing what to do or who to turn to. This sadly compounds the problem, as involving significant individuals and families is crucial in helping substance misusers change and maintain themselves afterwards.

In a section in the EATA report by John Marsden, from the National Addiction Centre, there is encouraging evidence gleaned from research that for a majority of people experimentation with drugs does not lead to dependency with all the difficulties that ensue. The most vulnerable population is among the young, with most people starting by the age of 20. However, the corollary of this is that if left untreated, people who develop major problems with substances are likely to get worse. Taking drugs has a clear impact on the individual's health but the problems go far wider and can affect finances, their personal situation and those of their family. When they 'burn their boats', it is very difficult to salvage relationships with families and the wider community, which in turn drives them further into seeking the company of other substance misusers. How is this vicious circle to be broken?

In terms of illegality, the New English and Welsh Arrestee Drug Abuse Monitoring (NEW-ADAM) is a national research programme of interviews and voluntary urine tests among arrestees. It showed that 65 per cent of arrestees tested positive for one or more illegal drugs and 30 per cent tested positive for two or more substances. Twenty-nine per cent tested positively for opiates including heroin and/or cocaine (including crack). The average amount an arrestee was spending on illegal drugs was £15,000 per year (Home Office, 2001). Drug taking at this level is likely to lead to severe community penalties or imprisonment, which further destroys the ability of the client to maintain their independence.

How do we motivate clients to change when they don't see a way forward?

We have evidence of what works, what sometimes works and what does not work. It is easiest to start with what does not work. Threatening the client with the foolishness of what they are doing to themselves. Scare tactics like 'if you carry on in this way you will kill yourself' are most unlikely to produce the intended change in behaviour. Confronting the client is likely to lead to a defensive reaction. Assuming the role of expert and telling them about the physical consequences of their substance misuse is also unlikely to work. Setting goals for change has to appeal to a shared higher aim that the client reaches in discussion with the social worker. Why should the client have the same thoughts and aspirations as the social worker? Finally, labelling the client as an 'addict' or 'substance misuser' is unhelpful and does not assist them to think about changing. It may merely confirm for them that they have failed and that change is impossible.

If we think about what sometimes works, we might utilise reflective listening and be empathic. We might be optimistic and try to inspire the client to change. They may indeed like the worker, but these qualities, admirable as they might be, are unlikely to be sufficient to promote long-term positive change. Personal disclosure is not recommended.

If we are to succeed with the client then certain basics should be present, namely being clear about the social worker's role and its inherent authority; being honest about the nature of the contact, the options available to the client as well as reinforcing and giving pro-social values (non-criminal, positive values and actions). Clients will need to make a judgement: are the positives in not taking drugs stronger than the positives in taking them? What do the drugs do for them?

ACTIVITY 7.1

You meet with a young man, just out of care, who takes drugs for recreation. The habit is getting out of control and he is missing work on occasion. As the social worker, you have concerns about his ability to cope. You draw a set of scales and ask him to write down on one side the benefits of taking drugs and on the other side the disadvantages. What do you think he will write down?

COMMENT

He might say that taking drugs gives him contact with other young people who also take them, so it is part of his social scene. He might add that he enjoys the effect that he gets from the drug, so it is a pleasurable activity. On the negative side he is missing work so it is affecting his ability to plan and keep control of his life outside of his social scene. He is likely to be feeling more than just tired on Monday mornings and he cannot limit the after-effects of the drugs to the weekend. He might be gaining a tolerance of the drug so that he is beginning to take more of it than he used to and he might be uneasy at this point about his ability to control his drug taking. There is a cost to his drug taking, including economic, physical, emotional and social. The important point is that if he is to change, he will need to make a decision that the scales are pointing downwards towards the disadvantages. If not, will he change his substance-misusing practices? The skill of the social worker is to make sure that he thinks through this exercise fully and while acknowledging for the client that there are aspects of substance misuse that he finds positive, he does not deny the cost side by minimising the negatives. It may require the social worker to explore alternatives to the social scene he has been using, to find other ways that he can go out and enjoy himself, without putting himself at risk from substances.

We will now move on to a case study that demonstrates the potential for dealing with substance misuse issues when as a social worker you might be based in a local authority setting.

A girl aged 10 lives in a family where there is a history of domestic violence and drug abuse. She has learning difficulties (her language development is not age appropriate) and is very withdrawn. She is subjected to playground taunts by older children and she is starting to refuse to eat.

Consider the aspects of the girl's life that might impact on her psychological well-being and consider why they may be having an effect on her.

Partly because perpetrators tend to justify their actions by reference to things their victims have done or not done, child and adult victims and/or witnesses of domestic violence often say that they blame themselves for the perpetrator's behaviour – 'it is my fault that they beat me up', 'it is because I am bad that this happens'. As well as experiencing periodic violence, the 10-year-old girl has also grown up in an environment in which she is competing, for affection and attention, with drugs. The refusal to eat is a form of self-harming that appears to be her way of coping with the insecurity, self-doubt and guilt that her family background has instilled in her. It can be seen from the example that the drugs issue may not be the initial reason why this family came to the attention of the social services, but following on from this it becomes clear that there is a drug problem that needs to be addressed.

The problematic drug use in the family could have further effects: inconsistent parental supervision might force the girl to take on responsibilities that she cannot understand or cope with, there may be lack of routine, and she might witness all the paraphernalia involved with drug taking. She might be worried about the effects of the drugs on her parents' health, not least because the media put out a message that 'drugs kill'. This could lead to her having a high level of anxiety about her future (Harbin, 2000).

The resolution of the girl's difficulties necessitates a holistic approach with the entire family and there are a number of problems to resolve. Let us consider this further by examining how this case progresses. Resolving the problems and pressures on the girl necessitates engaging with her parents and, in particular, attempting to resolve the problems that have been mentioned above.

CASE STUDY continued

The school is concerned with the welfare of the 10-year-old daughter and refers her to social services. The parents see the social worker and they are clearly worried about their daughter. The parents admit that their relationship has been rocky for some time, usually related to the father's drug problem. The drugs have caused debts. Debts cause tension, which results in domestic violence. The parents have nearly split up on several occasions and they feel stuck. There appears to be some motivation to change but it is not strong.

ACTIVITY 7.3

How will you engage with the family to create change? You know that you cannot force through change but you feel that in this instance there is potential, as the parents want to change their behaviour and the father has expressed a desire to stop taking drugs, although his motivation seems more pious than real.

COMMENT

In this case, it is important to work with the parents and for them to acknowledge that their relationship is having a damaging effect on their daughter. How sincere are they in wanting to save their marriage? The social worker might work with the couple or may refer them on to an organisation like Relate, which specialises in marital problems. They may benefit from family therapy, which may be available within the child and family consultation service. The father might benefit from one-to-one counselling and support from the local drug action team. He needs to learn how he can avoid situations that lead to him taking drugs as well as strategies to avoid relapse. If his motivation is not strong, then his attitude to change needs to be strengthened. Motivational interviewing is a technique usefully employed to achieve this. First though, let us consider the issue of domestic violence.

Some issues to be considered

Domestic violence is not an uncommon occurrence with alcohol and substance misuse. It is important to examine whether it is happening within the family before embarking on a treatment approach to change the substance and alcohol intake, so that this should not endanger the partner and other members. Smith and Meyers (2004) include a chapter in their book on this issue. They cite studies that show that where violence had taken place between partners, drink had been involved in two-thirds of the cases. In two other studies of women who had had to receive emergency treatment from injuries resulting from domestic violence, the perpetrators were four to five times more likely to have used drugs than partners of a non-violent control group.

While it is tempting to suggest that victims of domestic violence should leave their abusing partners, the evidence is that although many victims do leave their partners at the time of the attack, they may return to the relationship on more than one occasion, even if the domestic violence does not cease. Therefore caution needs to be exercised so that the social worker does not exacerbate the situation. Clearly, in our example, the domestic violence has had a damaging effect on the daughter in the family and one assumes on the mother. The mother may want to work with the social worker to break the substance misuse habit and may feel that this can be done without exacerbating the risk of further domestic violence.

Clients may not talk about wanting to change but their partners and family may well do so. It is important to draw on their support and encouragement to assist the client in changing. We will look at methods of how to engage with reluctant clients to start this process off (later in this chapter).

The first task is to identify areas of concern that will need to be discussed with the client. There is a need to engage with the client without dictating to them how they are to change – that is an approach that does not work. What follows is an approach that seeks to engage with the client to encourage them to want to change.

Motivational interviewing

The motivational interviewing approach emphasises the empowerment of the client and seeks to involve them in the work of changing their behaviour. This approach is one that has been developed by Miller and Rollnick (2002). The following quotations highlight the essence of this approach.

> *Motivational interviewing is a particular way to help people recognise and do something about their present or potential problems. It is particularly useful with people who are reluctant to change and ambivalent about changing . . . [For some] motivational interviewing is only a prelude to treatment . . . It creates an openness to change, which paves the way for further important therapeutic work.*

> *In motivational interviewing, the counsellor does not assume an authoritarian role. One avoids the message that 'I'm the expert and I'm going to tell you how you need to run your life.'*

> *Clients are always free to take our advice or not. Some research indicates that therapists exert a surprising amount of influence over whether or not clients change!*

> *The strategies of motivational interviewing are more persuasive than coercive, more supportive than argumentative.*

Important aspects of this approach include a de-emphasis on labelling in negative terms and instead an emphasis on personal choice and responsibility for deciding future behaviour. The social worker conducts an objective evaluation, but focuses on eliciting the client's own concerns. Resistance is seen as an interpersonal behaviour pattern influenced by the therapist's behaviour and it is met by reflection. Treatment goals and change strategies are negotiated between client and therapist, based on data and acceptability; the client's involvement in and acceptance of goals are seen as vital.

There are five general principles to motivational interviewing:

1. Express empathy
   - acceptance is a prerequisite to starting the process of change;
   - reflective listening is an essential response;
   - expect to be met with ambivalence;
   - the client should be seen as capable of changing.

2. Develop discrepancy (that the current lifestyle and future goals of the client do not match)
   - awareness of consequences of no change is important;
   - the counsellor needs to be directive;
   - a discrepancy between present behaviour and important goals will motivate change;
   - the client should put forward the arguments for change.

3. Avoid argument
   - arguments are counterproductive;
   - defending breeds defensiveness;
   - resistance is a signal to change strategies;
   - labelling is unnecessary.

4. Roll with resistance (an interesting phrase, essentially meaning move on and try other strategies)
   - momentum can be used to good advantage;
   - perceptions can be shifted;
   - new perspectives are invited from the client;
   - the counsellor does not put forward solutions for the client;
   - the client should provide the solutions to problems.

5. Support self-efficacy
   - the client will be motivated if they have a belief in the possibility of change;
   - the client is responsible for choosing how they will change;
   - the client needs to carry out their changes so that they are the driving force;
   - there is hope in the range of alternative approaches available;
   - the counsellor needs to believe in the client's ability to change.

Motivational interviewing is appropriate for all ages but are there differences when working with younger people? Gillian Tober (1991) suggested the following:

- *Time*: perhaps fewer sessions might be needed or they should be activity focused.

- *Low self-esteem and low self-efficacy*: the young person may realistically perceive that they are disempowered, therefore self-esteem may be bolstered within the interview with the therapist.

- *Reactions to authority figures*: expect disapproval and negativity, there is potential to increase self-esteem.

- *The need to apply motivation to change at a number of levels*: there may be different levels of change in terms of social functioning or interpersonal relations.

- *Peer group influences*: subcultural norms may be stronger influences in the young.

Problem-solving activities

Clients can be taught to problem solve. The psychologist Mary McMurran, whose work, while focused on combating addiction, can be applied to clients with a variety of needs, has developed problem-solving techniques. The therapist makes available a variety of potentially effective responses to problems and works with the client to increase the probability of selecting the most effective response.

There are five stages as follows:

1. *Orientation* – in which the client is taught to recognise when a problem occurs.

2. *Problem definition and goal setting* – the client learns to describe their situation accurately, including problematic factors, and to set achievable goals.

3. *Generation of alternatives* – the creation of different strategies for meeting goals.

4. *Decision making and action* – selecting the best option and forming an action plan.

5. *Evaluation of the action* – to see whether and how something has worked well or otherwise.

NB This process may be repeated a number of times.

Task guidelines

Miller and Rollnick suggest five early strategies for successfully engaging with clients:

- ask open-ended questions;
- listen reflectively;
- affirm;
- summarise;
- elicit self-motivational statements.

The questions used may be evocative or may focus on the positive and negative aspects of the client's present behaviour. It can be helpful to look back to times before the client's behaviour made problems worse, how the client would like life to be, and then to set goals in terms of these aspirations. It may also be helpful to use paradox as a means of creating a discrepancy between the present behaviour and how the client would like life to be. In eliciting 'self-motivational statements', the aim is for the client to recognise their problem, demonstrate some concern about it and express some intention to change. The skill, as stated by McMurran and Hollin, is to get the client to consider the negative effects of their problem behaviour and the benefits of change.

Example questions that you could try with a client include:

- What concerns you about...?
- What problems do you associate with...?
- What changes would you like to...?
- What are the pros and cons of...?

When answers are offered, you should seek elaboration and/or clarification. It may be worth trying role reversal – getting the client to play the counsellor and the counsellor to present the client's views. Use summaries to check accuracy of information and always aim to move the client forward.

There is a useful acronym that can serve as a reminder of ways of working with unmotivated, shy or inhibited clients: FRAMES:

- *Feedback* – personal to client about their behaviour.
- *Responsibility* – owned by the client for their actions.
- *Advice* – non-confrontational.
- *Menu of alternatives* – present possible goals and ways of achieving them.
- *Empathy* – raise self-esteem, client-centred positive style.
- *Self-efficacy* – encourage the client to believe they can change.

(Miller and Sovereign, cited in McMurran and Hollin, 1993)

Working with involuntary clients

Very often we work with clients as a result of a formal order, which means that the contact has not started with an agreed contract. It does not mean that nothing can be achieved. This might be the case with younger clients or with adults in child protection situations where they may feel that if they do not co-operate then they may lose access to resources or to their children. Chris Trotter (1999) has researched into this work and has produced the following approach to 'what works' as well as what sometimes works and what does not work.

Approaches that work include the following:

- Accurate role clarification: what are we here for?
- Discuss authority of the practitioner's position.
- Clarify the nature of the order that the offender is on, the rules and sanctions that can be applied.
- Be honest and clear about the nature of supervision and options available.
- Discuss the role of the client, giving them a clear idea of what is expected of them.
- Reinforce and model pro-social values in your contact with the client so that the client adopts positive attitudes and attributes. These are non-criminal values and actions, or those values and actions that are the opposite of criminal and/or anti-social.
- For the social worker this means promoting/modelling the positives and challenging the negatives – good anti-discriminatory practice.
- Adopt a collaborative problem solving approach, identifying strategies with the client to achieve goals – shared higher aims with the client as utilised in task-centred casework.

Approaches that sometimes work include:

- using empathy;
- reflective listening;
- humour;
- optimism;
- self-disclosure.

Among the approaches that do not work are:

- blaming;
- punishing;
- judging;
- threatening;
- scaring;
- focusing on social worker's goals rather than the client's;
- focusing on what the client is doing wrong;
- lack of clarity on role of authority;
- aggressive tactics;
- focusing on insight alone;
- uncertainty about the purpose of the intervention;
- viewing the client as the problem;
- having a pessimistic view of the client's capacity to change;
- failing to focus on the client in the family and social context.

Using authority to create and manage change in clients

Drug taking has taken root in many residential areas in the United Kingdom, especially in council estates and poorer areas. Alcohol consumption has also increased and has led to problems with under-age drinking and binge drinking (Burney, 2005). There is thus a link between incivilities and the problematic consumption of drugs and alcohol. Cherry (2005), when discussing the legitimate use of authority to challenge these incivilities, mentions developing a positive relationship with the client, and for the practitioner to act as a catalyst for change. Cherry draws heavily on the work of Trotter, Miller and Rollnick in drawing up a staged model for changing people's behaviour. In her eight-stage model the client firstly identifies the behaviour that needs to change. It is broken down into small parts that need to be addressed. The thinking processes of the client are discussed to find out why the inappropriate behaviour takes place. The client rehearses what pro-social behaviour would consist of. The client can then rebuild the small parts back into more complex behaviour, which can then be drawn on more generally. Finally, the need for positive reinforcements is lessened, ideally to withdraw dependency on the practitioner so that the client is able to deal with new and unexpected situations. This might include the possibility of relapse.

Two models for working with substance misuse

Let us take an example of therapeutic interventions from the field of addiction. It is helpful to consider two different models: the 'disease model' and the 'wheel of change', postulated by Prochaska and DiClemente (1994). In the first model, the first drink of alcohol or use of a substance returns the client to square one. They are back into the abyss and have lost the fight against the evil drink or drugs. This model, which works for some, is supported in self-help groups. Alcoholics Anonymous broadly supports it in their 12 steps programme. As a probation officer, I found that the disease model worked for some who needed to be able to meet with others who had been able to stop and to keep their guard up, possibly many years after their last drink of alcohol.

The disease model

John Wallace, in his chapter 'Theory of 12-step-oriented treatment' in Rotgers et al. (2003) usefully puts into context the notion of 'disease'. Newcomers to the programme are told by their sponsor that they have a disease that prevents them from controlling their drink or drug problem. As a consequence they need to avoid their former drinking associates and drinking situations. The programme has a biological dimension in that the drug is likely to make the person ill, but perversely they need to continue to take the drug to avoid the symptoms of withdrawal; for example, the alcoholic may get the 'shakes' if they attempt to stop suddenly without medical help and the drug user would go through what has been called 'cold turkey'.

The substances taken affect the functioning of the brain and are depressive. Thus the substances affect the mood of the user, resulting in psychological disturbance and a general feeling of negativity. Socially the user is likely to experience deteriorating personal relationships affecting partners, children, relatives and their friends. Their careers, finances and other social aspects of their lives are almost certainly going to be put under strain, with the potential to spiral out of control.

Finally, feelings of alienation might lead to a feeling of lack of moral purpose. Indeed the need to purchase drugs and alcohol might lead the user to follow a way of life that they feel is morally repugnant, with the consequent further loss of personal esteem, a vicious downward circle. For those with a religious or spiritual belief, they may feel cut off from their faith.

The 12-step model can be a source of strength for some substance misusers and indeed the author has seen it successfully change the lives of people who have led a tragic life wrecked by their need, for whatever reason, to take substances to excess. The model requires complete abstinence rather than controlled consumption. The first step is an admission of one's powerlessness over alcohol or chemical – that their life has become unmanageable. The second step is that the person has come to believe that a power greater than ourselves could restore us to sanity. While not wishing to embark on a discussion of religion, spirituality or indeed mysticism, it is worth pointing out that this method does work for many people and certainly should not be dismissed. The process requires the person to make a personal inventory and share this with others. It is a group therapy and individual therapy approach that increases the awareness of the individual. It is not for the social worker to be judgemental about its spiritual basis.

The 'wheel of change' model

The second model, the 'wheel of change', designed by Prochaska and DiClemente (1994), is an approach that is used in many drug support agencies in the community. In this model there is a cyclical process. It starts with a period of pre-contemplation. The client does not realise that they have a problem. They can cope with their lives, they proclaim, even if the substance misuse costs them their jobs, their health, their family or their freedom. Through techniques such as employing cognitive dissonance, they can be encouraged to see that they do not live life as they would like to. This phrase means that the social worker encourages the client to look back to a time before the addiction became a problem and to look forward to envisage how they would like their future to be. This will be in sharp relief to how their lives are actually lived. Pre-contemplation is the period when the client acknowledges that there is a problem with their dependency on substances. If they do not, then they do not try to change. It does not mean that they are written off. It means that they have not made the necessary mental leap to want to break from their habit and they are not ready yet to move on to the next step.

For those who do want to change, they move into the next period of contemplation. What would they like their life to be like? From here they make decisions to change and break from their old routine, associates, etc. It is not easy if much of their waking time has been spent with others who misuse substances. They may need a period of detox to cope with the withdrawal symptoms. Change does not occur overnight but has to be planned. Alternatives will need to be built into their lives to make up for the gaps. This can be exciting and draws on social work skills, perhaps via a task-centred approach, to achieve manageable goals that have eluded the client for a long time. These might be small steps in many ways but massive for the client. In our example of a family with marital problems, where the father has had a substance misuse problem, he might want to start taking his daughter to school regularly. By doing so, he would be demonstrating responsibility, which could at times be when he might often be high on substances. He is contemplating an action that replaces drug taking with something he would like to do, namely being responsible for his daughter.

Now the client needs to take action. This is the time when steps are made to put their decision into effect. It is difficult and the client will need support and encouragement. While it is important that the goals set are the client's, a degree of realism is important and so 'shared higher aims' discussed by the client and the social worker are the key to success. Can the client be trusted to carry out the action if it requires a responsibility for others as well as for themselves? Action may involve going for detox or getting a prescription so that there is no longer a reliance on illicit substances. But most of all it means the client gaining control over their life. This is a big step for them.

This has to be kept up and there is a period of maintenance for the changes. Maintenance is the period when the initial euphoria wears off, the recognition that life is tough. Bureaucracies can frustrate ambition, etc., and can drag the client down. Drawing on the resources of the family, if they have stuck by the client, can help. Indeed, one goal might be to use the change to re-establish a bond with the family. If the client can maintain their good intentions, then their problems are largely resolved and life may be better from this point on. However, not many clients can achieve this immediately.

This model allows for the possibility of relapse. Things go wrong. The client may go back and need to revisit the pre-contemplation stage again and be assisted to move on to fresh contemplation. Why might this happen? Some clients have 'skeletons' in their emotional cupboards and find it difficult to allow themselves to succeed. Others succumb to the temptation or think that they can control their drug habit. Links with former associates may not be conducive to maintaining their intention to remain off substances. It should not come as a surprise if this happens. The client may adopt the response of 'well, I've tried and failed, I can't do it', which puts them back at the pre-contemplative phase. They will need support to move forward again. The habit of substance dependency can be a really hard one to break. This is discussed in detail in a chapter in the book by Connors et al. (2001) where they talk about preparing clients for such a possibility, including a written list of actions that could be taken.

Pictorially the steps are shown below:

It can be seen as a dynamic process where the client is moving on. To describe this as a 'wheel of change' is misleading because the second pre-contemplation stage is different from the first. The client will have moved on and is not static in terms of their life and what they have tried to achieve in trying to get in control of their substance misuse. A more helpful pictorial expression is given below:

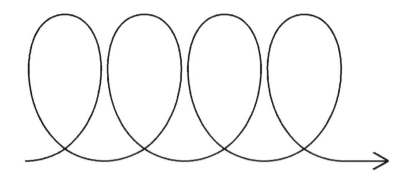

Here it can be seen that the client loops around in their progress, and their pathway is a series of successes and failures. Rather than achieving their goal in one circle, they will make a number of attempts, with support, until they achieve their goal.

Working with dependent clients of all ages is a difficult occupation as failure can occur and the client needs to start again. It is the skill of the therapist to recognise when this is happening and to work with the client to see why it has happened. It may be that there are very painful areas in their lives that they find hard to deal with. Cognitive methods of intervention help the client to work through better ways of dealing with difficult issues. The client can rehearse situations that have gone wrong to see how they could have handled them better. They may need to learn how to avoid being in the wrong place at the wrong time, for example, so that they are not tempted to have a drink or get into a fight. The social worker cannot make such decisions for the client, but a good relationship, based on trust, will encourage the child or young person to examine what went wrong and to learn from the experience.

CASE STUDY

Jim was living with his partner and their two young children. He was a former heroin user and he appeared to be doing well until he met some former acquaintances. He was persuaded to take some heroin. He started to use the drug regularly until he was given an ultimatum that he had to stop or his partner would throw him out.

As the social worker with the family, you are a little sceptical about his motivation but he seems very keen to stop again. You arrange for him to have a detox and then go into residential treatment. He appeared to settle in well and had almost completed the treatment programme when he appeared at your office very upset, having walked out of the programme. He had immediately relapsed. He tells you that he feels a complete failure and he does not know what to do. He wants to remain in his relationship and he loves his children but he does not think that his partner will take him back.

What do you do? How do you work with Jim to resolve the difficult situation he has got himself into? Should you involve his family and/or inform his partner that you have seen Jim? Has he reached the point of no return?

COMMENT

The Prochaska and DiClemente model builds in the potential for relapse. You need to work with Jim to understand why he left the treatment programme. It is not uncommon for the initial attempt to change to fail, as the client is moving from contemplating to implementing a complete break from their former way of life. Programmes are likely to be challenging, forcing the client to confront issues in their past that they have tried to run away from. It is not easy to cope with and if he does go back, he will be prepared for the regime and the expectations on him to work on his personal issues.

Gossop (2003) includes a very helpful discussion on detoxification, which may make substance misusers feel very anxious. The process itself may be extremely unpleasant and produce a number of physical symptoms including vomiting, stomach cramps, tiredness, insomnia and muscular pains. Detoxification is not a life-threatening process, although it can be intense for a period in excess of 72 hours. In itself, it is not a cure, but a step in the process of change.

When Jim left the residential placement, his reference point would have been his old associates and his old way of life. In the maintenance part of the programme Jim will need to put into place a new way of life that is likely to fail if it is not profoundly different from what he has done before. There is a difference between dependence on the drug of choice and the craving to take the drug.

In the above scenario, Jim had had the weekend to reflect on his flight away from the programme. He thought through where he wanted to be and resolved to return to the programme and start again. Support is very important here and it is possible that the client will need to reassess the positives and negatives of not returning to treatment. In Jim's case, he realised that he had a lot to lose and he wanted to go back. The return was organised. His partner was contacted and she was prepared to give Jim a second chance, although she would not have him back until he completed the programme. It is very important to take a holistic view of the family and to build in support for the family in addition to the client with the substance misuse problem.

Building in the maintenance component. Jim leaves the residential programme. What happens next? Jim will be physically over his need to take drugs but how do you help him not to relapse?

When Jim returns to the family home he will be at risk of relapsing again. As the social worker you can work with Jim to look at the situations when he might be at most risk of relapse. Is there a particular time of day when he is more tempted to take drugs? Are there particular areas that he should not go to, where for example he is known? How does he deal with stressful situations? You can role-play with him how he might deal in other ways with pressure. You could also role-play other pressure situations, such as how he could deal successfully with former associates who might try to persuade him to relapse – in fact anything that helps him to build up confidence to successfully maintain his resolve to remain off drugs.

Connors et al. (2001) comment that the therapist (social worker) needs to create an atmosphere where the client can feel comfortable, so that they can discuss the causes of their relapse. There is a need to quickly contain the substance-misusing behaviour so that the client can move around the circle again back to the maintenance phase. The analogy that Connors et al. use is that of a racing driver where driver and pit staff work together to refine and improve the car's performance in order to win the race. This invokes the notion of recycling rather than relapse. Positive thinking, working on strategies to avoid potentially dangerous situations, where the person could be put under danger of relapse, can be practised in advance. If things go wrong, the client needs to be able to trust the professionals, to be honest and to move the process on again.

Social workers have the knowledge and skills to be non-judgemental in their work with clients as well as the objectivity to work constructively with the client to formulate goals and work toward a shared higher aim. Whether a psychodynamic, task-centred, or cognitive behavioural approach is used, the essence of a positive relationship built on trust is within the professional ambit of the practitioner. Working with clients with low self-esteem and who do not expect to succeed is a challenge but it is achievable. What is positive is that the support networks in the community have been strengthened immeasurably in recent years, where drug action teams and other supports are geared for a much faster response to substance misusers than was previously the case. Possibilities for creative partnership work have been opened up.

The social worker needs to be clear on who their client is. If the social worker is working with the child in the family, then it is likely to be the case that a separate worker should be assigned to the parent with the substance misuse problem. The needs of the child may not be compatible with the needs and wishes of the adult. Role confusion could lead to the social worker missing important issues in the family and losing sight of the child.

The National Treatment Agency has sponsored research on the effectiveness of treatment approaches. Wanigarantne et al. (2005) evaluated the effectiveness of psychological therapies with clients with studies, where the methodologies varied from meta-analysis of random controlled studies (type I), evidence from at least

Continued

RESEARCH SUMMARY *continued*

one controlled trial without randomisation (type II), descriptive studies (type III), at least one well-designed observational study (type IV) and expert opinion, including the opinions of service users and carers (type V).

Brief interventions using motivational interviewing was found to be superior to all other interventions (type I). Cognitive behavioural therapy (CBT) figured highly in terms of effectiveness, including working on relapse prevention. It was particularly effective for alcohol problems. In terms of intensity there was no difference between twice weekly CBT and a more intensive five-day a week day programme (type I).

General alcohol counselling, including psycho-education and humanistic approaches, was effective in comparison to no treatment or those on waiting lists, but was less effective than CBT or 12-step approaches. Counselling with methadone maintenance produced significantly greater improvements in reducing illicit opiate use compared to methadone only (type I). The addition of other psychosocial services further improved outcome (type I). Family therapy produced very promising results, better than individual counselling, peer group therapy and family psycho-education (type I). A four-year follow-up showed that patients receiving individual counselling were four to five times more likely to be arrested for a substance abuse related offence than those in family therapy (type II). The family as a resource and strength is clearly valuable when clients have not lost this support.

The findings from the National Treatment Outcome Research Study (NTORS) were very encouraging in terms of showing that drug misusers in NTORS reported a substantial reduction in crime after entering treatment, both in acquisitive crime and drug-selling crimes. These fell to about a quarter of their starting level (Gossop, 2005). Gossop described coping behaviour for clients as the behaviour patterns that are used to deal with problematic situations. CBT approaches are used to help clients find approaches that do not rely on substances to help them when the going gets difficult and/or stressful:

> Treatment seeks to reduce the risk of relapse by teaching drug users to recognise high-risk situations and to develop and use coping strategies, to avoid returning to drug use. Those clients who made use of coping responses after treatment were less likely to return to illicit drug use. *(Gossop, 2005, p6)*

COMMENT

When the author was a probation officer at the start of his career he supervised a male on parole licence who had a very severe alcohol problem. When this man was drunk he was dangerous and violent. He earned very well as a carpenter on building sites and so received much cash in hand on a Friday night, which worried me. He had a supportive partner and he attended Alcoholics Anonymous, where he found the support of being with other former alcoholics very helpful. He would come to see me weekly and would say to me that he had been 'dry' for the previous week. As a new worker I wanted to do some in-depth work casework with him but was this my need, not his? What he wanted was to be able to say to an authority figure that he was remaining off alcohol and the weekly visits were important to him. I did a home visit and was reassured by his partner that indeed he was keeping his resolve, and the period of parole passed without problem. It was not my role to dictate what he needed to do. What he wanted was to demonstrate to an authority figure that he was being good and he was happy with the positive response that he received each week. An important consideration here was the continuity: he was not reporting to a receptionist or to a variety of officials but to a person who knew him and his circumstances. I would have recognised quickly if he had started to slip. Such a case illustrates the danger in reassessing this case as a low-priority one which could be allocated to a general response.

I wrote another report on a man who told me that he routinely drank around 10–15 pints of beer per day and more at the weekend. He also worked as a labourer and did not see the level of alcohol consumed as a problem even though he had got into trouble for disorderly conduct. I tried to get him to see that it must have been a problem or he would not have been up in court, but he would not accept it. He was stuck at the pre-contemplation stage and would not be shifted. In consequence he could not be worked with and there was no further contact between us. In more recent times, it is likely that he would have been placed on an alcohol education programme whether he was motivated or not. Whether this would have been beneficial is open to doubt.

CHAPTER SUMMARY

When tasks go wrong or do not work, it could lead to a constructive re-evaluation of the problem and should not be seen as failure. When children, young people and families have been dysfunctional for a long period of time, the solution is unlikely to happen overnight. Sadly there is no magic pill to make things better. Rather, it is hard work and commitment by all concerned, possibly over a long period of time. The pace has to be set by the client and the skill of the worker is to maximise their motivation, self-belief and preparedness and ability to change. Clients can inform themselves about drugs and get online advice by using the 'Ask Frank' website. This site contains much useful information on drugs, their effects, penalties for possession and supplying, etc. However, it is the skill of the practitioner that will encourage and facilitate change.

An article by Ashton (2005) gives encouragement to practitioners who are prepared to use the techniques highlighted in this chapter to motivate and work with substance-misusing clients. What does not work is 'pigeonholing' clients by labelling them, or working slavishly to a manual, i.e. being over-prescriptive. The approach, states Ashton, requires 'the application of sensitivity and social skills.' These are the attributes of a professional worker.

The Health and Social Care Act 2012 transferred responsibility for public health to local authorities from the NHS, with upper tier and unitary authorities becoming responsible for improving health in their area. This took place from the beginning of April 2013 so at the time of publication it is hard to assess the impact of this change. Anecdotally, it appears to have the potential to make delivery more responsive to local need. Public health grants are to be ring fenced with health and wellbeing boards influencing

Continued

CHAPTER SUMMARY *continued*

commissioning decisions. Health and wellbeing boards will be required to produce Joint Strategic Needs Assessments and Joint Health and Well Being Strategies. It will be instructive for readers to obtain and read these.

In terms of drug and alcohol services, these will become multi-agency partnerships, including local authorities, becoming responsible for commissioning and coordinating local services. Again, it is too early to form a judgement on these changes. While multi-agency approaches are in principle productive, agencies need to learn and understand each others' languages, structures and priorities, which takes time. One further change, which can be controversial, is the move towards payment by results (PbR). PbR is likely to become central to the way drug services are funded and has yet to be shown to be effective. Anecdotally, accusations have been made that it can lead to risk averse decision making, complex cases may be too difficult to demonstrate change in the time allowed, leading to a loss of service or 'cheating'. This may become clearer over time. What is clear is that the agenda is changing and this will mean that services will look different in a few years' time to the present.

FURTHER READING

All the titles suggested for further reading will expand on the techniques given in the chapter. Gossop considers a range of treatment options, including the use of methadone maintenance. The other recommended books focus on motivating the client to change, as well as what works and what doesn't work. These techniques are consistently used in drug treatment agencies and practitioners should be familiar with these approaches.

Gossop, M (2003) *Drug addiction and its treatment.* Oxford: Oxford University Press.

Miller, W and Rollnick, S (2002) *Motivational interviewing: preparing people for change,* 2nd edition. New York: Guilford.

Rotgers, F, Morgenstern, J and Walters, S (eds) (2003) *Treating substance abuse. Theory and technique,* 2nd edition. London: Guilford.

Smith, J and Meyers, R (2004) *Motivating substance abusers to enter treatment.* New York: Guilford.

Trotter, C (1999) *Working with involuntary clients: a guide to practice.* London: Sage.

WEBSITES

www.talktofrank.com/
Ask Frank.

www.drugscope.org.uk/
DrugScope. A really valuable source of information. In particular look at frequently asked questions (faqs).

www.homeoffice.gov.uk/drugs/
Home Office drugs page.

www.eata.org.uk
European Association for the Treatment of Addictions. This is a very useful site for information on the treatment of clients with substance dependence. In particular look at the publications, press releases and latest news.

www.local.gov.uk/c/document_library/get_file?uuid=ef73ac40-827e-4e7f-bb27-9b19fff157c0&groupId=10171
Changes to the delivery of services to drug and alcohol users after the Local Government Association paper on the new public health role from April 2013. This includes links to the latest drug and alcohol strategies, sites with useful information and examples of good practice across the country.

Chapter 8

Conclusion

Introduction

Make not thyself helpless in drinking in the beer shop.
For will not the words of thy report repeated slip out from thy mouth without thy knowing that thou hast uttered them?
Falling down thy limbs will be broken and no one will give thee a hand to help thee up. As for thy companions in the swilling of beer, they will get up and say 'Outside with this drunkard'. (Translation from the *Precepts of Ani* (*circa* 1500 BC) www.med.mun.ca/artistinresidence/pages/handshistory2.htm)

The purpose of this chapter is to draw together and conclude the themes that have run throughout this book and to link these to good social work practice. Central to this is client empowerment and a commitment to anti-discriminatory practice. The importance of structured assessments with substance-misusing clients will be considered and finally we will return to the theme of working in partnership.

Client empowerment

The quotation above highlights the negatives and perils of alcohol misuse, but not the reasons why a person might start to consume alcohol. Alcohol can make a person feel more relaxed and act as a disinhibitor. It works in a similar way to tranquillisers on the central nervous system. Many substance misusers have personal difficulties and issues that pre-date any drug/alcohol problems. Substances can often be used to blot out psychological and social problems (Gossop, 2003). The client is unable to deal with these problems, and substances are used as a shield. Why then is empowerment so important when working with substance misusers? These clients often feel that they have lost control over their lives and develop a dependency culture to live a hand-to-mouth existence, denying that they have a problem. The quotation is 3,500 years old but it puts into context in a way that is pertinent today that substance misuse places the individual outside of society and leaves them in an extremely vulnerable position. Davey puts this problem of social isolation very well:

> *People who are seriously disadvantaged in society rarely have single problems – they have multiple interlocking problems. They do not compete on a level playing field. They suffer a 'cycle of deprivation'. Empowerment must address all their problems together if it is to be meaningful. Poverty, poor housing and the nature of the social security system put a strain on relationships and lead to widespread demoralisation. Depending on the circumstances of individuals they can lead to physical and mental ill health, criminality, addiction and the persecution of individual or collective scapegoats: racism, sexism, picking on individuals who are 'different'.* (Davey, 1999, p37)

When working with substance misusers, the drug must not be the only focus for intervention and drug use must not be decontextualised from the wider world of the substance misuser. How do individuals learn how to take drugs? Is it an activity that can be separated from the people substance misusers associate with? When we see the person as their substance misuse problem or, worse, as the substance itself – an alcoholic, a 'junkie', a pill pusher – we are discriminating against them and ceasing to look beyond the label.

Edwin Sutherland described the concept of 'differential association' as meaning that people had to be taught how to become thieves and indeed white-collar (middle-class) criminals. Essential to this was the notion that crime was not an innate attribute to the individual but a learnt behaviour. The poor might have become thieves but the rich perpetrated crimes also within the corporations in which they worked (see Lilly et al., 1989). The social worker is unlikely to come into contact with the white-collar criminal but is likely to work with people who have a cluster of problems as described by Davey above. How do people get taught to take drugs? Who introduced them to drugs and what are the implications of this, if they want to stop taking them?

Labelling the client as a 'drug problem' while ignoring the other aspects of their lives implies a single-focus approach that is unlikely to succeed. It is disempowering. Helping the client to get over the physical dependency on drugs might take a couple of weeks in detox, but few people imagine that this would be sufficient for them to remain off drugs. What is needed is a holistic assessment with the intention of gaining a thorough appraisal of all the issues facing the client. Structured assessments, including checking out what substances they take, licit and illicit, are more likely to ensure that all key aspects of the clients' lifestyle are investigated. If the clients are not asked about substances, they are unlikely to tell you that they are taking them. It can be easy to obtain a prescription for anti-depressants and to become dependent on them. When these are mixed with alcohol, for example, the client may be putting their health in serious jeopardy.

You may be a surprised to learn that when a group of young European drug users was asked what would be the most difficult of substances that they were currently taking to give up, they answered: tobacco 40 per cent, alcohol 30 per cent, cannabis 22 per cent and heroin 15 per cent (Frischer and Beckett, 2006). The relationship between licit and illicit drugs is complex.

Links with social work and the realities of structured assessment

Social work has a theory base that enables practitioners to develop an understanding of human growth and development. What connections can be made between psychoanalytic theories and substance misuse? Early psychoanalytic theories saw addiction as a regressive act returning the client 'to an infantile pleasurable state' (Margolis and Zweben, 1998, p64). However, more recent theorists have seen substance misuse as a form of self-medication to manage deficits arising from early deprivation and faulty/ non-existent parent–infant relationships. Furthermore, the choice of drug is not accidental:

> *Patients experiment with various classes of drugs and discover that a specific one is compelling because it ameliorates, heightens, or relieves affect states that they find particularly problematic or painful.* (Khantzian, 1997, in Margolis and Zweben, 1998, p65)

Thus heroin addicts use opiates for their calming effects; amphetamines, which have a stimulant effect, enhance self-esteem; alcohol and other central nervous system depressants lower anxiety and tension. Khantzian drew his theory from his clinical work with substance misusers in the public and private sectors in Massachusetts. There is limited empirical evidence to support these hypotheses; however, that does not mean that they are without foundation, as they have been developed from clinical experience. The notion of self-regulatory impairment is relevant here – by this is understood that the substance misuser has deficits in their ability to form relationships, or to be tolerant in stressful situations, to care for themselves or in their low self-esteem. Substance misusers may not be able to cope with their emotions, nor be able to verbalise their feelings, and use drugs as a neutraliser. Such difficulties are likely to affect the ability of the client to form relationships, which may oscillate between over-dependence and hostility. Again, substances may be used to try to cover over these difficulties.

An interesting question here is whether difficulties in forming relationships and the disjuncture in parenting practice fall across the spectrum of social class in some sort of even pattern. As Frischer and Beckett (2006) point out, the evidence is that problematic drug use is linked to structural problems like accommodation, poor education and unemployment. They continue:

It might be argued that higher social classes are equally experiencing problematic drug use and corresponding criminality, but the likelihood is that their crimes are white collar and our justice system is inherently less able to identify them...what we have to work with is the current government premise that to effect desistence in problematic substance misusers, lifestyle work is vital. (Frischer and Beckett, 2006, p140)

Their approach mirrors Edwin Sutherland and is somewhat deterministic. It does not explain why some people undertake illegal activities while others do not. The same can be said for the consumption of drugs and although we might use a structured assessment to say that a person is highly likely to take substances or offend, we cannot say this conclusively. There must still be a large element of human nature and choice in decision making, which is where clinical judgement is important in risk assessment. Criminogenic factors, for example, associating with offending peers, do not guarantee a return to offending.

The probation service has moved much further than social work in relying on computerised assessment. The HM Inspectorate of Probation report on substance misuse (2006), found that in assessment reports (known as OASys) the level of problematic drug use varied from 16 to 23 per cent and some assessments were incomplete. Furthermore, even when a significant substance misuse problem had been identified in OASys, it did not necessarily translate into a supervision plan objective. Worryingly this was the case in 28 per cent of the cases that had been inspected, although it was significantly better for the 'prolific and other priority' offenders, when this figure dropped to 9 per cent. This highlights a warning for social work not to go down the road that probation has moved in, namely of client (offender) management target setting.

The report expressed concern that while there has been progress in getting offenders onto drug rehabilitation programmes, there has been a major problem in doing the same for offenders who have alcohol treatment requirements (ATRs). It comments:

- *Alcohol treatment was scarce in the areas inspected, although senior managers were aware of the level of need as indicated by assessments using OASys.*

- *In contrast, the provision of treatment for offenders with drug misuse problems was generally readily available.* (HM Inspectorate of Probation, 2006, p6)

The report found that twice as many offenders had alcohol misuse problems as had drug problems but alcohol treatment services were few and far between. For reasons that were not explained but clearly were inconsistent, court orders for probation work with alcohol problems referred to 'treatment' whereas for drug problems it referred to 'rehabilitation'. A further complexity was that:

it had been a key implementation difficulty for areas to reconcile the tensions between offence seriousness, offender management tier and treatment intensity. This resulted in inconsistent delivery between areas.
(HM Inspectorate of Probation, 2006, p6)

This meant that probation assessed offenders in terms of re-offending on one scale and the offence seriousness triggered the level of intervention required. The level of offender management this generated would determine whether treatment came from a qualified probation officer or probation service officer, and what programme of treatment the offender would be assigned to and the intensity of treatment. However, while the health service operated a four-tier treatment model, the drug rehabilitation requirement in a community order (Criminal Justice Act 2003) operated on three different levels, with low-, medium- or high-intensity treatment components. In some areas there was difficulty between probation and the drug alcohol advisory teams in agreeing to provide structured day programmes for drug offenders of sufficient intensity and duration to meet the level of seriousness of the offence. Ironically the inability in some areas to provide suitable alcohol provision for offenders was not seen as a problem as the probation service did not have 'performance targets to meet' (HM Inspectorate of Probation, 2006, p19). Clearly delivery of treatment needs to be predicated on the level of need and not to meet targets. Social workers, who work with individuals and families, need to know about probation practice with drug- and alcohol-misusing offenders in order to know what is likely to happen to them.

ACTIVITY 8.1

Formulating an assessment

Why is it important to make an accurate assessment of a person who has a substance-misuse problem? How would you go about this task?

COMMENT

In Chapter 2 we were introduced to the four-tiered model of care that operates in England. In this respect it was stated that all drug and alcohol misusers must have a drug assessment and care plan. The appropriate tier of support and services needs to be engaged, which requires an in-depth knowledge of the frequency and extent that substances are being taken. You should recall that tier 1 consists of services offered by a wide range of professionals – primary care medical services, generic social workers, teachers, community pharmacists, probation officers, housing officers, homeless persons units. These professionals need to be able to communicate with a common set of expectations of what can be offered to the client. The work is not just about substance misuse. Tier 2 provides open access services to substance misusers who can self-refer or be referred by professionals. This level is concerned with trying to get the client to engage and may not entail a high level of commitment by the client. It could be viewed as the contemplation stage, in the Prochaska and DiClemente model of the wheel of change. Thus harm reduction could be the outcome for the substance misuser, including needle exchange. In tier 3, structured programmes of care are provided specifically for substance misusers. This might include structured day care, methadone maintenance treatment, community detox and cognitive behavioural and other treatment counselling approaches, delivered as part of a day programme. Finally, tier 4 is for those with high levels of presented need, requiring inpatient treatment. This includes detox and residential rehabilitation.

If the client is given treatment that is more intensive than is required, it is likely to be counter-productive and unnecessary, as well as more expensive. Therefore the client needs to be accurately assessed for what level of treatment they both want and need. Doel and Shardlow (2005), commenting on assessment within the social work setting, are cautious about the assessment process, which they are concerned is often 'on' rather than 'with' the client. On the positive side they acknowledge that with good communication skills: 'an assessment can be transformed from a formalized checklist to a genuine partnership of enquiry' (Doel and Shardlow, 2005, p85). The social worker is required to see the person in front of them, rather than concentrating on the questions they have to answer on the form. In terms of social work practice, the assessment must be used as a starting point for further action, which works well with the task-centred approach. In Chapter 7, motivational interviewing was used as a mechanism to get the client ready for change. Comment was made that this approach requires the social worker to be more directive than is often the case, but no change would result in the client remaining unstable in their substance misuse.

How the task of formulating the assessment is undertaken depends on the agency the social worker is operating in. In youth offending teams, in England and Wales, there is a structured risk assessment profile called ASSET, which includes substance misuse as a category to be considered. What is required is knowledge of what substances are taken, how often and when, what circumstances might trigger taking the substance, whether they are taken alone or with others present – in short, as much detail as possible so that the client can make an informed decision on how and when they would like to change. The social worker should also be conscious of the links between substance misuse, the client's general health and their mental health. The social worker might ask the client to keep a diary of what they took, when they took it, why they did so, and over time a pattern may well emerge. The client might not have faced up to the level and frequency of use and the diary may become a useful tool in helping the client to control their use of substances. The more often the social worker asks about the use of substances, the more their confidence will grow in dealing with this part of the client's lifestyle.

RESEARCH SUMMARY

In 2000 a research programme to run over four years was announced, the Drugs Misuse Research Initiative (DMRI), costing £2.4 million. The goal was to expand knowledge on:

Continued

- *effectiveness and cost-effectiveness of treatment and care modalities;*
- *the impact of waiting lists for drug treatment on uptake, completion rates and outcomes, and how to use time on the waiting list positively to increase the likelihood of treatment success;*
- *co-morbidity of substance misuse and mental health problems;*
- *the impact of drug use on young people's psychosocial development;*
- *prevention and treatment interventions aimed at young people;*
- *long-term heavy cannabis use.*

(MacGregor, 2005, pp1–2)

Susanne MacGregor (2005) was the programme co-ordinator for the DMRI and her article is an overview report of Phase One of the DMRI, which consisted of 14 projects linked to the 1998 10-year drug strategy. A systematic review of longitudinal studies commented that cannabis use 'showed consistent associations with lower educational attainment, increased risk of use of other drugs, and increased reporting of psychological problems' (MacGregor, 2005, p10). However, there is an important caveat to this regarding 'confounding factors'. Two factors may not be causally related but they may have common antecedents. The example given is that 'early life adversity' may increase the risk of drug use as well as harm through other life pathways. Care must be taken therefore not to make assumptions about the long-term effects of drugs, for example, cannabis.

In this respect, a further study of prolonged heavy cannabis use found that this was 'non-intrusive, non-destructive and controlled' (MacGregor, 2005, p14). Caution does need to be exercised here as often cannabis is smoked with tobacco so there are likely to be issues related to lung health. This study was based on adults who were mature enough to avoid activities like driving while taking cannabis. A different study among 10–12 year olds, in Glasgow and Newcastle, found that by the age of 12 just under 10 per cent had been offered illegal substances. Cannabis was the drug most used in this young age group. Within the survey group of 2,318 children, almost 4 in 100 had used illegal drugs previously, but only 1.5 per cent in the previous month when surveyed. More worryingly, almost 29 per cent had been in situations where illegal drugs had been used, supporting the 'normalisation' thesis discussed in earlier chapters. There was lack of support for children whose families were users and in general, the closer the relationship between the child and the person offering the illicit drugs, the harder it was to refuse. Many of these families had a plethora of problems and cannabis use was one among many difficulties experienced. These families are likely to come to the attention of social workers for many reasons and professionals should ensure that substance misuse is not forgotten in the initial and continuing assessments being made on and with the families. There is clearly a further role here for the social worker to help young people rehearse strategies for politely

Continued

declining illicit substances when offered to them. In this respect the children wanted 'the involvement of other experts rather than, or in addition to teachers, especially those with relevant real life experience' (MacGregor, 2005, p13).

An evaluation of brief intervention with 342 young (16–22 years) non-injecting stimulant users in London and Kent found that there were high rates of offending in the sample group. Most were using ecstasy (202), cocaine (73) and crack (67). Those who took crack as their first-choice drug had poorer health than the others. What was encouraging from this research was that brief motivational intervention was acceptable to all the users and frequency of using all the major substances declined. However, training peer workers to deliver this was somewhat problematic and many of those trained did not actually take part.

ACTIVITY **8.2**

What does the above information tell you about the challenges of growing up in the twenty-first century?

COMMENT

In Chapter 2 there was a discussion about the normalisation of drug use among the young. The DMRI research in Glasgow and Newcastle confirmed that many young people are likely to be in situations where drugs are available and possibly offered to them. Education about drugs is essential for young people, their parents and carers, and professionals. The symptoms of substance use need to be recognised and young people need to be aware of the consequences of taking substances.

Two further areas examined were co-morbidity and treatment outcomes, including the effects of waiting times for treatment. In terms of mental health, it was stated that there was 'a robust relationship between tobacco, alcohol, and drug dependence and other psychiatric disorders' (MacGregor, 2005, p21). A national epidemiological study drew on data from 1.4 million patients in England and Wales between 1993 and 1998. It found that the numbers of co-morbid individuals being treated by general practitioners was increasing by 10 per cent each year, especially for serious psychiatric disorders. Co-morbid patients, especially those with personality disorders, have a higher rate of unmet need than others with substance-misuse difficulties. There was a particular message for professionals and this is salient to the social work profession:

> *There is an urgent need for training since staff demonstrated lack of competence in assessment and diagnosis. The need for staff development and training is evidenced by the inability of services to identify substantial numbers of co-morbid disorders in all but a minority of cases.*
> (MacGregor, 2005, p30)

ACTIVITY 8.3

What knowledge should social workers have about the impact of substance misuse on mental health?

COMMENT

Having read this far, you should have an understanding that there is a strong link between substance misuse and mental health. Without getting into a 'chicken and egg' discussion (that is, what comes first), the two issues are clearly closely interlinked. Social workers need to be aware of this, and that mental health must be included in the assessment process.

Waiting times for treatment

Research on opiate misusers revealed that waiting times did not impact on take-up or retention in treatment three to six months later. Mostly clients are lost between referral and assessment. However, this is a complex area and organisations use different definitions, measuring their waiting times differently. Some are more able than others to retain clients, perhaps by maintaining some contact in the interim period. In a further study some service users were unhappy that they were unable to access services until they had become offenders also. In terms of treatment outcomes the DMRI research commented that treatment, as described in research literature and the subject of evaluations, did not accord with what was currently being delivered. Thus the effectiveness of treatment needed further exploration and evaluation.

The DMRI was completed in 2009 with 10 projects that are of major interests to social workers. Executive summaries can be accessed at: **http://webarchive.nationalarchives.gov.uk/20091116140310/http://dmri.lshtm.ac.uk/execs.html** The level of investment in drug treatment services had grown to £1.5 billion in 2005, a one-third increase in three years. The main emphasis is on Class A drugs and supporting 'vulnerable groups and communities' (MacGregor, 2005, p51). As this includes the young, women, black and minority ethnic groups and both rural and urban areas, it is focused squarely on the communities with whom social work engages. The need for this further research tells us that there is more to learn about effective interventions with substance-misusing clients. Motivational interviewing gives us the confidence to work with clients to encourage and empower them to change.

At the time that this book is being completed profound changes are occurring in the delivery of public health, with the aim of closer partnership with offender services. Joint papers are being produced between the Ministry of Justice and the Department of Health. The intention is to ramp up the level of inter-agency sharing, commissioning, liaison and diversion, substance misuse, health and changes in justice delivery. The catalyst for this is the Health and Social Care Act 2012. There is a cross-departmental programme board, with representatives from the Department of Health, Ministry of Justice (Home Office), Department for Education, Ministry of Justice (National Offender Management Service), Youth Justice Board and Public Health England. Time will tell if these major changes are going to be effective.

Effective sharing between agencies

How agencies communicate with each other and at what level is of central importance to good practice. In youth justice, the key agencies – social work, probation, police, health and education – are physically together under one roof, enabling good practice to take place in terms of both referring clients on to treatment and for preventative work. In some areas, with the use of Children's Fund money (25 per cent of this is allocated to crime prevention), multi-agency discussions take place within Youth Inclusion Support Programmes (YISPs) for children aged between eight and 13 years.

The YISP involves a number of key agencies: police, youth offending service, education, welfare, health, housing and possibly voluntary agencies in the local authority. It is a way that agencies can informally share concerns before they become so entrenched that child protection and other serious issues force major action like triggering the removal of the child or eviction from the home due to serious social nuisance. The YISP might have dedicated workers attached to it who can work with the parents and other carers to produce an integrated support plan (ISP) for the young people concerned. This can be very effective and can trigger service provision at a lower level of need than is often the case in social services.

For adults the drug action team can be the locus for information, diagnosis and treatment. It has the facility for quick triage assessment and for entry into any of the four tiers for treatment. In my discussions with DAT managers it was clear that the potential for the DAT to work with clients is not always fully utilised and practitioners should acquaint themselves with what the DAT can offer. They usually have useful leaflets for the clients and these can be left for easy access in reception and waiting areas.

What is clear is that the problems of substance misuse are still only slowly being recognised and as social workers we have a responsibility to be well informed in this area. We have the techniques to engage effectively with clients who misuse substances. As professionals we have the confidence and commitment to see beyond the label to the person underneath.

Susanne MacGregor (2005) produced her DMRI overview report in a special edition of the journal *Drugs: Education, Prevention and Policy* (December 2005) volume 12, Supplement 1. This edition is dedicated to the report and there are also executive summaries from the projects themselves, so the entire journal is worth reading.

If at this stage you would like to read a detailed book on understanding drugs and what they do to you, then read **Parrot et al**. (2004) *Understanding drugs and behaviour.* Chichester: Wiley.

For government policy on young people see: **Home Office**: *Tackling drugs: changing lives. Every child matters: change for children: young people and drugs* (2004b). London: Home Office.

www.homeoffice.gov.uk/drugs/

For the most up-to-date information on government drugs policy.

www.dh.gov.uk/health/category/policy-areas/social-care/offender-health/
Offender health

http://healthandcare.dh.gov.uk/the-health-and-caresystem-in-april-2013-infographic/
Health and social care from 2013

http://healthandcare.dh.gov.uk/guide-system
The new health and care system

http://healthandcare.dh.gov.uk/category/publichealth/hwb/
Health and wellbeing boards

Appendix 1 Professional Capabilities Framework

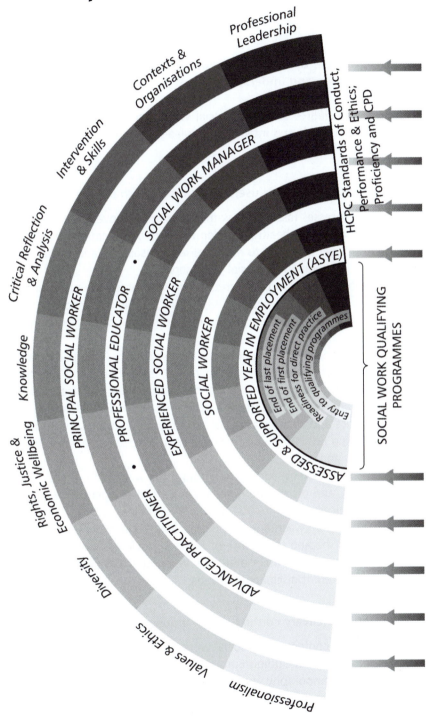

Professional Leadership

Contexts & Organisations

Intervention & Skills

Critical Reflection & Analysis

Knowledge

Rights, Justice & Economic Wellbeing

Diversity

Values & Ethics

Professionalism

PRINCIPAL SOCIAL WORKER

ADVANCED PRACTITIONER

PROFESSIONAL EDUCATOR

SOCIAL WORK MANAGER

EXPERIENCED SOCIAL WORKER

SOCIAL WORKER

ASSESSED & SUPPORTED YEAR IN EMPLOYMENT (ASYE)

End of last placement

End of first placement

Readiness for direct practice

Entry to qualifying programmes

HCPC Standards of Conduct, Performance & Ethics; Proficiency and CPD

SOCIAL WORK QUALIFYING PROGRAMMES

Appendix 2 Subject Benchmark for Social Work

Subject knowledge, understanding and skills
Subject knowledge and understanding

5.1 During their degree studies in social work, honours graduates should acquire, critically evaluate, apply and integrate knowledge and understanding in the following five core areas of study.

5.1.1
Social work services, service users and carers, which include:

- the social processes (associated with, for example, poverty, migration, unemployment, poor health, disablement, lack of education and other sources of disadvantage) that lead to marginalisation, isolation and exclusion, and their impact on the demand for social work services;
- explanations of the links between definitional processes contributing to social differences (for example, social class, gender, ethnic differences, age, sexuality and religious belief) to the problems of inequality and differential need faced by service users;
- the nature of social work services in a diverse society (with particular reference to concepts such as prejudice, interpersonal, institutional and structural discrimination, empowerment and anti-discriminatory practices);
- the nature and validity of different definitions of, and explanations for, the characteristics and circumstances of service users and the services required by them, drawing on knowledge from research, practice experience, and from service users and carers;
- the focus on outcomes, such as promoting the well-being of young people and their families, and promoting dignity, choice and independence for adults receiving services;
- the relationship between agency policies, legal requirements and professional boundaries in shaping the nature of services provided in interdisciplinary contexts and the issues associated with working across professional boundaries and within different disciplinary groups.

5.1.2 **The service delivery context**, which includes:

- the location of contemporary social work within historical, comparative and global perspectives, including European and international contexts;
- the changing demography and cultures of communities in which social workers will be practising;
- the complex relationships between public, social and political philosophies,

policies and priorities and the organisation and practice of social work, including the contested nature of these;

- the issues and trends in modern public and social policy and their relationship to contemporary practice and service delivery in social work;
- the significance of legislative and legal frameworks and service delivery standards (including the nature of legal authority, the application of legislation in practice, statutory accountability and tensions between statute, policy and practice);
- the current range and appropriateness of statutory, voluntary and private agencies providing community-based, day-care, residential and other services and the organisational systems inherent within these;
- the significance of interrelationships with other related services, including housing, health, income maintenance and criminal justice (where not an integral social service);
- the contribution of different approaches to management, leadership and quality in public and independent human services;
- the development of personalised services, individual budgets and direct payments;
- the implications of modern information and communications technology (ICT) for both the provision and receipt of services.

5.1.3
Values and ethics, which include:
- the nature, historical evolution and application of social work values;
- the moral concepts of rights, responsibility, freedom, authority and power inherent in the practice of social workers as moral and statutory agents;
- the complex relationships between justice, care and control in social welfare and the practical and ethical implications of these, including roles as statutory agents and in upholding the law in respect of discrimination;
- aspects of philosophical ethics relevant to the understanding and resolution of value dilemmas and conflicts in both interpersonal and professional contexts;
- the conceptual links between codes defining ethical practice, the regulation of professional conduct and the management of potential conflicts generated by the codes held by different professional groups.

5.1.4
Social work theory, which includes:

- research-based concepts and critical explanations from social work theory and other disciplines that contribute to the knowledge base of social work, including their distinctive epistemological status and application to practice;
- the relevance of sociological perspectives to understanding societal and structural influences on human behaviour at individual, group and community levels;
- the relevance of psychological, physical and physiological perspectives to understanding personal and social development and functioning;

- social science theories explaining group and organisational behaviour, adaptation and change;
- models and methods of assessment, including factors underpinning the selection and testing of relevant information, the nature of professional judgement and the processes of risk assessment and decision-making;
- approaches and methods of intervention in a range of settings, including factors guiding the choice and evaluation of these;
- user-led perspectives;
- knowledge and critical appraisal of relevant social research and evaluation methodologies, and the evidence base for social work.

5.1.5
The nature of social work practice, which includes:

- the characteristics of practice in a range of community-based and organisational settings within statutory, voluntary and private sectors, and the factors influencing changes and developments in practice within these contexts;
- the nature and characteristics of skills associated with effective practice, both direct and indirect, with a range of service-users and in a variety of settings;
- the processes that facilitate and support service user choice and independence;
- the factors and processes that facilitate effective interdisciplinary, interprofessional and interagency collaboration and partnership;
- the place of theoretical perspectives and evidence from international research in assessment and decision-making processes in social work practice;
- the integration of theoretical perspectives and evidence from international research into the design and implementation of effective social work intervention, with a wide range of service users, carers and others;
- the processes of reflection and evaluation, including familiarity with the range of approaches for evaluating service and welfare outcomes, and their significance for the development of practice and the practitioner.

References

4Children (October 2012) *Over the limit. The truth about families and alcohol.*

About.com (2004) *Alcoholism* http://alcoholism.com/

Addenbrooke, M (2011) *Survivors of addiction. Narratives of recovery.* London: Routledge.

Advisory Council on the Misuse of Drugs (2003) *Hidden harm. Responding to the needs of children of problem drug users.* London: Home Office.

Alcoholics Anonymous Sterling Area Services (1952) *Twelve steps and twelve traditions. How members of Alcoholics Anonymous recover and how the society functions.* New York: Alcoholics Anonymous World Services.

All Party Parliamentary Group on Alcohol Misuse (2009) London: Alcohol Concern.

Ashton, M (2005) The motivational hallo, *Drug and Alcohol Findings,* 13, 23–30.

Audit Commission (2004) *Drug misuse 2004. Reducing the local impact.* London: Audit Commission.

Barnard, M (2007) *Drug addiction and families.* London: Jessica Kingsley Publishers.

Barton, A (2003) *Illicit drugs: use and control.* London: Routledge.

Barton, A and Quinn, C (2002) Risk management of groups or respect for the individual? Issues for information sharing and confidentiality in drug treatment and testing orders, *Drugs: Education, Prevention and Policy,* 9 (1), 35–43.

Bean, P (2004) *Drugs and crime,* 2nd edition. Cullompton: Willan.

Bell, J and Sim, M (2007) Meeting placement challenges: one local authority's response. In Phillips, R (ed) *Children exposed to parental substance misuse.* London: British Association for Adoption and Fostering.

Bennett, T and Holloway, K (2005) *Understanding drugs, alcohol and crime.* Buckingham: Open University.

Bennett, T, Holloway, K and Williams, T (2001) *Drug use and offending: summary from the first year of the NEW-ADAM research programme.* Findings 148, Research, Development and Statistics Directorate. London: Home Office.

Berridge, V. (ed) (2002) *AIDS and contemporary history.* New York: Cambridge University Press.

Best, D, O'Grady, A, Charalampous, I and Gordon, D (2005) *Tier 4 drug treatment in England: summary of inpatient provision and needs assessment.* Research Briefing 7. London: National Treatment Agency for Substance Misuse.

Biestek, F (1957) *The casework relationship.* London: Unwin University Books.

Black, C, Bucky, S and Wilder-Padilla, S (1986) The interpersonal and emotional consequences of being an adult child of an alcoholic. *International Journal of the Addictions*, 21, pp213–321.

Blackman, S (2004) *Chilling out. The cultural politics of substance consumption, youth and drug policy.* Buckingham: Open University Press.

Bloor, M and Wood, F (eds) (1998) *Addictions and problem drug use. Issues in behaviour, policy and practice.* London: Jessica Kingsley.

Brady, K, Back, S and Greenfield, S (eds.) (2009) *Women and addiction. A comprehensive handbook.* New York: The Guilford Press.

British Association of Social Workers (BASW) (2003) *Consultation response to 'Every child matters'.* Birmingham: BASW.

Buchanan, J (2006) Understanding problematic drug use: a medical matter or a social issue?, *British Journal of Community Justice*, 4 (2), 47–60.

Buchanan, J and Young, L (2000) The war on drugs – a war on drug users?, *Drugs: Education, Prevention and Policy*, 7 (4), 409–422.

Burney, E (2005) *Making people behave. Anti-social behaviour, politics and policy.* Cullompton: Willan.

Cherry, S (2005) *Transforming behaviour. Pro-social modelling in practice.* Cullompton: Willan.

Cleaver, H, Unell, I and Aldgate, J (1999) *Children's needs – parenting capacity. The impact of parental mental illness, problem alcohol and drug use, and domestic violence on children's development.* London: The Stationery Office.

Connors, G J, Donovan, D M and DiClemente, C C (2001) *Substance abuse treatment and the stages of change.* London and New York: Guilford.

Cox and Jackson Consultancy (1998) *Drugs in the deaf community: an issue ignored. Summary of key findings of a survey.* Cheshire: Cox and Jackson Consultancy.

Crawford, K and Walker, J (2003) *Social work and human development.* Exeter: Learning Matters.

Crome, I, Christian, J and Green, C (2000) The development of a unique designated community drug service for adolescents: policy, prevention and education implications, *Drugs: Education, Prevention and Policy*, 7 (1), 87–106.

Cullen, F, Wright, J and Applegate, B (1996) Control in the community. The limits of reform?, in Harland, A (ed.) *Choosing correctional options that work.* London: Sage.

Cusick, L, Martin, A and May, T (2003) *Vulnerability and involvement in drug use and sex work,* Home Office Research Study 268. London: Home Office.

Davey, B (1999) Solving economic, social and environmental problems together: an empowerment strategy for losers. In Barnes, M and Warren, L (eds) *Paths to empowerment.* Bristol: The Policy Press.

Department of Health (1996) *The task force to review services for drug misusers: report of an independent review of drug treatment services in England.* London: Department of Health.

DiClemente, C (2003) *Addiction and change. How addictions develop and addicted people recover.* New York: Guilford.

DIP E-bulletin (March 2006) *The monthly E-bulletin for the drugs interventions programme* No 22. London: Home Office.

Doel, M and Shardlow, S (2005) *Modern social work practice. Teaching and learning in practice settings.* Aldershot: Ashgate.

Downes, D and Rock, P (2003) *Understanding deviance,* 4th edition. Oxford: Oxford University Press.

DPAS (1999) *Drugs and young offenders. Guidance for drug action teams and youth offending teams.* London: Home Office.

Drug and Alcohol Education and Prevention Team (2004) *Drug education for young deaf people. A briefing paper for practitioners working with young deaf people.* London: Alcohol Concern and DrugScope.

Drugs Interventions Programme (DIP) *Developing a comprehensive rent deposit model (CRDM) to inform practice in selected DAT partnership areas* (Oct-Dec 2005). London: Home Office.

Drummond, C, Oyefeso, A, Phillips, T, Cheeta, S, Deluca, P, Perryman, K, Winfield, H, Jenner, J, Cobain, K, Galea, S, Saunders, V, Fuller, T, Pappalardo, D, Baker, O and Christopoulos, A (2004) *Alcohol needs assessment project.* London: Department of Health.

Duke, K (2003) *Drugs, prisons, and policy-making.* Basingstoke: Palgrave Macmillan.

EMCDDA See website for annual reports on the state of the drugs problem in Europe. **www.emcdda.org**

Evans, K and Alade, S (2000) *Vulnerable young people and drugs; opportunities to tackle inequalities.* London: DrugScope.

Forrester, D and Harwin, J (2007) Social work and parental substance misuse. In Phillips, R (ed) *Children exposed to parental substance misuse.* London: British Association for Adoption and Fostering.

Fountain, J, Bashford, J, Winters, M and Patel, K (2003) *Black and minority ethnic communities in England: a review of the literature on drug use and related service provision.* London: NTA.

Frischer, M and Akram, G (2001) Prevalence of comorbid mental illness and drug use recorded in general practice: preliminary findings from the general practice research database, *Drugs: Education, Prevention and Policy,* 8 (3), 275–280.

Frischer, M and Beckett, H (2006) Drug use desistance, *Criminology and Criminal Justice,* 6 (1), 127–146.

Goodman, A, Hurcombe, R, Healy, J, Goodman, S and Ball, E (May 2011) *Teenage drinking and interethnic friendships.* York: Joseph Rowntree Foundation.

Gossop, M (2000) *Living with drugs,* 5th edition. Aldershot: Ashgate.

Gossop, M (2003) *Drug addiction and its treatment.* Oxford: Oxford University Press.

Gossop, M (2005) *Drug misuse treatment and reductions in crime: findings from national treatment outcome research study.* Research Briefing 8. London: National Treatment Agency for Substance Misuse.

Gossop, M, Trakada, K, Stewart, D and Witton, J (2006) *Levels of conviction following drug treatment – linking data from the national treatment outcome research study and the offenders index.* Findings 275. London: Home Office.

Graham, J and Bowling, B (1995) *Young people and crime.* Home Office Research Study 145. London: Home Office.

Green, R and Ross, A (June 2010) *Young people's alcohol consumption and its relationship to other outcomes and behaviour.* Research Report DFE-RR005. London: Department for Education.

Hackland, F and Baker, B (2004) *Substance misuse. Professional certificate in effective practice.* London: Youth Justice Board.

Hagell, A (2002) *The mental health needs of young offenders. Bright futures: Working with vulnerable young people.* London: Mental Health Foundation. **www.mentalhealth.org.uk/html/content/young_offenders.pdf** (available as a download).

Hajra, M (12 May 2006) *Friday focus: drug education for young deaf people.* London: DrugScope.

Hammersley, R, Marsland, L and Reid, M (2003) *Substance use by young offenders: the impact of the normalisation of drug use in the early years of the 21st century.* Home Office Research Study 261. London: Home Office.

Harbin, F (2000) Therapeutic work with children of substance misusing parents. In Harbin, F and Murphy, M (eds) *Substance misuse and child care. How to understand, assist and intervene when drugs affect parenting.* Lyme Regis: Russell House.

Harris, P (2005) *Drug induced. Addiction and treatment in perspective.* Lyme Regis: Russell House.

Hearnden, I, Harocopos, A and Hough, M (1999) *Problem drug use and probation in London: an evaluation. Final report, November 1999.* Criminal Policy Unit, South Bank University. **www.kcl.ac.uk**

Heather, N and Robertson, I (1999) *Problem drinking.* 3rd edition. Oxford: Oxford University Press.

HM Government (September 2012) *Government response to the House of Commons Health Select Committee Report of Session 2012–13: Government's Alcohol Strategy.* Cm 8439. London: The Stationery Office. **www.wp.dh.gov.uk/publications/files/2012/09/Cm-8439-Accessible.pdf**

HM Inspectorate of Probation (1993) *Offenders who misuse drugs. The probation service response. Report of a thematic inspection.* London: Home Office.

HM Inspectorate of Probation (1997) *Tackling drugs together. Report of a thematic inspection on the work of the probation service with drug misusers.* London: Home Office.

HM Inspectorate of Probation (1998) *Delivering an enhanced level of community supervision. Report of a thematic inspection on the work of approved probation and bail hostels.* London: Home Office.

HM Inspectorate of Probation (2006) *Half full and half empty. An inspection of the National Probation Service's substance misuse work with offenders.* London: Home Office.

HM Prison Service (1999) *Home Secretary announces big expansion in drug treatment services for prisoners.* **http://hmprisonservice.gov.uk/news/newstext.asp?59**

Hoare, J (2009) *Drug misuse declared: findings from the 2008/9 British Crime Survey, England and Wales.* 12/09, July. London: Home Office.

Holloway, K, Bennett, T and Farrington, D (2005) *The effectiveness of criminal justice and treatment programmes in reducing drug-related crime: a systematic review.* Home Office Online Report 26/05. London: Home Office.

Home Office (1998) *Tackling drugs to build a better Britain: government 10 year strategy for tackling drug misuse.* Cm 3945. London: The Stationery Office.

Home Office (2001) *Drug use and offending: summary results from the first year of the NEW-ADAM research programme.* Findings 148. London: Home Office.

Home Office (2002) *Updated drug strategy.* **www.drugs.gov.uk/publication-search/drug-strategy/updated-drug-strategy-2002.pdf**

Home Office (2004a) *Tackling drugs: changing lives: delivering the difference.* London: Home Office.

Home Office (2004b) *Tackling drugs: changing lives. Every child matters: change for children: young people and drugs.* London: Home Office.

Home Office (2004c) *Tackling drugs – changing lives. Keeping communities safe from drugs.* London: Home Office.

Home Office (2005a) *Tackling drugs – changing lives. Delivering the difference.* London: Home Office.

Home Office (2005b) *Tackling drugs – changing lives. Turning strategy into reality.* London: Home Office.

Home Office (2008) *Drugs: Protecting families and communities. The 2008 drug strategy.* London: Home Office.

Home Office (2010) *Drug Strategy 2010. Reducing demand, restricting supply, building recovery: supporting people to live a drug free life.* London: Home Office.

Home Office (2012) *Drug Strategy 2010. Reducing demand, restricting supply, building recovery: supporting people to live a drug free life. Annual Review – May 2012.* London: Home Office.

Home Office (March 2012) *The government's alcohol strategy.* Cm 8336. London: Home Office.

Home Office Development and Practice Report (2002a) *Probation offending behaviour programmes – effective practice guide.* London: Research, Development and Statistics Directorate.

Home Office Development and Practice Report (2002b) *Training in racism awareness and cultural diversity.* London: Research, Development and Statistics Directorate.

Home Office Development and Practice Report (2003) *The substance misuse treatment needs of minority prisoner groups: women, young offenders and ethnic minorities.* London: Research, Development and Statistics Directorate.

Home Office Development and Practice Report (2004) *On-charge drug testing: evaluation of drug testing in the criminal justice system.* London: Research, Development and Statistics Directorate.

Hopkins Burke, R (2001) *An introduction to criminological theory.* Cullompton: Willan.

Horner, N (2003) *What is social work?* Exeter: Learning Matters.

House of Commons Committee of Public Accounts (2005) *The drug treatment and testing order: early lessons.* 9th Report of Session 2004–05. London: House of Commons.

Hunt, N (2003) *A review of the evidence base for harm reduction approaches to drug use.* **www.neilhunt.org/**

Hunt, N, Lenton, S and Wilton, J (April 2006) *Cannabis and mental health: responses to the emerging evidence.* London: International Drug Policy Consortium.

Hurcombe, R, Bayley, M and Goodman, A (July 2010) *Ethnicity and alcohol. A review of the UK literature.* York: Joseph Rowntree Foundation.

Inaba, D S and Cohen, W E (1993) *Uppers, downers, all rounders,* 2nd edition. Ashland: CNS.

Jones, R (2006) Social work must brace itself, *Community Care.* **www.communitycare.co.uk**

Karvinen-Niinikoski, S (2004) Social work supervision: contributing to innovative knowledge production and open expertise. In Gould, N and Baldwin, M (eds) *Social work, critical reflection and the learning organisation.* Aldershot: Ashgate.

Keller, D (2003) Exploration in the service of relapse prevention; a psychoanalytic contribution to substance misuse treatment. In Rotgers, F, Morgenstern, J and Walters, S T (eds) *Treating substance abuse. Theory and technique.* London and New York: Guilford.

Kendrick, N (1999) *Drugs and substance misuse.* Leeds: TOPPS.

Klee, H, Jackson, M and Lewis, S (eds) (2002) *Drug misuse and motherhood.* London: Routledge.

Klee, H and Lewis, S (2002) Preparing for motherhood. In Klee, H, Jackson, M and Lewis, S (eds) *Drug misuse and motherhood.* London: Routledge.

Kothari, G, Marsden, J and Strang, J (2002) Opportunities and obstacles for effective treatment of drug misusers in the criminal justice system in England and Wales, *British Journal of Criminology,* 42 (2), 412–432.

Kroll, B and Taylor, A (2003) *Parental substance misuse and child welfare.* London: Jessica Kingsley Publishers.

Lewis, S (2002) Concepts of motherhood. In Klee, H, Jackson, M and Lewis, S (eds) *Drug misuse and motherhood.* London: Routledge.

Lilly, J R, Cullen, F and Ball, R (2007) *Criminological theory. Context and consequences.* 4th edition. London: Sage.

London Probation Area (2003) Evaluating drug treatment and testing orders, *Probation,* 7, 5.

MacDonald, Z, Collingwood, J and Gordon, L (08/06) *Measuring the harm from illegal drugs using the drug harm index – an update.* Online Report. London: Home Office.

McGrath, Y, Sumnall, H, Edmonds, K, McVeigh, J and Bellis, M (2006) *Review of grey literature on drug prevention among young people.* London: National Institute for Health and Clinical Excellence.

MacGregor, S (2005) Summary of key messages from the drugs misuse research initiative, *Drugs: Education, Prevention and Policy,* 1–55.

MacGregor, S and Smith, L (1998) The English drug treatment system: experimentation or pragmatism? In Klingemann, H and Hunt, G (eds) *Drug treatment systems in an international perspective, drugs, demons and delinquents.* London: Sage.

Mair, G. (1988) *Probation day centres.* Home Office Research Study 100. London: HMSO.

Margolis, R D and Zweben, J E (1998) *Treating patients with alcohol and other drug problems: an integrated approach.* Washington: American Psychological Association.

Marlow, A and Pearson, G (1999) *Young people, drugs and community safety.* Lyme Regis: Russell House.

Mather, M (2007) Finding out about the past to understand the present: working with the medical adviser in adoption and foster care. In Phillips, R (ed) *Children exposed to parental substance-misuse.* London: British Association of Adoption and Fostering.

Matthews, S, Brasnett, L and Smith, J (2006) *Underage drinking: findings from the 2004 offending, crime and justice survey.* Home Office Findings 277. London: Home Office.

May, T, Duffy, M, Few, B and Hough, M (2005) *Understanding drug selling in communities. Insider or outsider trading?* York: Joseph Rowntree Foundation.

McIntosh, J and McKeganey, N (2000) The recovery from dependent drug use: addicts' strategies for reducing the risk of relapse, *Drugs: Education, Prevention and Policy,* 7 (2), 179–192.

McIntosh, J and McKeganey, N (2001) Identity and recovery from dependent drug use: the addict's perspective, *Drugs: Education, Prevention and Policy,* 8 (1), 47–59.

McMurran, M and Hollin, C R (1993) *Young offenders and alcohol-related crime. A practitioner's guidebook.* Chichester: Wiley.

McNeill, F, Batchelor, S, Burnett, R and Knox, J (2005) *21st century social work. Reducing re-offending: key practice skills.* Edinburgh: Social Work Inspection Agency.

Meikle, J (2013) NHS staff 'writing off' alcoholics who have liver disease. *Guardian,* 14 June.

Miller, W R and Rollnick, S (2002) *Motivational interviewing. Preparing people for change.* London and New York: Guilford.

Mott, J and Bean, P (1998) The development of drug control in Britain. In Coomber, R (ed) *The control of drugs and drug users. Reason or reaction?* Boca Raton: OPA.

Mwenda, L (2005) *Drug offenders in England and Wales 2004.* Home Office Statistical Bulletin 23/05. London: Home Office.

National Treatment Agency (2009) *Getting to grips with substance misuse among young people. The data for 207/08.* London: National Treatment Agency for Substance Misuse (available on *www.nta.nhs.uk*)

National Treatment Agency (2009) *The story of drug treatment.* London: National Treatment Agency for Substance Misuse (available on *www.nta.nhs.uk*)

Newbury-Birch, D and 11 other authors (2009) *Impact of alcohol consumption on young people. A systematic review of the reviews.* Research Report DCSF-RR067. Department for Children, Schools and Families.

Newham Substance Misuse Partnership Board (2004) *A guide to Newham alcohol and drug services.* London: Newham Drug Action Team.

NOMS (National Offender Management Service) (2005) *Strategy for the management and treatment of problematic drug users within the correctional services. NOMS drug strategy.* London: Home Office.

Nordt, C and Stohler, R (2006) Incidence of heroin use in Zurich, Switzerland: a treatment case register analysis, *The Lancet,* 367 (9525), 1830–1834.

NTA (2002) *Models of care for the treatment of drug misusers: Part 2: full reference report. Overview and action required. What is models of care?* London: National Treatment Agency.

NTA (2005a) *NHS Business plan 2005/06: towards treatment effectiveness. More treatment, better treatment, fairer treatment.* London: National Treatment Agency.

NTA (2005b) *Women in drug treatment services.* Research Briefing 6. London: National Treatment Agency.

NTA (2005c) *Retaining clients in drug treatment: a guide for providers and commissioners.* London: National Treatment Agency.

NTA (2006) *Directory of residential services for young people.* London: National Treatment Agency.

Office of National Statistics (ONS) (2013) *General Lifestyle Survey overview – a report on the 2011 General Lifestyle Survey.* **www.ons.gov.uk/ons/rel/ghs/general-lifestyle-survey/2011/rpt-chapter-2.html**

O'Hare, P, Newcome, R, Matthews, A, Buning, E C and Drucker, E (1992) *The reduction of drug-related harm.* London: Routledge.

Parker, H, Aldridge, J and Measham, F (1998) *Illegal leisure. The normalization of adolescent recreational drug use.* London: Routledge.

Parrott, A, Morinan, A, Moss, M and Scholey, A (2004) *Understanding drugs and behaviour.* Chichester: Wiley.

Patel, K (2000) The missing drug users: minority ethnic drug users and their children. In Harbin, F and Murphy, M (eds) *Substance misuse and child care.* Lyme Regis: Russell House.

Payne, M (1997) *Modern social work theory,* 2nd edition. Basingstoke: Macmillan.

Petersen, T and McBride, A (2002) *Working with substance misusers. A guide to theory and practice.* London: Routledge.

Phillips, R (2007) Telling it like it is. In Phillips, R (ed) *Children exposed to parental substance misuse.* London: British Association for Adoption and Fostering.

Phillips, W (2007) A brief introduction to the effects of psychoactive drugs. In Phillips, R (ed) *Children exposed to parental substance misuse.* London: British Association for Adoption and Fostering.

Pike, A, Coldwell, J and Dunn, J (2006) *Family relationships in middle childhood.* London: National Children's Bureau for the Joseph Rowntree Foundation.

Prime Minister's Strategy Unit (2004) *Alcohol harm reduction strategy for England.* London: Cabinet Office.

Prochaska, J and DiClemente, C (1994) *The transtheoretical approach. Crossing traditional boundaries of therapy.* Malabar, FL: Krieger Publishing Company.

Pudney, S (2002) *The road to ruin? Sequences of initiation into drug use and offending by young people in Britain.* Home Office Research Study 253. London: Home Office.

Quinney, A (2006) *Collaborative social work practice.* Exeter: Learning Matters.

Raistrick, D, Hodgson, R and Ritson, B (1999) (eds) *Tackling alcohol together. The evidence base for a UK alcohol policy.* London: Free Association Books.

Reitox National Focal Point (2004) *National report to the European monitoring centre for drugs and drug addiction* (EMCDDA) **www.emcdda.eu.int/**

Rotgers, F, Morgenstern, J and Walters, S T (2003) *Treating substance abuse. Theory and technique.* London and New York: Guilford.

Ruggiero, V and South, N (1995) *Eurodrugs. Drug use, markets and trafficking in Europe.* London: UCL Press Ltd.

Runciman Report (2000) *Drugs and the law. Report of the independent inquiry into the Misuse of Drugs Act 1971.* London: The Police Foundation.

Schön, D (1991) *The reflective practitioner. How professionals think in action.* Aldershot: Arena.

Seaman, P, Turner, K, Hill, M, Stafford, A and Walker, M (2006) *Parenting and children's resilience in disadvantaged communities.* York: Joseph Rowntree Foundation.

Seddon, T (2006) Drugs, crime and social exclusion, *British Journal of Criminology,* 46 (4), 680–703.

Sharp, C, Baker, P, Goulden, C, Ramsay, M and Sondhi, A (2001) *Drug misuse declared in 2000: key results from the British crime survey.* Findings 149, Research, Development and Statistics Directorate. London: Home Office.

Sims, B (2005) Treating the substance-addicted offender: theory and practice. In Sims, B (ed) *Substance abuse treatment with correctional clients. Practical implications for institutional and community settings.* New York: The Haworth Press.

Smith, J E and Meyers, R J (2004) *Motivating substance abusers to enter treatment. Working with family members.* London and New York: Guilford.

South, N (2002) Drugs, alcohol and crime. In Maguire, M, Morgan, R and Reiner, R (eds) *The Oxford handbook of criminology,* 3rd edition. Oxford: Oxford University Press.

The Lancet (2006) A second chance for the UK to reduce drug-misuse deaths, *The Lancet, Editorial,* 367 (9525), 1792.

Thom, B (1999) *Dealing with drink. Alcohol and social policy: From treatment to management.* London: Free Association Books.

Tober, G (1991) Motivational interviewing with young people. In Miller, W R and Rollnick, S (eds) *Motivational interviewing. Preparing people for change,* 1st edition. London and New York: Guilford.

Travis, A (2002) 'Tough love' policy at heart of new drugs strategy. *Guardian,* 4 December.

Trotter, C (1999) *Working with involuntary clients: a guide to practice.* London: Sage.

Turnbull, P, McSweeney, T, Webster, R, Edmunds, M and Hough, M (2000) *Drug treatment and testing orders: final evaluation report.* Home Office Research Study 212. London: Home Office.

Turner, S, Petersilia, J and Deschenes, E (1994) The implementation and effectiveness of drug testing in community supervision: results of an experimental evaluation. In Mackenzie, D and Duchida, C (eds) *Drugs and crime: evaluating public policy initiatives.* London: Sage.

UK Focal Point on Drugs provides the latest information on drug use in the UK and reports it to the European Monitoring Centre on Drugs and Drug Addition (EMCDDA).

University of Stirling (March 2013) *Health first. An evidence-based alcohol strategy for the UK.* Stirling: University of Stirling. **www.stir.ac.uk/media/schools/management/documents/Alcoholstrategy-updated.pdf**

Valentine, G, Skelton, T and Butler, R (2003) *Towards inclusive youth policies and practices: lessons from young lesbians, gay men and deaf people*. London: National Youth Agency.

Velleman, R and Orford, J (1999) *Risk and resilience*. Australia: Harwood Academic Publishers.

Velleman, R (2011) *Counselling for alcohol problems*. 3rd edition, London: Sage.

Walker, R and Logan, T K (2005) Setting the stage for treating drug court clients: how to initiate treatment. In Sims, B (ed) *Substance treatment with correctional clients. Practical implications for institutional and community settings*. New York: The Haworth Press.

Wanigaratne, S., Davis, P, Pryce, K and Brotchie, J (2005) *The effectiveness of psychological therapies on drug misusing clients*. Research Briefing 11. London: National Treatment Agency.

Ward, J, Henderson, Z and Pearson, G (2003) *One problem among many: drug use among care leavers in transition to independent living*. Home Office Research Study 260. London: Home Office.

Washton, A and Zweben, J (2006) *Treating alcohol and drug problems in psychotherapy practice*. New York: The Guilford Press.

Wild, T C, Newton-Taylor, B, Ogborne, A, Mann, R, Erickson, P and Macdonald, S (2001) Attitudes toward compulsory substance abuse treatment: a comparison of the public, counsellors', probationers' and judges' views, *Drugs: Education, Prevention and Policy*, 8 (1), 33–45.

Wilson, C and Orford, J (1978) Children of alcoholics: report of a preliminary study and comments on the literature. *Quarterly Journal of Studies on Alcohol*, 39, pp121–42.

Wincup, E, Buckland, G and Bayliss, R (2003) *Youth homelessness and substance use: Report to the drugs and alcohol research unit*. Home Office Research Series 258. London: Home Office.

Wintour, P (2013) No 10 set to drop minimum alcohol pricing in face of cabinet revolt. *Guardian*, 13 March.

Working Party of the Royal College of Psychiatrists and the Royal College of Physicians (2000) *Drugs. Dilemmas and choices*. London: Gaskell.

Yates, R (2002) A brief history of British drug policy, 1950-2001, *Drugs: Education, Prevention and Policy*, 9 (2), 113–124.

Young, J (1971) *The drug takers: the social meaning of drugtaking*. London: Paladin.

Index

Drug Rehabilitation Requirement (DRR) 32, 41, 138
drug smuggling 33
drug strategy 53, 54, 86, 106–8
drug testing 74, 79, 94
  see also Drug Treatment and Testing Orders
drug treatment 96–9
  adult substance misusers 18
  conflict over outcomes 95
  disease model 125–6
  drug-misusing parents 50–1
  effectiveness 42–3, 90–1, 131
  eligibility matrix 10
  entry to 34
  expenditure 65, 106
  investment in 142
  local systems for monitoring 24–5
  offenders 34, 38, 72, 95, 137
  reconvictions following 89
  requirement 41
  services 19–22, 28, 138
  waiting times 142–3
  wheel of change 51, 126–32
  young offenders 42, 75
  young people 29
  see also alternative therapies; harm minimisation/reduction; Models of Care
Drug Treatment and Testing Orders (DTTOs) 32, 39, 40, 41, 42–4
drug use x
  black and ethnic minorities 95
  care leavers 80
  costs 116
  gender 88, 98
  normalisation 5–6, 16, 140
  prevalence 2–3, 79
  psychiatric conditions 75–7, 140
  recreational 5, 7, 60, 84
  related social problems 36–7
  risk factors 27, 84
  socio-economic deprivation 17, 72, 79, 90–1, 95
  subculture 5, 7
  in the UK
    information 2
    nature and extent of 16
  vulnerable groups 18, 84, 88, 116, 135
  young people 2
  youth homelessness 81
  see also poly drug use
Drug Use 2004 (Audit Commission 30, 93
drug wise 59
drug-misusing parents
  children of 48, 51
  numbers 17
  treatment 47–8
drug-related deaths 23, 62
DrugData Update report (2006) 18
Drugs: Protecting families and Communities (2008) 46

drugs
  commonly used 59–64
  and crime 33, 35, 72, 83, 89–90, 95–6
  education 18, 87–8, 141
  experimentation with 116
  major initiatives 55
  market and local communities 96
  'maturing out' 80
  misuse 16–17, 18, 38–9, 51, 52
  see also illegal drugs; individual drugs; prescription drugs
Drugs Act (2005) 32, 42, 94, 97
Drugs and Alcohol National Occupational Standards (DANOS) xi, 13
Drugs Intervention Programme (DIP) 93, 94, 98
Drugs Misuse Research Initiative (DMRI) 84, 140, 141, 142
Drugs Prevention Advisory Service report (1999) 27–9, 74, 75
Drugs Prevention Initiative 75
Drugs Strategy (2008) 53, 54, 77, 78, 87
drugs tsars 38
DrugScope x, 18
dual diagnosis 61, 75–7

early intervention 75
Early Intervention Grant 107
Early Morning Restriction Orders 103
ecstasy 61, 62
  effects 64
  outrage at arrival of 5
  penalty for possession 35
  use 3, 4, 37, 59, 65, 80
empowerment 8, 54, 134–6
ethnic minorities see black and ethnic minorities
European Association for the Treatment of Addiction report (2003) 115
European Monitoring Centre for Drugs and Addiction (EMCDDA) 2, 53, 57, 65
Every child matters 25, 29–30, 74, 84
exchange needles 11–12
experimentation 116

families, working with 46–53
Families for Children Team 50
Family Intervention Projects 47
family relationships 48, 92
father-child relationships 72
female offenders
  and probation service 38
  substance misuse 37, 98
foetal alcohol syndrome 63, 104
foster care, children in 50
four-tiered model, service provision 19–22, 138
FRAMES 123
Frank 61, 87, 133
funding, treatment of young people 26

gender
  alcohol 85–6

alcohol consumption 86, 103, 112
choice of drug 16, 59
drug use 2–3, 26–7, 59, 65
'maturing out' of drugs 80
needs and risk assessment 27–30
participation, drugs market 96
substance misuse 16–17
targeting those at risk 77, 78
see also children

youth homelessness, drug use 81
Youth Inclusion Support Programmes (YISPs)
    143
youth justice 143
    and child welfare 74–5
Youth Justice Board 25, 73, 143
Youth Justice, the Next Steps 74
youth offending teams (YOTs) 27, 73–4